THE EVERYTHING® ETIQUETTE BOOK

The Everything® Series

The Everything® Baby Names Book
The Everything® Bartender's Book
The Everything® Bicycle Book
The Everything® Cat Book
The Everything® Christmas Book
The Everything® College Survival Book
The Everything® Dreams Book
The Everything® Games Book
The Everything® Golf Book
The Everything® Home Improvement Book
The Everything® Pasta Cookbook
The Everything® Study Book
The Everything® Wedding Book
The Everything® Wedding Checklist
The Everything® Wedding Etiquette Book
The Everything® Wedding Vows Book
The Everything® Wine Book
The Everything® Etiquette Book

THE
EVERYTHING®
ETIQUETTE
BOOK

Mind your manners, with family and friends,
announcements and invitations, business, travel,
the Internet and every other awkward situation

Nat Segaloff

Adams Media Corporation
Holbrook, Massachusetts

An Everything® Series Book. The Everything® Series is a registered trademark of Adams Media Corporation.

Published by Adams Media Corporation
260 Center Street, Holbrook, MA 02343

ISBN: 1-55850-807-4

Printed in the United States of America.

J I H G F E D C B A

Library of Congress Cataloging-in-Publication Data
Segaloff, Nat.
The everything etiquette book / Nat Segaloff.
    p.   cm.—(The everything series)
Includes index.
ISNBN 1-55850-807-4 (pbk.)
1. Etiquette. I. Title. II. Series.
    BJ1801.S44   1997
    395—dc21   97-24584
                         CIP

Illustrations by Bill Morrison and Barry Littmann

This book is available at quantity discounts for bulk purchases.
For information, call 1-800-872-5627 (in Massachusetts, call 781-767-8100).

Visit our home page at http://www.adamsmedia.com

*To Mr. and Mrs. Louis T. Nealon—my beloved
Aunt Helen and Uncle Neal—who
taught me how to have good fun
as well as good manners.*

Author's Note: A Word on Gender

In previous generations it was the wife who ran the home and the husband who held the job. Needless to say, that is not always the case any more. Although in the strictest tradition the woman is still the keeper of her family's social obligations, more and more responsibility is now falling to the man.

In the case of single men and women living alone, of course, there is no question of assignment. A more egalitarian age, however, calls for a more equitable approach. Therefore, except for the most obvious cases (such as bridal showers or bachelor parties), this book will use pronouns of both genders.

CONTENTS

CONTENTS

ACKNOWLEDGMENTS

Pamela A. Liflander suggested and edited this book, and Agnes Birnbaum of Bleecker Street Associates agented the deal. They both possessed patience and humor on those occasions when I did not.

Additional thanks go to Robert W. Abramoff, Liane Brandon, Christopher Darling, John de Lancie, Gayle Kirschenbaum, Stan Levin, Emily Lockman, Marnie Mosiman, Pamela A. Perry, Steve Sherwin, Nancy Ross Simon and Fred Spring for offering counsel and confidence. Finally, virtual thanks to Loren Rose and to Ontrack Data International, Inc., for resurrecting my dead hard drive.

Grateful acknowledgement is made to *The Everything® Wedding Book* by Janet Anastasio and Michelle Bevilacqua (©1994 Adams Media Corporation).

INTRODUCTION

"Pinkies out!"

Quick, wasn't that the first thing you thought of when you heard the word *etiquette*? Most of us regard manners as a collection of silly rules that snotty people use to make everybody else feel out of place. Consequently, etiquette is widely (and incorrectly) regarded as a social barrier, something that only snobs care about, and certainly nothing for the rest of us to follow, right?

Well, think about it again the next time you look for your knife and fork and find them right beside your plate. Or when you hold the door for somebody and he or she says, "Thank you." Or when your phone call is returned, you receive a thank-you note, or somebody lets you go ahead of him in the checkout line. All of these are examples of that so-called nasty, stuffy, class-conscious convention called "etiquette."

Simply defined, *etiquette* is the way civilized human beings behave around one another to minimize conflict.

Over the span of civilization, humans have developed ways of talking, acting, living, and moving, as well as resolving and—especially—*preventing* conflict. In the broadest sense, this is etiquette.

But there's a catch, and one that this book will repeatedly stress: etiquette isn't a set of legally enacted laws. It's an informal

> "The great secret, Eliza, is not having bad manners or good manners or any other particular sort of manners, but having the same manner for all human souls: in short, behaving as if you were in Heaven, where there are no third-class carriages, and one soul is as good as another."
> —George Bernard Shaw, *Pygmalion*

agreement among people, a distillation of human behavior over the years, and it differs from country to country and even neighborhood to neighborhood. It also can change, not in importance, but over a few fine points, such as hemlines, slang, dress codes, or gender roles.

What doesn't change is the assumption that people who interact in a society agree to follow its customs. If they don't know what the customs are, they can either learn by observing or by asking questions. If they happen to make a few mistakes, well, etiquette even tells us how to correct them without insult.

As a voluntary system of behavior, etiquette presumes that a person wants to act correctly. If someone is rude on purpose, however, (I am thinking of several well-known Hollywood celebrities as I write this), that person no longer deserves society's polite tolerance. Across the country, it seems that an effort to return to simple good manners is an evolving trend. There is a frustration that we all feel at the increasing coarseness of American society. Surprisingly, this trend does not seem to be traceable to the so-called "permissive" sixties; if anything, that was an era in which people cared about each other's feelings, sometimes to a fault. No, modern vulgarity seems rooted in the "greed is good" era of the eighties, where people judged each other not by the content of their character but by the size of their portfolio.

At one time, societal disdain was to be avoided at all costs; one's social position was sacred. Today, social scorn is to be courted on the theory that squeaky wheels get the oil—or at least ink in *Entertainment Weekly*. Perhaps this is just a phase, like a child who has just learned the word "poop" and uses it to get a rise out of adults.

But behavior that is precocious in a seven-year-old is boorish in a twenty-seven-year-old. Immaturity has derailed its share of careers (except for radio disc jockeys), and it sure isn't any way to be taken seriously as an adult. Public opinion can be mercurial, and those who delight in offending others— whether through mere ignorance or crass intent—generally discover, to their disgrace, that society eventually gets even.

This is particularly true as we plow head-long into the twenty-first century. By any measure the last 100 years have been a century of progress: electric cities, telecommunication, space travel, and medical breakthroughs head the list of human achievements. Note that these are technological advances, however; humankind has made less headway as a civil species, as a survey of manners will reveal.

Legislation has come to take the place of good deportment: what are civil rights laws except what should have been basic decency from the very beginning of the U.S. republic? What is the women's movement but a means of replacing the bad manners of repression with the good manners of equality? What is Social Security if not a way to mandate what used to be automatic respect for elders?

America is a country defined by its litigation. If we can't get an apology from someone, we sue him. Life has become a free-for-all: nobody needs to take responsibility for his own actions any more because we were all abused as kids or driven insane by TV or rock music. Every criminal is a victim of another criminal. As Dana Carvey's Church Lady says, "how conveeeeeeeenient."

We need etiquette today more than ever. Not laws, but beliefs. Not sanctions, but simple decency. Because rules, if well written and consistently observed, do not repress, they liberate. Children raised knowing clear limits develop into adults who respect the rights of others. Society can better spend its energies catching and rehabilitating criminals than making fashion arrests.

Good manners are not a sign of weakness, they are a symbol of strength. They mark the person who uses them as someone who treats others with respect (and commands it in return). On a practical level, etiquette shows people the way out of social jams; on a metaphysical level it helps us all appreciate each other for our positive reasons, not the bad ones.

George Bernard Shaw observed, "A gentleman is someone who never insults someone else unintentionally." *The Everything® Etiquette Book* is designed to reduce the risk—and, to be quite frank about it—to close the gap.

(By the way, sticking the pinky "out" while drinking tea is considered pretentious. When holding a teacup, one curves the pinky with the other fingers while the index finger is inserted into the handle and the thumb steadies it.)

—Nat Segaloff
Los Angeles, California

CHAPTER ONE

CHILD'S PLAY:
From Birth Through Puberty

It has long been unfashionable to say so out loud in our society, but the truth is that having—and raising—children is the first duty of parents. Period.

Although peers, schools, and employers may assume some of these responsibilities after the child is old enough to leave the house, it is Mommy and Daddy who are supposed to start the ball rolling. Some courts even hold parents legally responsible for their offspring, such as the enterprising judges who haul parents into court when their kids are truant. In one case the parents of a teenager living at home were successfully sued for damages when their son had a car accident.

Why are we suddenly punishing the lax parent instead of the incorrigible child? Part of it may be modern society's mania for placing the blame on somebody, anybody. But at heart it's also the belief that mommies and daddies ought to teach their progeny to be decent, functioning, respected members of society.

That responsibility cuts across social lines. Certainly the demoralizing effects of welfare, gangs, and commercialism make the task tougher for, say, single, inner-city parents. But wealth and privilege do not automatically confer parenting skills.

The fact remains that if a child does not learn the accepted way of getting what he wants by the time he becomes an adult, he will likely become a burden, not only to himself but ultimately to us all. Children must be taught how to survive in mainstream society, for it is there that they will spend the rest of their lives.

It starts at birth. Kids are not just miniature adults but separate entities that demand special attention—even before they are born. Accordingly, the rituals surrounding the birth of a baby are among the most enduring areas of etiquette.

> *When you grow up and have children of your own, I only hope that they give you as much pain and heartache as you've given your father and me.*
>
> *—a mother's prayer (anonymous)*

CONCEPTION AND PREGNANCY

Although some religions and lawmakers insist on having a presence in the bedroom, there is no "right" or "wrong" way for a man and woman to procreate—biologically, at least.

Etiquette doesn't enter the bedroom, but it does stand guard at the door. Culturally, the custom is for a man and woman to be

BABY SHOWER GIFTS

Good baby shower gifts include:

- Baby care book (e.g., *Baby and Child Care* by Dr. Spock)
- Baby carriage
- Baby carrier
- Baby hat
- Bassinet
- Blanket
- Board books
- Booties
- Bottles/nipples
- Bounce seat
- Car seat
- CDs or tapes specifically geared for children (e.g., Raffi)
- Changing table
- Clothes
- Comb and brush set
- Crib
- Crib mobile
- Cup
- Diaper bag
- Feeding bowl
- Frame for photos or birth announcement
- Gift certificate to diaper service
- High chair
- Intercom/monitor
- Jogging stroller
- Music box
- Night light
- Nursing pillow (if you know the mom is planning to nurse)
- Photo album
- Portable crib
- Silver rattle
- Stroller
- Swing
- Toys

married at the time they conceive a child. Any departure from this custom—whether by illegitimacy, common-law marriage, artificial insemination, egg donation, surrogate motherhood, and so on—begs the question of how to explain it should it eventually become necessary to do so, such as to relatives, doctors or, more important, to the child herself.

That doesn't mean that a single woman who has chosen to have a child on her own has to take out ads. But it does mean that people who have chosen to have children by atypical means should not be surprised when the subject comes up, even though raising it is rude. Such questions as "Who's the father?" and "Was it a planned pregnancy?" are as out of place as counting back the weeks between the birth and the wedding. However, human nature is such that people will ask them anyway; etiquette dictates that they keep the answer to themselves.

Pregnancy Announcements

Desi Arnaz used to joke that when Lucille Ball was carrying Desi Jr. during the filming of *I Love Lucy* in 1952, CBS wouldn't let them use the word *pregnant* on the air. Instead, recalled Arnaz, "We had to say she was 'expecting.'"

Nevertheless, although a woman's pregnancy is rarely a secret by the fifth or sixth month, it still isn't a suitable topic for casual discussion outside of family and friends, unless the woman who is "expecting" raises it herself.

Conversely, parents who are expecting a child should remember that not everybody is as excited about the impending event as they are and that social gatherings that turn into a seminar on pregnancy will very likely be the last to which the impending parents are invited.

Playwright George S. Kaufman once sent a telegram to a new mother who had discussed her pregnancy to the extent that the birth was anticlimactic. His wire read, "Congratulations. We always knew you had it in you."

Smoking, Drinking, Drugs, and Pregnancy

Aside from the tangible dangers to the developing fetus from a mother-to-be who ingests drugs, tobacco, or alcohol, it is not polite for friends to smoke around her or flaunt their freedom to revel in substances she cannot—or, rather, should not—consume.

Pregnancy and Travel

Airlines and cruise ships may refuse to accommodate women in the later stages of pregnancy either for fear that the stress of travel may induce labor or because they do not have adequate medical facilities should the baby arrive. To avoid inconvenience to other passengers, women beyond their seventh month should check ahead with their doctor and their transportation carrier.

Baby Showers

Notwithstanding the foregoing, friends of the expectant mother can help lighten the financial burden of parenthood by throwing a baby shower (the concept derives from "showering her with gifts," not with babies).

A shower is scheduled anywhere from four to six weeks before the due date (for the pragmatic reason that miscarriages and questions of fetal viability are settled by the third trimester), usually in the afternoon. It is hosted by a close friend at the friend's home or the function room of a club or restaurant. More and more, men are also being invited to showers.

Only one baby shower need be held, and then only for the first child, as subsequent children will have the benefit of hand-me-downs. In the case of a couple who adopt a child, shower invitations should include the child's gender and clothing sizes.

The shower hostess may coordinate gift giving among the guests; this allows several guests to pool their resources to buy more expensive gifts such as strollers or cribs. Some department and baby specialty stores now offer registry services.

(In the tragic event of a stillbirth or crib death, the parents, if they offer to return the gifts, should be encouraged to "please keep them for your next baby.") Invitations for baby showers are available in most card shops or can be written by hand.

Baby Showers for Unwed Mothers

Unwed mothers are just as much in need of baby items as married mothers are. It would be considered rude to exclude them from any prebirth rituals.

Videotaping the Childbirth

It's ironic that people who would think it pornographic to show the conception of a baby would advocate the idea of videotaping that same baby's messy birth. Okay, the ordeal of having a baby may quickly yield to the joy of holding the newborn in one's arms, but why relive it in full color and sound? Opinions vary, but the ultimate question should be, Who are you ever going to show it to?

Instead of making a medical film, why not tape greetings of various relatives welcoming the baby and play them back when the child has grown up enough to appreciate them? As some of the taped relatives may have died in the intervening years, it will stand as a lovely memorial.

Birth Announcements

In the old days, members of polite society tolerated their names in the paper only on four occasions: birth, debut, marriage, and death. Much has changed since then. Specifically, an entire industry is now devoted to babies and all that surrounds them, such as books containing thousands of baby names, diaper services, customized toys, silver combs, rattles, and cups, or framed baby footprint certificates.

But first things first: telling the world that the baby has arrived. Birth announcements are appropriate for the first and all subsequent births.

Our Home Has New Joy!

Name: Charlotte Ann MacGregor
Weight: Six pounds, ten ounces
Length: Twenty inches

Carole and Addison MacGregor
49 Shawn Drive
Wheaton, MD 20902

When a Child Is Adopted

Parents who adopt a child are bestowing the greatest of all gifts they can give: love. Now that the stigma of adoption has lifted, it is absolutely correct to issue an announcement.

> Mr. and Mrs. Addison MacGregor
> as pleased to announce
> the adoption of
> **James Michael**
> **Age:** *eighteen months*

As for discussing adoption, the prevailing wisdom is that the child should be told that he is adopted as soon as he is old enough to ask the question. Many parents are fond of telling an adopted child, "We wanted you so much we chose you." When the child asks the thornier question, "Why did my real mommy give me away?" a good placating response is, "We don't know, but whatever the reason, we are thankful that it brought us together."

The question is bound to arise again. And it should; as scientists discover more and more traits carried by the genetic trail, it may be a matter of life and death for a child to learn more about his birth parents.

The law is no more up to date in this area than etiquette is.

If a legitimate third party (teacher, doctor, lawyer) asks about adoption, he should be told the same information that the adopted child has received.

Birth of a Sick Child or a Child with Disabilities

No unusual notation should be made in the birth announcement of a child who is disabled or in some way different. Parental love knows no qualification.

Good manners dictate that friends and family make no untoward remarks that invade the privacy of a family still coming to terms with the added responsibilities of a "challenged" child. Indeed, quiet support may be needed all the more.

BABY GIFTS

There is no obligation to send a baby gift in response to a birth announcement, although it may be a kind gesture to do so. At the very least, a note of congratulations is due.

When choosing a toy for a newborn child, make a special effort to buy one that meets safety requirements. Although plush animal toys are cute, they often contain plastic eyes or other parts than can pull off and pose the risk of choking. If in doubt, check the label for age appropriateness.

The time has passed when a proud father handed out cigars to announce the birth of a son or daughter. For one thing, smoking is now considered an insult; for another, do you know how much a good cigar costs these days?

NAMING

A name is something a child carries with him or her for life, and the responsibility of choosing one weighs heavily on the parents. Often a male child will carry his father's or grandfather's name, as in "Jr." or "III." Increasingly, girls are being named after their mothers. Creative parents have even coined new names by combining their own, such as "Aleva" (Alan and Eva).

Some religions hold that names contain magic and that choosing the right one is a spiritual event. Catholic tradition suggests including the name of the saint whose celebration day occurs on or near that of the child's birth. Greek Orthodox practice accords the child a single given name. Jewish custom is split: Ashkenazic Jews name their children to honor a dead relative, whereas Sephardic Jews may name their offspring after living relatives, including the father, thereby allowing for a "Jr."

At no time is it ever polite to comment humorously on a person's name. Even if it was, the chances are slim that the person hasn't heard the joke before, and nothing is as coldly received as a tired wisecrack made at the expense of someone's most personal possession. (My name is "Nat," not "gnat.")

If the name is known at the time of birth, it is entered on the birth certificate at the hospital and thereafter may be published in the "births" column that appears in local newspapers.

Ritual Circumcision

This Jewish tradition (otherwise known as *Bris or B'rith Milah*) is performed eight days after the birth of a male child. It involves the removal of the foreskin of the penis as a reminder of the biblical covenant (*b'rith* means covenant) between God and the Jews. There also is anecdotal medical evidence that circumcision may reduce the occurrence of penile cancer, and of cervical cancer in female partners of circumcised men.

Among Christians, the practice historically has gone in and out of favor; there is debate about the fact that it is performed without anesthetic on a child who cannot refuse. In some non-Western cultures, female children are frequently circumcised by removing the clitoris.

In the Jewish *B'rith Milah* ceremony, the boy's godfather holds the baby on his lap while the *mohel* performs the rite and the congregation (including invited friends and family) prays. This is where the child's name is formally affirmed. It is a comparable custom to hold a "baby naming" party for female Jewish children or for members of any other non-Jewish culture.

Rarely are written invitations sent out for circumcisions, as they follow the birth so closely. A baby naming may occur up to a month after delivery and may involve a written invitation combined with a birth announcement.

UNWED MOTHERS

*D*an Quayle vs. Murphy Brown aside, the shame once attached to unwed mothers has diminished somewhat in some circles. Coldly put, the deciding factor seems to be whether the mother is capable of supporting her child herself.

Thankfully, times have changed when a single woman "in a family way" had to "go visit her aunt in Kansas" until she delivered. Nevertheless, an unmarried mother and her child may have to endure occasional moments of embarrassment. Fortunately, these are mitigated by modern society's divorce rate, which has made the stigma of broken families virtually moot. That's why it's best to bring the child up knowing the score, such as:

1. When people ask the mother "Who's the father?"
2. When kids ask the child, "Where's your daddy?"
3. If the school nurse needs hereditary data
4. If the child's last name differs from the mother's
5. If the mother's new fiancée suggests adoption
6. When a birth certificate is needed for a passport or other ID
7. When there are racial differences

Regardless of whether she has a tummy or doesn't have a wedding ring, it is impolite for anyone to make such a personal inquiry as "Who's the father?" Small children cannot be prevented from unleashing their natural curiosity, but adults are supposed to know better.

If some grownup has the impertinence to ask, the expectant single mother might consider replying, "I'm sure you didn't mean to be rude with your question, but that's between the baby and me."

Baptism

The soul of a newborn Christian child is sanctified through the biblical ritual of baptism, a rite of both spiritual rebirth and "christening," or naming. Often churches will hold a special christening ceremony, which involves the parents and godparents as well as the congregation and guests, when the child is one month old. In the case of a desperately sick infant, the baptism may occur earlier, and privately, as last rites.

In some congregations the child is completely immersed in water, although, more commonly, his forehead alone is gently bathed with holy water in a font designed for the ceremony. For this he is cradled by the godparents, and the worshippers reavow their own faith while welcoming the child into the fold. The specifics can vary from church to church and denomination to denomination, and the officiating clergy can instruct the participants beforehand.

Godparents

Unlike guardians, godparents are not financially or legally responsible for the children they honor. Yet being a godparent is an important responsibility. Its purpose is to extend the influence of the immediate family and offer the child moral guidance.

Determining who the godparents shall be should be done before the birth of the child, and the delicate choice should be made from among close friends or family. The Catholic church requires that only Catholics serve as godparents.

No compensation is given godparents; the honor alone is sufficient. Godparents should, however, give a commemorative gift to the child, such as a name-tag bracelet or (for Catholics) a saint's medal.

Forms of Address for Children

Males under twelve are usually referred to on formal occasions as "Master" (as in "Master John Jones"). When they turn twenty-one, they may be called "Mr." In between, just use their full name. It's too precious to call a teenage boy "Mr." Modern custom indicates that females are formally referred to as "Miss" until the age of sixteen, after which they may be called "Ms."

DRESS AND DONATIONS

On occasion, B'rith and baptism ceremonies can be held in the home. Receptions following them may be held at home, in a restaurant, or in a facility in the church or synagogue. Dress is the same as for a regular religious service. Gifts are not generally exchanged, although an honorarium ($50 to $100 or as negotiated) may be extended to the officiant. If a circumcision is performed by a medical doctor, a professional fee should be expected through normal billing channels.

NURSING

If the nursing mother cannot arrange to be alone at feeding time, she might consider withdrawing into privacy, asking her visitors to leave, or nursing as discreetly as possible. Nursing in public places should be done discreetly as well.

DIAPERS AND OTHER BABY MESSES

Many airplanes, restaurants, department stores, and other public businesses now have defined areas (often in the ladies lavatory, but seldom in the men's lavatory) for changing diapers.

As the only thing worse than changing diapers is *not* changing them, asking the proprietor, "Excuse me, may we use your restroom?" should do the trick without embarrassment.

Sometimes there may be no specially designed area to change a soiled diaper, such as at a beach, park, outdoor concert, or fast-food restaurant. First, try asking someone in charge for permission to use the employees' washroom. If that fails, find a secluded area: behind a shade tree, in a corner of the room, surrounded by friends, on your lap (as opposed to the dining room table), or a similar shielded area. Try going through channels first, then use common sense.

If you're changing a disposable diaper, remember to discard it properly so as to leave no residue (including aroma).

Because nascent systems are only just finding a natural schedule, infants are apt to burp, bubble, sneeze, cough, drool, and spit up without warning. Don't call the exorcist; this is what babies do. Parents grow accustomed to having their clothing soiled by these little occurrences; some even tote along plastic bibs or towels. If a child makes a mess on somebody else's blouse, rug, or sofa, however, the parent may help clean it up. If there is staining or damage, the parent should offer to pay for the cleaning.

CHILDREN IN PUBLIC PLACES

Believe it or not, not everybody thinks that your child is holy. Some adults—for various reasons—prefer the company of adults or at the very least find children a nuisance. This is why society generally excludes children from such venues as business offices, theaters, fine restaurants, courtrooms, and other public areas, or at least insists that any child who is admitted to them must behave while there and be accompanied by an adult.

This is because children automatically dominate any room they enter. A group of adults can be having a perfectly mature conversation when a baby enters, and immediately the level of conversation plummets to the "goo goo" variety.

This is why society has devised the adage that "children should be seen and not heard" and etiquette demands that the parents of children enforce it. There are exceptions:

- In the child's home or when specifically invited to another's home
- At playgrounds, beaches, and family recreation areas
- At "family" restaurants or similar public gathering spots
- At public events specifically designated for children, such as the circus or matinees of G-rated

movies. Performances of R-rated films, into which a baby is carried by a parent who couldn't get a sitter, do not qualify.

One baby's giggle is another person's foghorn. Yet in a world whose population needs to get along, children must be allowed to be, well, kids, without infringing on the rights of others. Here's a short list of kiddie dos and don'ts:

- *Airplanes*. Children should keep quiet and in their seat as much as possible on airlines. A noisy child—and the parent who tolerates him—is an attack on the hundreds of other passengers who have no recourse other than to glare. If an adult made the commotion that some children make on flights, the air marshals would arrest him the instant the plane landed. Until the airlines specifically designate which seats a child will occupy (so as to allow others to sit elsewhere), the problem will persist. Parents can help by bringing along a favorite, silent toy to engage the child's attention.
- *Restaurants*. Unless the restaurant is known for having a family atmosphere, children should not be allowed into dining spots unless they are well behaved, and should be removed the instant they are not.
- *Theaters*. Any patrons, including children, who create a disturbance should be ejected (with a refund) if they talk, cry, or run up and down the aisles during movies, concerts, plays, ballets, or any other public performance other than a specifically designated kiddie matinee.
- *Places of worship*. It is important for a child to receive spiritual instruction, but not at the expense of others in the congregation. This is why a child must be at least six or seven before receiving communion or confirmation, or thirteen before being called to the Torah. A child who misbehaves during a religious ceremony (including weddings and funerals) should be removed by a parent and kept out of earshot of the rest of the worshippers.
- *School*. Nowhere does it say that a disruptive child must be allowed to remain in a classroom, day care center, playschool, or sandbox if he or she behaves in a manner that corrupts other children who may be present.
- *Other People's Kids*. Naturally, your child is perfect; it's always somebody else's kid who picks on people, shouts, and runs around like a Tasmanian devil. Children should be kept from playing with disruptive children. If you have prohibited your child from hanging around with a "bad influence," extol his own polite behavior and contrast it with that of the uncouth friend.

It is educative for children to have contact with adults, but such contact should be a positive experience for both parties. Setting limits and establishing accepted behavior go a long way toward allowing both sides to feel comfortable, with the parents serving as guides.

CHILD CARE ISSUES

Au Pairs and Nannies

In an age when both parents work, the old-fashioned convention of hiring a nanny or *au pair* has returned to American life. These positions are frequently (but not always) held by a woman, whose job is to care for the child. Often, moderate housework associated with caring for the child is also included.

A nanny is an employee, but not a maid. She may live in or live out and has established hours, which must be agreed on in advance of hiring. An *au pair* (pronounced "oh-pare") is usually a young woman who lives with the family, takes meals with them, and travels with the family in the same class of service (meaning if you fly first class, so does she). Au pairs generally attend school part-time and are only expected to work a certain number of hours per week.

Engaging a nanny or au pair is a major decision for parents. Fortunately, specialized employment agencies can make the task easier, although not foolproof. It is absolutely incumbent on the parents to check references and, if they are acceptable,

to observe the child together with the nanny or au pair for an indication of how they will get along.

A live-in nanny or au pair must be accorded privacy in his or her own room. The employer must knock before entering. She is called by her first name, although she should refer to her employers as "Mr." or "Mrs." unless otherwise permitted. Live-out nannies are customarily addressed by their last names unless they prefer otherwise. Remember that Mary Poppins was always called "Mary Poppins" regardless of who was speaking to her.

Remember to fill out the appropriate Social Security and tax forms and to report and pay withholding taxes from any home employee you may engage. You also should check whether your prospective employee is legally allowed to work in the United States prior to hiring—even if you never intend to run for political office.

Baby Sitters

For families who cannot afford or do not need a nanny or au pair, a baby sitter is hired for a number of hours at a time to watch the child, provide a presence in the house, and be prepared to summon help or parents if needed.

Historically, baby sitters have been neighborhood teenagers or older women known to the parents through the community. Depending on their age, baby sitters are addressed on a first-name basis, even by the child, who should be allowed to feel comfortable around them.

Handling Awkward Questions

Mystery writer Gregory Mcdonald (*Fletch*), citing his journalistic roots, once stated, "There are no wrong questions." Surely he was referring to reporters, not children. Why, television host Art Linkletter built his career by getting kids to "say the darnedest things." His technique was brilliant: he simply asked them to repeat what their parents had warned them not to tell anybody. This is how he extracted such gems (from eight-year-olds yet) as "Alimony is a disease you get from marriage" and "I'm expecting a baby."

Alas, children today are more precocious. They are apt to ask awkward questions, usually at the wrong time, and always in front of the wrong person. Examples include:

- Why is that man bald?
- Why is that woman in a wheelchair?
- Why does Uncle Morris smell bad?
- Why is her nose so big?
- Where do I come from?

The usual way of handling this (without stifling the child's curiosity) is to answer the question broadly and nonjudgmentally ("You come from Mommy and Daddy's love"). If the child persists, tell him evenly that you will explain later when you get home—and remember to do so because if you don't, the child invariably will. The general rule is to tell the child no more than he or she specifically asks.

As for assuaging the party whom the child may have offended, it occasionally works to offer, in an apologetic tone of voice, "I'm terribly sorry; he didn't mean anything by it." People will cut kids a lot of slack. On occasion the recipient of the child's scattershot inquisitiveness may answer the question herself or himself. This can result in a miraculous exchange, such as when a person in a wheelchair tells a youngster, in an honest and nonthreatening manner, why she cannot walk.

Intercoms and Monitors

What a wonderful invention! A wireless device that lets Mom or Dad work downstairs while listening to their sleeping child in the upstairs nursery.

Unfortunately, anybody with a CB tuner can also listen, not only to the baby but also to any personal conversations you have around her, including your credit card number if you happen to give it out on a telephone within earshot of the monitor's sensitive mike. Use with caution.

If you have guests while using your monitor, be aware that anything you say while out of earshot of your guests may be overheard by them.

MANNERS IN CHILDREN

It was once observed that when an adult acts as a child he is immature, but when a child acts as an adult he is a juvenile delinquent. Although children are the equal of adults in the cosmic equation, they are not equal in such everyday matters as manners. Children may not enter a private room without

CHILDREN AND DEVELOPMENT

It is easier to teach children good manners than to un-teach them bad ones.

Just as a boy's or girl's character is generally set by the time he or she reaches sixteen, so is his or her respect for good manners.

Children need to be taught "yes" as well as "no." After all, etiquette stands for as many things as it discourages. A child should be told "no" if he or she attempts something dangerous; wants to do something that you don't think he ought to do (such as go swimming after a big meal); attempts to hurt someone or destroy property; or says something wrong or hurtful.

Be consistent. A "no" today should not become a "yes" (or silence) tomorrow. Never change a "no" to a "yes" if the child begs, throws a tantrum, or sulks. He or she will learn to push your buttons if you do.

If you make a mistake, tell the child why. Encourage the child with "yes" when he does something that pleases you or others, when he shows respect, when he completes an activity you appreciate, or when he shows affection. A child who feels appreciated and secure will grow into an adult who upholds tradition and is dependable.

If you want a child to do something, let her pick from among two or three things, any of which you want her to do anyway. She will have made a choice, and you will have gotten her to cooperate.

The following words are from an old volume on etiquette:

It is not enough to give children the material things of life. There are some things that money cannot buy, and this thing we call "culture" is one of them. It is a part of the heavy responsibility of parents to lead the children in their charge into the paths of right thinking and right living and the task should be a joyous one. For every child born into the world has infinite possibilities and at its very worst the task is illuminated by the way of hope. Even the ugly duckling became a swan.[1]

[1] Eichler, Lillian, Book of Etiquette, New York: Nelson Doubleday, Inc., 1921.

knocking and being admitted; they may not interrupt conversations, except in a true emergency; they may not eat with their hands once they have mastered silverware; they may not shout or run wildly in a public place of business. In short, children must behave as adults when they are in an adult context.

Children Answering the Phone

Children should be taught to say, "Hello, Jones residence," and not to hang up until the conversation is over. They should be taught how to use the telephone in emergencies, such as dialing 9-1-1; how to give their name and address to authorities; and not to speak with callers whom they don't know or who do not identify themselves.

Other than that, the telephone is not a toy, and children should be discouraged from answering it while an adult is present or an answering machine is on.

The Children's Table

It is regarded as a badge of honor when a child is graduated from sitting at the children's table to the adults' table at family gatherings. Maturity, however, not chronology, should be the determining factor in such a move.

Children are not generally invited to formal meals. They are fed beforehand and left at home in the charge of a sitter or nanny. Children whose parents are hosting a formal dinner party will also be fed ahead of time (as customarily a late dinner is served) and put to bed, with the parents taking turns checking in on them as they sleep.

On informal occasions when a child accompanies his parents to a dinner table, he is seated (usually in a high chair) immediately beside the parent who will be responsible for feeding and cleaning him. A parent bringing a finicky eater to someone else's home for a meal should check the menu ahead of time and, if necessary, bring alternate food.

Playground Etiquette

A child's earliest meaningful interaction with peers is likely to be at the local playground, at first under parental supervision and later without it. Any child who behaves badly toward another child will soon be chastised either by his or her own parent, the parent of the other child, or the targeted child. A child who throws sand, hits, pushes another child off of the seesaw, or refuses to share toys will isolate himself from others.

Remember that preschool children sort out right from wrong only when they comprehend that some things win parental approval while others garner disapproval. Therefore, it is vitally important for a child not to be overdisciplined for minor infractions, yet still be firmly and *consistently* advised that hitting, sand throwing, and the like are inappropriate.

Bullies

You have to wonder whether trial lawyers and Hollywood agents were bullies when they were little or whether they acquired the skill. Or maybe the romantic wisdom is true after all: school bullies are just insecure wimps who use their prematurely large size to win the approval their puny brains will never achieve.

If a child is a bully, the parents will hear about it eventually, either from teachers or other parents or because the child will soon have no one to play with. Bullying behavior, although unfortunate in and of itself, usually is an indication that there is a greater problem, and the child or parents should be counseled professionally.

The issue of the child who is tormented by a bully is far more complex because it usually involves issues of self-image, personal safety, and even guilt. A child who is unwilling to confess his fear of a school bully may become distanced from his parents or suffer a crisis of trust. If the situation cannot be resolved through school mediation, it is no longer a matter of etiquette; police authorities may be summoned—and parents are frequently held legally liable for the actions of their delinquent children.

SCHOOL DAYS

From the time he or she begins going to school, the greatest influences on a child's upbringing are her friends, not her parents (remember what happened to Pinocchio). Parents must, therefore, prepare a child for the apparent contradiction of their values by peer encounters. Only a solid foundation in manners will keep a child on track from the age he enters kindergarten—even earlier if he attends nursery school or day care.

Two generations ago, schools were places where parents sent their children to prepare them to function within society. It was there that they learned mathematics, history, writing, and reading skills. They also developed the ability to think critically, express themselves in interactions with others, and codify the skills they would use in seeking jobs and maintaining good citizenship.

Nowadays some schools seem more like day care centers for adolescents. Grades in public school and universities have become inflated to the point where an "A" in the 1990s is worth what a "C" was worth in the 1950s; textbooks have been "dumbed down" or cut to fit the pattern of trendy values. Nowadays, the educational system seems more concerned with making kids "feel good about themselves" than teaching them how to write a functional memo.

It is against this background that young men and women today come of age and develop the manners that will help them survive. That is why it's best to establish acceptable habits when children are young.

Classroom Decorum

Talk about mixed signals: the class brown-nose who sits in the front row, raises her hand every time, and politely calls the teacher "Mr." or "Ms."—in other words, behaves flawlessly—is exactly the person the other kids in class want to beat to a pulp. On the other hand, a kid who defies authority may aggrandize himself with his friends but run afoul of the school authorities. What to do, what to do?

There remains the assumption that when the teacher enters the classroom, the real world enters, too. Students may grumble at the need to raise their hands before speaking, remove their hats, unplug their personal stereos, stow away chewing gum, or ask permission to go to the bathroom, but the convention is that the classroom is the place to learn, not to strut.

At least it is in polite society.

The teacher is referred to as "Mr.," "Mrs.," "Ms.," or "Dr." (as appropriate) by students, and the students are generally called by their first names by the teacher. This is not because the teacher doesn't respect the students, but because the teacher is a grown-up and the students are not. Teachers refer to each other as "Mr.," "Mrs.," "Ms.," or "Dr." in front of students, even if they call each other by first names in the teachers' lounge.

Lending or Borrowing Homework

It is both unethical and illegal for one person to lend homework to someone else or to borrow it. Even asking to do so provokes a moral dilemma. It also is wrong to cheat on tests, to submit a thesis written by someone else, or to accept credit for a term project completed by another. The fact that this must be said at all is a statement about modern ethics.

If asked to borrow homework, the student should politely, but firmly, decline with a simple, "I'd rather not. I worked very hard on it and I don't think it's right to let somebody else use it." If that doesn't dissuade the mooch, suggest that he get the teacher's permission first. This also preempts the subject of snitching. Where does it say that "just say no" only applies to sex and drugs?

Intentional Failing

Educators have noted a regrettable trend in the African-American community in which good students will intentionally fail courses or perform below their skill level in order not to appear "white" to their peers. In these instances, academic achievement is seen as synonymous with a desire to succeed in what is perceived as an overwhelmingly "white" world. Teachers are aware of this phenomenon and try to keep an eye on students of color whose grades plummet for no apparent reason other than a desire to belong.

"Just Say 'No.'"

Although it embodies the essence of politeness, "Just say 'no'" reflects the fallacy that merely declining to do something is enough to rebuff its temptation. The frequent rejoinder to "Just say no" is likely to be, "Oh, come on, you know you really want to."

The best response to "Oh, come on, you know you really want to" is a better phrase, something popularized by the feminist movement: "What part of 'no' don't you understand?"

Parent–Teacher Conferences

There was a time when parents actually attended parent-teacher conferences; that was before both parents had to work and conferences turned into scheduling nightmares. When they occur today, the likelihood is that the parent will arrive—if at all—already in a confrontational frame of mind. At least, that's what teachers are reporting.

Unless they also are friends, teachers address parents as "Mr.," "Mrs.," or "Ms.," just as the parents should address them. If there is a professional title, such as "Doctor," "Reverend," "Sister," or "Father," (the latter two for the teacher, obviously), it should also be used.

School Colors

A generation ago, "school colors" meant the crepe paper or bunting that decorated the gym or festooned the stadium. Nowadays it is a fashion statement that can quite literally mean life or death.

The modern concept of school colors began with the red of the "Bloods" and the blue of the "Crips," the two Los Angeles–based gangs whose feral influence has spread internationally since the late eighties. A child wearing something as innocent as a dark blue t-shirt into a blood-red "hood" may face intimidation or violence.

As a result, many school systems have instituted dress codes that forbid gang colors, gang-favored insigne, "gangsta"-style loose-fitting clothes, jewelry, and sculpted haircuts displaying gang symbols. Some have even mandated uniforms. The practice has caused civil liberty concerns not dealt with by etiquette. But the situation forcefully raises the issue of how etiquette can address

behavior that is widely observed, yet nevertheless incorrect. Well, it doesn't. Etiquette survives improper behavior. It maintains its own standards in the hope that, once the bad behavior passes, propriety will once again be observed.

DISCIPLINE

Your Own Children

It is never pleasant to have to punish your children, let alone in a public setting, but sometimes it is unavoidable. Errant children should be taught that they have transgressed in a manner befitting the level of transgression and to an extent that it will not recur.

Doing so in front of others, however, is to place your child, yourself, and the others in potentially embarrassing positions. Child psychology aside, etiquette frowns on any display that lowers the dignity of another person.

Other Children

"We take care of our own" is a nice public service motto—provided, of course, that it is accurate. What do you do when somebody else's child misbehaves in your presence? Do you tattle on him or handle it yourself?

Legally, of course, it is a parent's sole right and responsibility to discipline his own child. But when a mother sees her little

Jason being pummeled by the nasty bully from across the street, a simple "Now cut that out" seems hideously deficient.

First, break up the fight and send the bully home, phoning ahead (if you know the parents' number) to let them know what you saw. Ask your child what happened. It doesn't matter who started it; parents will take their own child's side anyway. Tell the other parent that you will not allow the two children to play together if they cannot get along.

If, on the other hand, you try to break up the fight and the bully starts swinging at you, attempt to escape with your child; if he persists, do not attack, but use self-defense techniques. Then call the police.

Tips for Children: What to Do When Friends Misbehave

"Is that the way you behave in your own home, young man?" is hardly an endearing question, but one that parents will eventually want to ask one of their child's (especially a teenager's) buddies. Young people behave the way they were raised to behave, and, until they learn to observe and adopt appropriate behavior, they are apt to repeat it.

It is easier and more effective for your son or daughter to correct a friend's bad habits in your home ("My mom doesn't like us to drip on the carpet, okay?") than for you to attempt to do it. Nevertheless, if a child's friend doesn't respond to his peer's suggestion, the parent has every right to do so. It should be done as a discreet aside so as not to unduly embarrass the guest (e.g., "Bobby, please flush the toilet after you've finished using it"). It is proper to educate a young person in etiquette, provided one is not overbearing about it.

CHILD ABUSE

*W*hether child abuse itself is increasing or only how frequently it is reported, nothing is as chilling as the possibility that a defenseless young person is being mistreated. Doctors, social workers, day care specialists, and teachers are constantly on the lookout for signs of abuse, yet they are also too well aware of the catastrophic effect that false charges can have on innocent people's lives.

If you suspect that a child is being abused, there is no polite way to raise the question. Call your local police department's child abuse hotline and ask to speak with a counselor who can advise you of the safest, least invasive way of determining the truth. Or call the Childhelp USA IOF Foresters National Child Abuse Hotline at (800) 422-4453.

A parent should not embarrass a young person by scolding him in front of one of his friends. If scolding is required, it should be done privately. If another child's parent does not observe this rule, however, what should your child do while this is going on and afterward?

Your child might venture, "Are you okay?," but nothing more. If the disciplined youngster voices a tirade against parental authority in general and his own parents in particular, it is polite for your child to nod his or her head but not comment otherwise.

The one exception is if the discipline becomes abusive. If there is physical injury involved or prolonged verbal abuse in excess of what seems tolerable, let alone reasonable, action should be taken. A young person witnessing this level of punishment to a friend should discuss it immediately with his own parents who should provide counsel on a course of action.

CHILDREN'S APPEARANCE

Manners of Dress

Oh, how trends change! The same black garb, leather accessories, chains, studs, and body piercing that young people wear today would have, a generation ago, opened them to a wide variety of highly personal offers in Times Square.

Although such eccentric dress can be stylish to people young enough to wear it with élan, it looks downright perverse on anyone over the age of, say, thirty. In any event, it is never appropriate business attire unless one happens to be in the pop music or leather trades, and it certainly is not accepted on formal occasions.

Hair Length

Hair has become as much of a fashion statement as clothing, jewelry, and tattoos in terms not only of length (or shortness), but also of color.

Tradition holds that, as long as one's hair is kept clean and away from food or heavy machinery, it is improper for others to comment upon. The only self-censoring rule for clothing, haircuts, tattoos, and body piercing should be, "Am I going to look stupid ten years from now in snapshots?"

CHAPTER TWO

THE DATING GAME:

*Chastity
to Chaperones*

Poets have denuded whole forests filling books with musings about love; fortunately, etiquette is neither as ambitious nor as prolific. But it is more exact—not so much about what love means but about how men and women should behave while pursuing it.

MAKING INTRODUCTIONS

In the past, a lady and gentleman did not meet each other on formal social occasions without being introduced by a third party known to both. A gentleman might have initiated conversation with a lady (with a tip of his hat, of course), but would never have presumed to call upon her without at least presenting a letter of introduction to her and her parents. These days, a bartender who introduces one customer to another can be charged with pimping.

Present American society, fraught as it is with mixed signals and the threat of litigation, suggests that it is best to learn modern displays of "availability":

- A presence at a singles' bar or other well-established public meeting place
- Friendliness in a sober person
- "Have you got a light?"

> *Children know such a lot now.*
> —Sir James M. Barrie, <u>Peter Pan</u>

- "Is this seat taken?" (in an empty hall)
- "May I buy you a drink?" (This question usually comes from a man—ironically, a woman asking a man to buy her a drink may suggest another kind of commerce.)
- "Lovely weather we're having."
- In a business context: "Why don't we go to lunch and discuss the presentation for the Amberson account?" (Note the choice of a daytime, office-hours meeting in a public place, first to get actual work done then to break the ice.)

ASKING SOMEONE OUT

The time has thankfully passed when only the man was permitted to broach the subject of a date, but that doesn't make it any easier for a woman to ask a man out. A lot may depend on where they met each other: office versus school versus bar versus airplane versus party, and so forth. Only the intensity of the first meeting will determine how fiercely to pursue a second.

A woman desirous of going out with a man should be able to come right out and ask him. In reality, however, the process is more complicated. If she knows his interests, she might suggest that they both attend a previously scheduled public event (concert, lecture, nature walk, etc.). This falls somewhere between a "date" and "entertainment." Should he accept her invitation, they will then work out the logistics: who calls for whom, who buys the tickets, and so on.

Male to Female

In general, society permits a man to ask after a woman's social availability, subject entirely to her interest, and affording her the room to decline with no further obligation.

Female to Male

The women's movement liberated more than women; men, too, have been freed of social stigma when a woman asks them for a date. As when a man approaches a woman, the man asked out by a woman should respond with a clear yes or no.

Male to Male

The prevalence of homophobia in American society—and the bigotry associated with it—has made it more convenient for a man to ask another man out if they both meet under circumstances that are clearly gay-themed, such as a gay bar, gay pride event, or mutual gay friend's house. Otherwise, sexual preference is nobody's business.

If it turns out that the man being asked out is not gay, a simple, "No thank you, I'm straight" should suffice. There is apt to be some embarrassment, not to mention the possibility of a challenge ("What's the matter, do I look gay or something?").

Whatever either party's decision or persuasion, politeness must be the rule.

Female to Female

As with gay men, it is helpful to assume that one's presence in a lesbian bar is a pretty safe indication of sexual orientation or at least an intelligent ability to deal with approaches. The same rules apply for woman to woman advances as for man to man advances, except that the music is more apt to be k.d. lang than Judy Garland.

What to Ask

No matter who does the asking, a specific question containing enough information to permit a considered answer is the only proper invitation for a date. "Would you like to go to a movie on Saturday night?" or "How about dinner tomorrow night if you're free?" are preferable to "What are you doing Saturday night?" or "Maybe I'll call you tomorrow night."

What to Respond

The same consideration is required when accepting or declining a date. If you have already committed yourself to a date with one person, you must not cancel it to go out with someone else. Even hedging is the same as saying no and can verge on insult.

For example, the best response is, "No, thank you, I already have plans." On the other hand, answering, "I'm waiting to hear back from my Cousin Shirley who is due in town and may want to stay with me" (even if true) is the same as saying, "I'll take a chance that somebody better than you asks me out."

When the invitation is welcome, but the timing is not, one may politely decline with, "I'm afraid I'm busy, but I would love to see you another time." If a date is out of the question now and forever, a pleasant but firm, "No, thank you, I am not available" will do the trick, although it may have to be repeated on one or two subsequent occasions until the other person gets the idea.

Letting the Other Person Know That You Want to Be Asked Out

When people routinely carried handkerchiefs, a sure signal that a lady was interested in a gentleman was that she dropped hers near him; if he picked it up and returned it to her, the door was open for introductions.

But people don't use hankies so much any more, and how can a man retrieve a tissue with a straight face? Since nobody wants to be shot down asking for a date, how does one semi-ask a non-question?

First, the presumption must be that the two of you know each other at least well enough to support the possibility of a deeper friendship. Then cover one base by checking for an engagement or a wedding ring. If that's no help, ask a mutual friend whether the object of your affection is available (it is not incumbent on the mutual friend to act as go-between).

The only polite tactic is to be observant. Does the other person know you're alive? Do you meet regularly at the water cooler or speak in the elevator? Has this person acted flirtatious or struck up a conversation with you? Are you coming from equal positions of influence (not, for instance, a male supermarket customer asking out a female register clerk or—even more odious—a male boss hitting on a female employee).

Once discourse is established, the direct question is always the best one: "May I ask you out?," followed by particulars.

Married Men and Women

Ann Landers's advice remains the best, as well as the most cynical: if a husband or wife cheats on his or her spouse in order to be with you, he or she is capable of doing so again. It is not only improper legally and morally to become involved extramaritally, but also extremely intricate socially (as in: "Let me introduce you to my new girlfriend—uh, Mrs. Smith").

Blind Dates

When a mutual friend (or a newspaper ad) brings together two people who would not otherwise ask each other out, it's called a blind date. It's also a lighted fuse that disregards all the social conventions, including the old-fashioned concept of matchmaking, because matchmakers paired people for a living, not for sport. Other than the basic courtesies extended between individuals, blind dates are a breach of etiquette.

THE FIRST DATE

When two people agree to go out on a first date, correctness dictates that the male arrive at the female's residence at the agreed-upon time to "collect" her. (In cases where a woman has any doubts about the character of her date, she may elect to meet him in a public place for safety's sake. He should always offer to pick her up, however.) If he has a car, he should park as close as possible; if he hires a taxi, the driver should wait in front while the man rings the bell; if the man and woman must take public transportation, the man should arrive at the woman's residence and they shoud then leave together for the bus or subway stop. It is the man's responsibility to return the woman safely home at the agreed-upon hour.

If the woman is living at home with one or more parent, the man should introduce himself to them before leaving with the woman. In practice, there is usually a time lapse between these two events: while he is in the living room uncomfortably getting the once-over from Mom and Dad (plus siblings), the daughter is taking one last moment in her bedroom making herself presentable.

If the woman maintains her own residence or is living with roommates, the man should still call for her there and be invited inside (roommates can be even more brutal in their appraisal of his worth).

In no event should a first date involve a man pulling into the driveway and honking the car horn for the woman. Such behavior is cheap and insulting—not to mention noisy—on subsequent dates, too. It also is improper for two young people to arrange to meet secretly for their first date.

Kissing

In *Annie Hall,* Woody Allen had a clever way of getting past the issue of kissing Diane Keaton on the first date:

> "Gimme a kiss . . . because we're just gonna go home later, right, and, there's gonna be all that tension: you know, we never kissed before, and I'll never know when to make the right move or anything. So we'll kiss now, we'll get it over with, and we'll go eat."

Historically, women who kissed on the first date were considered "easy." In practice today, the question of whether to kiss remains the man's to ask, the woman's to answer, and will be settled well before the man returns the woman home by how enjoyable the evening has been up until then. There is no longer any stigma attached to people who kiss on the first date—as long as they both want to.

Inviting Your Date Inside

"Saying goodnight" is a metaphor for what the lady told the gentleman after he escorted her safely home after a date. She did not invite him into her home on their first date, on subsequent dates if nobody else was home, or if doing so would encourage him to pursue an intimacy she did not want.

THE TEN COMMANDMENTS OF DATING

1. *Thou shalt keep a date once you have agreed to go out with somebody, even if someone "better" subsequently asks you out.*

2. *The male shall call for the female at her family's home and meet her parents, unless both of you are on your own, in which case you can make other meeting arrangements.*

3. *Thou shalt agree beforehand who will pay (or share) the restaurant tab, the concert tickets, and so forth.*

4. *Thou shalt not expect sexual favors in proportion to the amount of money spent during the date. The two are separate issues.*

5. *Thou shalt not show disrespect—verbal, physical, or metaphysical—toward your partner at any time.*

6. *Thou shalt end the date at the previously agreed-upon time unless thou hast made other arrangements with any third parties who may be concerned.*

7. *Thou shalt kiss on the first date only if both parties want to.*

8. *One party shall not touch or otherwise invade the person of the other party without specific permission, and then must be prepared to stop if that permission is withdrawn. This is easier said than done, and is most accurately achieved in the absence of intoxicating substances.*

9. *Thou shalt deliver, either verbally or in writing, a heartfelt "thank you" following the successful completion of a date and, if another date is desired, may say so at that time.*

10. *The first party shall not discuss the specifics of the aforementioned date with any third party without the permission of the second party.*

Either adult may suggest coming in for a post-date coffee or nightcap, but at the woman's house it is her prerogative to ask. If the man is the one who asks, the woman is under no obligation to accede—to coffee, borrowing the bathroom, or anything else. If the woman announces that she prefers to be left alone to rest for work tomorrow, the man is expected to go home.

THE SECOND DATE

If either party desires a second date, the best time to bring up the subject is at the end of the first one. "Let's get together next week" is a convenient indication of interest; a "Sorry, I'm busy next week" is a clear example of lack of it. If the woman does not want the man to follow her inside but does want to see him again, she should say, "Not tonight," or "I have work tomorrow, but I would like to see you again. Why don't we speak on Monday and arrange something?"

THANK-YOUS

Either the woman or the man—preferably both—is expected to telephone or write the other with thanks for a pleasant date as quickly as possible following the occasion. The man also may send flowers or candy to amplify his thanks.

Sending a more personal gift (apparel, perfume, jewelry, etc.) would be inappropriate so early in a relationship.

WHO PAYS?

The formula is not rigid, but it is consistent: the man pays on the first assignation no matter who suggested it. From that point onward, the general rule is that the person who does the inviting also does the paying. The notable exception is for dating couples on a limited budget, in which instance the

man and woman may agree ahead of time who will pick up what charges. The woman, for instance, may spring for the concert tickets while the man pays for dinner.

Should an ongoing relationship develop, the two can share the bills. There is a subtle code that can signal the difference: if one partner says, "Let's go out," it means splitting the tab. If one of them asks, "May I take you out?," it means that he or she intends to pay. (Please note that the expression *Dutch treat*, meaning "each pays his own way," is considered offensive to people of Dutch ancestry.)

SEX

Sex is the first reason human beings become involved with each other and the last reason they admit to for doing so. It stands to reason, then, that a great deal of etiquette is devoted to expressing desire for sex in ways that are acceptable in public.

For two people to have sex with each other, both of them must be willing to do so. "Willing" means a sober, informed, participatory, and voluntary decision. The alternative is not a matter for etiquette, but for the police.

Any person who engages in sexual intercourse without using a condom might as well chew on razor blades. AIDS and other sexually transmitted diseases (STDs) are passed between people by the exchange of bodily fluids, primarily blood, semen, and vaginal discharge, either through sexual contact or by sharing needles (hypodermic or tattoo—any invasive device that is not properly sterilized between uses).

Before engaging in any sexual activity that may expose one person to the fluids of another, it is important to discuss whether the risk of HIV or another STD exists, and what you are *both* going to do about it. This almost always means raising the subject of condoms.

There is nothing ill-mannered about discussing AIDS or using condoms, and here's why: if you are intimate enough to talk about having sex, you are intimate enough to talk about condoms.

PUBLIC DISPLAYS OF AFFECTION

The following rules apply:

- *Hugging.* Women and men (any combination) may briefly hug each other when greeting or parting.
- *Two-cheek kissing.* Women and men (any combination) may also "smack air" (casually kiss on both cheeks) when greeting in public, but it seems less affected if they are European.
- *Casual kissing.* A simple, quick kiss on the cheek or mouth is a sweet and accepted way for two people (male/female and female/female but not male/male) to greet each other if they are at least slightly more than friends. Long, wet, open-mouth kisses involving tongues are never appropriate in public.

- *Kissing the hand.* A gentleman bends down and kisses the air above a lady's hand while holding it lightly in his own. This invariably looks pretentious among Americans and should be avoided unless one is in the theater or trying to be British.
- *Hand-holding.* Two people holding each other's hands, if it doesn't prevent getting past street signs or turnstiles, is an accepted, if awkward, demonstration of a relationship. This is equally true for homosexual and heterosexual couples.
- *Kissing strangers.* Television game shows notwithstanding, it is never appropriate for two casual acquaintances to do any more than shake hands.
- *Kissing relatives.* A quick peck is fine, but anything more passionate is taboo. This includes uncles who think it is funny to give whisker burns to nieces, or aunts who pinch the cheeks of nephews. Such displays are not affection, they are bordering on child abuse.
- *Kissing and telling.* This refers to one party in a relationship who discusses intimate details of that relationship with a third party. It is vulgar and says more about the person doing the talking than the one being talked about.
- *Parents kissing children in front of other children.* Starting at about age ten, a child regards parental tenderness as embarrassment, not affection.

CHIVALRIC CODES

During the Middle Ages, English knights obeyed a strict code of chivalry. That code placed well-born women on a pedestal and decreed that titled warriors accord them not only respect but also an allegiance that approached fealty. A knight would do battle for the honor of his chosen lady (who could even be married to someone else!), and no eyebrow was ever raised to question the purity of his devotion.

From these chivalric codes have come our modern notion of chivalry, further illustrating the maxim that "a lady is a woman around whom a man behaves as a gentleman":

- A gentleman may hold a door open for a lady to pass through first, although this has ceased to be a hard-and-fast rule. Practically speaking, the first person to arrive at a door should hold it open for the next, and that person should smile or say "Thank you" at the gesture.
- A gentleman allows a lady to enter and exit the elevator first and holds the door to prevent it from closing on her. In a crowded elevator, those at the front may step onto the landing to permit ladies at the back to exit.
- The gentleman walks ahead of a lady coming downstairs.

- A gentleman walks on the curb side of the sidewalk with the lady on the building side to prevent her from being splashed by passing cars.
- The taller of two people sharing an umbrella should hold it.
- A gentleman removes his hat in the presence of a lady unless religious observance specifies he keep it on. Military men in uniform should remove their hats.
- Men's hats are not worn indoors (malls, lobbies, and public transportation are considered "outdoors"), unless religious observance specifies they keep them on. Baseball caps are considered men's haberdashery, even when worn by women, and should likewise be removed indoors.

MORE CHIVALRIC CODES

- A firm handshake is believed to be a Native American symbol of peace that derives from the idea that a man doing it is unarmed. Men remove their gloves when shaking hands; women need not. If shaking hands with someone who has a prosthetic hand, one may grasp the hand itself (if articulated), the hook, or the wrist (if the hand is missing). Some people without a right hand prefer to offer their left hand, sometimes inverting it to permit it to be held more easily. People who are fully able to shake hands but for some reason refuse to do so are considered rude.

- Gentlemen rise when a lady enters or leaves the room or when she leaves or returns to the table (ladies will invariably say, "Oh, don't get up," but not before the gentleman extends the courtesy). The only exceptions are if the man is in a wheelchair or is seated in a booth from which it is physically difficult to stand.

- A gentleman follows the lady to their table in the restaurant (because the maitre d' precedes her) and steadies her chair as she sits (although the maitre d' will likely do so).

- In movie (or other) theaters or sports events, the man allows the woman to walk ahead of him into the row; he sits on the aisle. If two or more couples attend together, the women sit between the men.

- When driving a car, a gentleman unlocks the passenger door from the outside, helps the lady to her seat, then closes the door before opening his own. He also gets out first on arrival to help her from the car. (Note: according to dating lore, if the woman reaches over and unlocks the man's door before he gets to it, she likes him.) If the woman drives the car, the man still helps her in before taking his passenger seat.

- A gentleman yields his seat to a lady on public transportation, and young persons of any gender yield their seats to older ones of either gender. That doesn't mean that the other person must accept it; a courteous, "No, thank you, I'd rather stand" or "Thanks, my stop is coming up soon" conveys appreciation without obligation. It is also polite to offer one's seat to a pregnant woman or someone trying to cope with small children. Allowing a dating couple to sit together is also a gracious gesture.

- *Necking.* A couple may kiss and hold each other in seclusion if both of them want to, but doing so in a public place (movies, bus, Times Square) is considered rude and distracting.
- *Office affection.* It is never proper to force affection on someone in an office setting, even at Christmas parties under the mistletoe.
- *Padiddle.* When a dating couple is driving at night and an oncoming car has one headlight missing, whoever says "padiddle" first gets to kiss the other. In Canada this is known as "One-Eyed Jack."

CONVENTIONS AND CAVEATS

Parietals

Some colleges and boarding schools act "in loco parentis"—"in the place of parents"—by restricting the rights of the students dwelling under their purview. When these restrictions are administered by a college, they are called parietals. In theory, colleges try to control the rights of their resident students so that they will not be held legally accountable by the students' real parents for failing to do so. Parietal rules generally apply to university-owned housing and may curtail contact between the sexes, establish curfews, and provide punishment if the rules are broken.

Parietals have been almost entirely eliminated in these days of coeducational resi-dences and enlightened enrollment. Nevertheless, as incidents of assault and date rape (or perhaps just their reporting) increase, it is a term with which students might do well to become reacquainted.

Chaperons

A chaperon is an adult who supervises a social gathering of young people. To the young people, therefore, a chaperon is a killjoy; to the parents of the young people, however, a chaperon is a welcome proxy.

In point of fact, chaperons can be a mother and father who host their teenager's party at home. They need not stand guard with a ruler to make sure that all couples dance a foot apart, but they should be in the house somewhere in case of emergency.

When the boy and girl are underage, a chaperon is usually involved in driving them to and from the movies or a party at some-body else's house. Teenagers owe it to their chaperon not to be late or rowdy; chaperons owe it to their teenage charges to extend them trust and not to bring up, in the presence of a date, how they used to wet the bed when they were little.

Age of Consent

In some states (chiefly those with large rural populations) the age of consent for sexual relations between a man and woman may be under sixteen. In most areas, how-ever, it is seventeen.

Furthermore, even if both parties are under seventeen, the age of consent usually specifies no more than a four-year age difference between them. If this is flouted, it is a matter for the sheriff, not etiquette.

Coming Out

When a homosexual man or woman publicly declares his or her sexual orientation, it is called "coming out." The term derives from the phrase "coming out of the closet," the "closet" being slang for engaging in furtive same-sex activities. It has no connection with a debutante's presentation to society (see Chapter 3).

Although coming out may be curious and sometimes threatening to heterosexuals, it is a profound and emotional decision for the gay or lesbian person going through it. Any discussion of sex is, strictly speaking, inappropriate except among intimate friends, but the public declaration of coming out commands respect and compassion not only by fellow gays but also by straights. It also demands discretion and consideration from the person coming out, in that not everybody will be as fascinated with the subject as he or she is.

Only when a homosexual avows his or her homosexuality is it permissible to publicly refer to his or her sexual preference. The tactic of "outing" someone—that is, forcing a man or woman to attest to his or her homosexuality by making it a public issue—is highly controversial and of questionable legal wisdom, however important it may be to the gay equality movement.

Unless a gay man or lesbian has openly acknowledged his or her sexual preference, it is acceptable only to refer to his or her marital status as "single," "unmarried," or, in more elegant times, "a confirmed bachelor," if at all.

Companions

When age or incapacity dictate the need for someone to help a man or woman on a day-to-day basis, a companion—usually of the same sex and of a mature age—may be retained. In addition, a single man or woman may engage the temporary services of a companion or escort to accompany him or her on social or business occasions, in which instance the age of the escort and the employer may be similar.

A companion travels with his or her employer in the same class of service, takes the same meals, and must be accorded a reasonable amount of private, free time (agreed upon in advance). Because of the infirmity of many such employers, a companion may be under a great deal of stress.

Escorts, on the other hand, are a different matter. Frequently hired for their attractiveness and knowledge of the social graces, male escorts and female companions sometimes carry an expectation of providing sexual favors. In such instances, other terms for them are *gigolo*, *call girl*, and any number of others, some less flattering. The sexual orientation can vary. When a paid escort or companion accompanies a man or woman to a formal social event, the man or woman hiring the escort assumes all expenses and responsibilities.

CALLING CARD ETIQUETTE

One custom of yore that has, alas, been abandoned by everyone except Japanese businessmen is the calling card. Precise rules governed their use, which atrophied by the end of the 1960s (along with many other proprieties), except in diplomatic circles.

They grew from the pretelephone practice of people making social calls on one another between certain hours (4 to 6 P.M. in the city; 10:30 A.M. to 1 P.M. in the country) on specific "at home" days and from the general awareness that individuals had for another individual's privacy.

A simple white calling card (measuring $2\,^5/_8$" x $1\,^3/_8$" for men and $2\,^7/_8$" x $1\,^7/_8$" for ladies) bore the visitor's name in black ink and plain type. It was presented at the door to the butler or maid and was then carried in to the host (yes, on a silver platter), who would decide whether to admit the caller. It was not unusual for a lady, irritated with a gentleman caller, to have her servant dispatch him with a firm, "Miss Abigail is not at home for you today, sir."

Although calling cards always carried their bearer's names, they might also include a professional title or, in the case of military callers, one's rank. Mothers and daughters calling together would present double cards.

The possibility for confusion in some situations was reduced thus: a widow would use her late husband's name (Mrs. John Smedley) until her eldest son was married and carried the name of the deceased father (John Smedley Jr.), at which time the widow, if she had not remarried, would revert to using her own Christian name (Mrs. Charlotte Russe Smedley).

Calls were made for other reasons than social. A visitor wishing to acknowledge a family in mourning might merely leave his card on the tray or half-table (or with the servant) and depart without disturbing the grieving family inside. New neighbors might also wish to announce their presence without staying. Salesmen would leave their business cards (name plus line of work) without expecting admittance. Wives might also leave their husband's cards in addition to their own when making a first social call.

MORE CALLING CARD ETIQUETTE

A gentleman could leave his card for a lady, but if she was unmarried, he would leave a second card for her mother (who would be present if her daughter was receiving callers) and a third card for her father (who presumably would be away at work). A lady would never leave her card for a gentleman. She might, however, leave it for the gentleman's mother if she was in residence.

If a card was left for only one member of a household, that member's name was written on the top of the card in pencil. In some quarters, it was fashionable to bend one corner of a calling card if the purpose of the visit was business, although in most quarters the personal card and the business card were never used at cross-purposes.

Before an extended trip, a lady or gentleman might leave a card with "P.P.C." written on the corner. <u>Pour prendre congé</u> means "to take leave" and indicates a desire to see friends prior to departure. While someone was abroad, his or her card may have borne a temporary address, which explains the calling card Truman Capote specified for his bewitching heroine:

> Holly Golightly
> Travelling

One-sided Friendship

Nothing is more tragic than the person whose affection for another is not reciprocated. Etiquette demands that such people accede to their inamorata's wishes by withdrawing. It also insists that the uninterested party be definitive, yet polite, in stating that he or she is not interested in a relationship.

Spousal Abuse

It is never acceptable for one party in a relationship to assault, beat, verbally accost, or otherwise abuse the other. This is not a matter of etiquette—it is a question of human decency and, ultimately, the law.

If you ever find yourself at either end of such a situation, walk away and defuse it. There are shelters for abused women and there is counseling for abusive men, and even a growing (if begrudging) recognition that women can abuse men as well.

The first rule is also the truest: a person who abuses once will likely do it again, and no amount of apologizing, kowtowing, accommodating, or affection will change anything. Get out now.

CHAPTER THREE

BEHAVING AT HOME:

Family, Friends, and Formalities

The British monarchy and Hollywood aside, most families don't air their dirty linen in public. That doesn't mean that people related by blood don't try to spill it from time to time, only that families have ways of containing divisive issues. By contrast, when friends or business rivals feud with each other, the rift is frequently permanent. But somehow families stick together.

Now, that doesn't mean that every home is filled with cuddly-sweet Waltons, Bradys, or Cleavers. It means only that warring kin tend to cut each other some slack before they cut each other physically. Is it love, DNA, or a clearly defined set of traditions that preserves family unity? Perhaps the maxim holds true that "Your friends like you *because* of yourself while your family likes you *in spite* of yourself." Maybe the rituals of weddings, anniversaries, birthdays, holidays, reunions, and other occasions establish codes of behavior that carry over into family relationships.

It's worth noting that good manners begin in the family. However much time we may spend away from home, the family remains not only a source of knowledge and support, but frequently of judgement:

- "Where on earth did you pick up that awful word?"

> *Be it ever so humble,*
> *there's no place like home*
> —*John Howard Payne*

- "If all of your friends jumped off the edge of a cliff, would you jump off, too?"
- "If all the other kids are dyeing their hair that color to look different, then won't they all end up looking alike?"
- "Are you leaving the house dressed like *that*?"
- "I don't care what the other parents let their children do. *My* child doesn't go out until the homework is finished."
- "You may criticize me now, but in later years you'll see that I was right."

And so forth. On the other hand, friends can also exert influence in ways they believe to be in one's best interests (but rarely are):

- "Oh, come on, just one more kamikaze before last call."
- "I know for a fact she wants you to ask her out. She told her best friend who knows my sister who told me to tell you."
- "Never mind the parking signs; they never tow around here."
- "If I were you, I'd give that cop a piece of my mind."

And, finally, here is the killer question that lights the fuse in all relationships: "Does this dress make me look fat?"

This chapter contains a guide for what to do if you're a stranger in a strange land and also when things get a little too familiar. It's about blood being thicker than water and nobody being thicker than a bore.

KIDS PARTY ON!

Children's Birthday Parties

As a practical matter, the number of children at a child's birthday party should not exceed the child's age in years.

Invitations should be sent to the very young guests directly, or in care of their parents, who should phone the hosting parent to accept or decline. At that time the logistics of travel, gift giving, dress, and food may be discussed at "the executive level."

All children under five should be accompanied by a parent. It is a wise host parent who provides for the needs of the other parents as well as the child invitees. Food should be simple and broad-based: pizza, barbecue, chips, cake, ice cream, and soft drinks are always fashionable, although too much sugar can sometimes cause behavior problems.

It has become the social fashion for parents to try to outdo each other devising creative parties for children. From year to year it could be a clown (along with balloon animals), a magician, backyard carnival rides, pony rides, go-carts, squirtgun battles, or environmentally friendly restaurants.

If old enough to understand, a guest child should shop with his parent for the appropriate gift to give to the birthday boy or girl. This may call for some diplomacy on the part of the buying parent, for invariably the child will want to give the kind of gift he would like to receive. An estimate of $2 to $3 per year of age of the birthday child is a fair spending goal.

Kids love opening presents and should do so in front of their friends, who will take pride in noting how their choice was received. The parent may remind the recipient ahead of time to be excited and to thank each giver at the time of the party; a verbal thank-you is adequate unless a guest who could not attend has sent something over in his absence.

A child's party should run no more than three hours. It should be a morning affair for preschoolers (who usually nap in the afternoon), but youngsters of school age can enjoy an afternoon celebration.

As a final note, remember to explain to a very young child that the present is for the friend having the birthday, and must be given up!

Sweet Sixteen Parties

It seems that only girls have Sweet Sixteen parties, a coveted event that marks their passage into adulthood—or at least young ladyhood. Thrown by a girl's parents or close aunt, usually at home, they offer a last chance to be, well, naive.

Sweet Sixteen parties can be all-girl, although boys can be invited with proper chaperons. Invitations are sent in advance.

In fact, this may be the first formal occasion to which the girl herself is invited directly, and not through her mother.

Dress is at the option of the girl-of-honor and should be specified on the invitation. Because it's also a birthday party, it is appropriate to expect gifts. Although a written thank-you note afterward is always appreciated, a verbal thank-you may suffice if the presenter is in the room at the time her gift is opened.

Teenagers' Birthday Parties

Teenagers love to party casually, but if they are at an awkward age (say, between thirteen and sixteen) they may require a special "occasion" to get together and dress up. A birthday party is as good an occasion for this as any other.

With parents as hosts, a boy or girl will probably enjoy inviting friends over to the house for a birthday party. If that seems like too much of a fuss, combining several friends' nearby birthdays into a group party is a good way to spread the attention.

Invitations may be written but are often phoned, and accepted the same way. It is bad manners to fail to show up as promised, but somehow teenagers run into obstacles at the worst times (grounded, can't get the car, got a zit, etc.). Gift giving should be expected unless "no gifts" is stressed at the time of the invitation.

Teen parties provide the opportunity to build new friendships and try new things. For those reasons, it behooves the celebrant's parent or parents to be on hand to chaperon as well as to arrange a ride for anyone whose transportation (read: parent) may become unavailable as the evening wears on.

Customary refreshments include soft drinks, chips, pizza, and other informal finger foods. Formal sit-down parties for teenagers are rare (a notable exception is society debuts) and would be considered stuffy. Unless there is money to provide a live band, recorded music is the norm; just make sure a well-informed member of the peer group chooses it.

Gift-giving can be awkward at teen birthday parties, especially where the celebrant is beyond the toy stage, doesn't want anything as utilitarian as clothing, and a new car is out of the question. In such cases CDs are always a safe bet, as are gift certificates, video games, books, and sports items.

Parties are where young adults learn social interaction, but can also be a forum where they try to push the limits. This is where chaperons can set limits and provide a safety valve. At no time should the hosting adult provide or condone the use of intoxicating substances, or permit friendships to go beyond the talking stage.

Pajama Parties

Getting into 'jammies . . . sharing toenail polish . . . drinking hot cocoa . . . making s'mores in the microwave . . . playing old Moody Blues records . . . reading out loud from teen magazines . . . phoning for pizza 'cause the delivery boy has a nice butt . . . WHOA! Girls' pajama parties ain't what they used to be!

Neither are guys' sleepovers—sometimes called "camping out parties" because they involve sleeping bags, pitched tents, ghost stories, and, nowadays, even portable TVs and video games.

But the ritual of the sleepover itself continues: kids between two and ten years of age camp out in the living room or backyard on a non-school night and pretend to be asleep while the parental figures toss and turn in the upstairs bedroom worrying about them.

Sleepovers are like any party, only more so. The parents of the hostess or host must be in residence and should assure the guests parents that they will remain present. They maintain a list of emergency numbers "just in case."

Sleepovers should be same-sex only, and siblings of the opposite sex should be discouraged from invading.

Stock up on cocoa, sodas, chips, and frozen pizzas—and then *trust your child.* Finally, plan on not getting into the bathroom until Memorial Day.

Proms

A high point of a teenager's high school social life is the senior prom (some schools also hold a junior prom, which is more like a class dance than the more formal senior prom). Attending the prom is often a cherished moment in a school career—frequently more so than graduation.

The school itself hosts the prom through a "prom committee" comprised of student leaders and faculty sponsors. The location can vary—school gymnasium, field house, hotel, or country club—but the ritual does not.

Once a prom is announced, tension can be palpable. The boy generally invites the girl to be his date for the prom, but this, too, has begun to shift. Even students who are "going steady" do not assume that they will automatically accompany each other to the prom, and until "the question" is popped there may be coy speculation among classmates.

Whoever does the inviting pays for the tickets, but the boy is expected to provide transportation—his own car or Dad's. Some parents pool resources to rent a limousine and driver for their kids, pragmatically realizing that illicit drinking may occur. The young man also will buy his date a corsage—which she is obliged to wear no matter how ugly it is. If the flowers clash with her dress, she can always pin it to her handbag or clip it around her wrist. She may buy him a boutonniere.

Dress is usually formal or semiformal (see Chapter 11) and always announced in advance. The strict days of the solid black tux and white dinner jacket have long passed and boys now wear any kind of fabric imaginable just as long as it is at least vaguely tuxedo-shaped.

Once the prom, which is supervised by faculty chaperons, is over, students usually adjourn to private "after prom" parties. Parents should expect to wait up for their children. The same rules of dating for regular occasions apply to proms. If a girl from one school invites a boy from another school to her prom, she is expected to pay for his ticket.

Two-School Proms

Two or more small schools in adjacent communities may hold combined proms to allow their students the excitement of a larger crowd. In such cases, even if the boy and girl come from different schools, the standard etiquette of proms applies.

Debuts

In many communities the tradition of "coming out"—in which an eighteen-year-old girl makes her social debut—has been preserved and, in fact, launches the annual social season. Becoming a debutante is an important introduction to polite society and involves a strictly observed set of rules. (Another form of "coming out"—the proclamation of one's homosexuality—is discussed in Chapter 2.)

Debutante balls reflect the financial ability of the deb's family, ranging from a large, privately funded affair to a group debut, called a cotillion, held en masse for a number of eighteen-year-olds from the same social set. These larger assemblies, at which attendance is by invitation or ticket sales to benefit a charity, feature live music and dancing. Because they are often held after a private dinner, food is not usually served. Young men of a similar social class or a nearby military college may be invited, not by the debuting girls but by the organizing committee who has screened the names ahead of time and deems them acceptable.

At charity cotillions, the girl (or her family) is expected to purchase the ticket for the boy as well as the other guests they invite. In all cases a formal invitation is extended and responded to promptly.

There is no similar debut for young men.

An invitation to the deb and her family might read:

> The Port Hampton Cotillion Commitee invites
> Mr. and Mrs. Donald C. Claypool
> to present
> *Miss Margaret Claypool*
> at the Cotillion
> on Friday, the 10th of October
> at ten o'clock
> Port Hampton Yacht Club

This invitation is generally a formality since debutantes and their families already know who they are. A handwritten reply is nevertheless expected.

When the Port Hampton Cotillion Commitee invites the social set at large to the cotillion it may be done with the following invitation sent four to six weeks in advance of the event. Since such balls are usually charity events, a list of patrons, debutantes, and beneficiaries will be enclosed along with a note stating how much the tickets cost. A self-stamped acceptance envelope is included. Because this is a paid event, it is only necessary to respond (by sending the check) if you plan to attend.

*The Port Hampton Cotillion Commitee
requests the pleasure of your company
at a Ball
to be held at the Grand Hampton Room
on Friday, the 10th of October
at ten o'clock
Port Hampton Yacht Club*

*Single ticket: $50
Couple: $100*

Black tie

ADULT FESTIVITIES

The Big Four-O

Years ago the caution was, "Never trust anybody over thirty." Now that baby boomers are getting older, the battle cry has become "Never trust anybody *under* thirty." Somewhere in the middle of that skirmish is the fortieth birthday and, with it, the fortieth birthday party.

Self-help babble aside, you're as old as younger people make you feel. Hitting "the big four-o" can be a devastating event for some people, and a party calling attention to it can be worse. Before throwing a fortieth birthday party for a friend, make sure he or she wants one.

The rest is just like any other adult party, except that one should expect a lot of cards saying, "You're so old that . . ." and joke gifts of Geritol®, Depends®,

Grecian Formula™, and prune juice. However, many people consider age references to be in poor taste. This is always a judgement call based upon the people involved. Even though the birthday recipient might smile and accept such a card politely, he or she can still feel insulted. In general, cards that call attention to a person's age—or are otherwise vulgar or cruel—demean the giver as well as the getter. In the end, the nicest card is the one you write yourself, not just sign.

Surprise Parties

By definition, surprise parties involve deception and betrayal by all of one's close friends—what an atmosphere for a festive occasion. Not surprisingly (!), surprise parties can be a highly controversial decision and recipients of them sometimes feel foolish and manipulated—until they get over the shock and begin to relax.

The liability of surprise parties is that word sometimes leaks out ahead of time or that people are invited whom the recipient would not want to come. On top of that, some people (especially in the business world) do not want their co-workers or employers to be able to guess their age.

On the positive side, people love conspiring in such a benign way against someone they all like. Often the gathering in anticipation is as much fun as the party that follows. Bottom line: once the guest arrives, a surprise party is run just like any other party. Just make sure the person wants one.

Anniversary Parties

As if the joy of marriage isn't enough, there is the added occasion of the anniversary party. Invitations to an anniversary party are sent by the couple themselves for the first few years, and later (twenty-fifth onward) by their children. Formal invitations follow the standard procedure (see Chapter 11).

If the gathering is planned as a small party, only family or intimate friends of the couple should be invited. These may be held at home or in a private dining room of a good restaurant. If a larger affair is desired (involving casual friends or business associates), then a restaurant, hotel ballroom, or club may be hired.

Unless age or infirmity precludes it, the honored couple should be stationed near the door to greet guests themselves. Musicians may also be appropriate, although not required (if they are used, be sure they know the tune the couple considers "our song").

It is entirely permissible for the couple to write "No gifts, please" on the invitation. If they choose to accept gifts, custom holds certain ones to be traditional. Gifts should be placed on a table at the reception and opened with great flourish at an appropriate time, usually after the meal but before dancing. If the party is being held in a public place, appoint someone to watch over the gifts or carry them to a safe place.

Anniversaries: Special Circumstances

Interim anniversaries celebrated by the two people involved—(one-month, six-month, anniversary of engagement, etc.) are not formal observances. Indeed, the best way to enjoy them most is probably alone.

If a divorced couple remarries, their anniversaries are counted from the date of their original marriage, as though they had never untied the knot.

Although a man or woman whose spouse has died is not, technically speaking, still married, the sense of loss and memory of the deceased will linger. It is a thoughtful gesture to remember the surviving spouse on the anniversary date by sending a brief, uplifting note, not mentioning death, but reminding her or him that you are "thinking of you."

Class Reunions

High school and college can be tough experiences in the present tense, but usually seem more glorious as time goes by. Accordingly, school reunions become a mixed bag: you want to find out what happened to the classmates you knew "back when," but at the same time you secretly hope you are doing better than they are.

This is why high school and college reunions are both the best and the worst of times. And it probably explains why an entire industry has sprouted since the mid-eighties, an industry that, for money, will arrange class reunions. Such companies can track down missing graduates with the tenacity of a loan collector.

Reunion committees (commercial or homegrown) usually locate people via Internet sites such as http://www.switch-board.com, by contacting parents who are still in the local phone book,* or by circulating a "have you seen" list to the people they did manage to contact. Travel agent affiliates will arrange for transportation and hotel accommodations, reunion tickets can be charged, and all that's left to do is lose weight. Think of class reunions as a senior prom with stretch marks.

Name tags with old yearbook photos are provided for people who don't look the same or cannot recognize each other, and a journal is often handed out (with ads, of course) containing names, addresses, phone numbers, and biographical updates. Photo albums and home videos may also be taken during the reunion for souvenir purposes (also for sale).

The etiquette for reunions is the same as for any other large party with the exception that you are not meeting new people, you are renewing acquaintances. Memory lapses are to be expected; in fact, they provide part of the fun. Unless you married your high school sweetheart, your spouse will be about as interested in attending your reunion as you would be looking at a stranger's dental X-rays.

Thank-you notes are not usually sent; the canceled check to the reunion company is sufficient. Finally, reunited friends frequently promise to keep in touch with each other, and the pledge of a letter or lunch should be kept with the same degree of honesty and enthusiasm as it was extended.

Introducing People at Social Occasions

It is the host's job to introduce people at a party because, obviously, he knows them.

Lapel name tags may be convenient for modern business functions, but they have no place at a social gathering.

On highly formal occasions, guests are announced to the room by the butler as they enter: "Mr. and Mrs. Hubert Fitz-Hugh." This may help people on the floor remember their names.

In all introductions, the gentleman is presented to the lady, e.g., "Miss Langley, may I present Mr. Hillandale. Mr. Hillandale, may I introduce you to Miss Langley." A host, hostess, or mutual acquaintance of either gender may do the presenting. A younger person is always presented to an older person, e.g., "Mr. Wheaton, I would like you to meet my nephew, Joey Whiteoak." A lady is never presented to a man unless he is a monarch, a high elected leader, or a church official.

Years ago it was just not done for a woman, especially a young one, to speak with a gentleman to whom she had not been formally introduced. In modern situations it is still expected that strangers will be introduced by a mutual acquaintance, although there is far less stigma attached to someone who boldly extends his hand and introduces himself (or herself). It is never permissible upon introduction to refer to an adult by his or her first name only.

What to Do When You Forget Names

There is no substitute for a proper introduction. On the other hand, some people are good at remembering names and faces

ANNIVERSARY COMMEMORATIVES

Theater critic Alexander Woollcott once wrote the following message to his friends George and Beatrice Kaufman on the occasion of their fifth wedding anniversary: "I've been looking around for an appropriate wooden gift and am pleased to present you with Elsie Ferguson's performance in her new play." Woollcott was correct in noting that the fifth anniversary is the "wooden" one that may be honored with an item crafted from wood.

Like Mother's Day, Father's Day, Secretary's Day, and other contrived occasions, the aligning of anniversaries with precious metals, gems, and other substances has become more of a commercial concern than a social one. It's usually the silver (twenty-fifth) and golden (fiftieth) anniversaries that get most of the attention, anyway. But for people who want to celebrate earlier mileposts, here's the Marital Periodic Chart (items underlined were popular decades ago and may still be presented):

1   Paper or plastic/<u>clocks</u>
2   Calico or cotton/<u>china</u>
3   Leather or vinyl/<u>crystal, glass</u>
4   Linen, silk, or synthetic fabric/<u>electrical appliances</u>
5   Wood
6   Iron
7   Copper or wool/<u>home office finery</u>
8   Electrical appliances/<u>linen</u>
9   Pottery
10 Tin or aluminum/<u>diamonds</u>
11 Steel
12 Table linen/<u>pearls</u>

13 Lace/<u>furs</u>
14 Ivory/<u>gold jewelry</u>
15 Crystal or glassware/<u>watches</u>
20 China/<u>platinum</u>
25 Silver
30 Pearl/<u>diamond</u>
35 Jade
40 Ruby or garnet
45 Sapphire
50 Gold
55 Emerald
60 Diamond
75 Diamond

and others are not. It takes real effort (not to mention mnemonics), and is considered an attribute both socially and professionally.

Occasionally everyone forgets a name (first, last, or both). Some people try and weasel out of their embarrassment by saying, "Oh, everybody go and introduce yourselves." This is effective, though tacky.

It is a great courtesy to come to the rescue of someone who has had a momentary name blackout. This also is a swift business tactic to perfect, as with, "Mr. Bragg, did I ever introduce you to Mrs. Deguerre?" Public figures who meet literally thousands of people a year and should not be expected to remember everybody's names will often hire aides who prompt them.

Sometimes it happens that one has casually noticed someone for years (such as in the office) but has never learned his or her name. If suddenly cornered, there is nothing amiss with stating, "I'm terribly embarrassed, but I don't believe we've ever really been introduced."

A bluff can sometimes backfire. If one remembers a first name only, there is the ploy of asking, "By the way, how do you spell your last name?" This works unless the person responds coolly, "S-M-I-T-H."

Cleaning Up after a Party

When a party is held in a restaurant or other professional facility, there is never a question of who cleans up. Yet occasionally a guest at a home party may offer to stay and help clean. If the host or hostess has servants or caterers, of course, this is not an issue, but in other situations, is it an insult to deny a helpful guest the chance to clear the table or empty the ashtrays?

In a sense, the real insult is to the hostess if a guest presumes that she cannot handle the duties of her own party. Apart from clearing the table after each course or busing cluttered coffee tables, a host without professional assistance should save the cleaning chores until after the guests have departed. Some hosts even prefer winding down in solitude, elbow deep in suds. The guest who offers to help clean up may be told, "Oh, that's all right, let's just leave this stuff and go into the living room."

RELIGIOUS OCCASIONS

People of one faith invited to attend religious observances of friends of another faith are expected to follow the tenets of the host's beliefs as long as they do not interfere with their own. There is a more detailed discussion of this in other chapters, but here are tips for attending the basic non-wedding celebrations.

Jewish Religious Observances

Christians attending Jewish religious services may be made to feel out of place by some of the traditions they encounter. At such times they might do well to remember that such traditions predate their own.

The synagogue or temple is the place where Jews gather for formal worship, although, strictly speaking, any gathering of ten Jewish men (*minyan*) is sufficient to hold a public service. In Orthodox services the women are segregated from the men.

On entering a temple, men cover their heads with a *yarmulke* (skullcap) to show respect for God. Absent a yarmulke, a hat will do, and it remains on while inside. Jews do not kneel when they pray; they stand, and on occasion may bow rhythmically or take a step if prescribed by scripture.

A Christian visitor, of course, is expected to cover his head when visiting a Jewish religious ceremony and may stand for prayer. Dress is businesslike.

Bar Mitzvah. In the Jewish faith a boy is considered a man at the age of thirteen. This is the point at which he is permitted to wear certain articles of religious clothing reserved for adult males, is counted among the ten men who constitute a *minyan*, and—most important—is permitted to join the men in reading the *Torah*, the collection of laws that define Judaism.

The tradition of the bar mitzvah is not a ritual from the Old Testament but is a celebration of faith and a deeply treasured one. It is held in a synagogue on the Saturday (Sabbath) immediately after the boy's thirteenth birthday. In times past, the "bar mitzvah boy" was expected to give a discourse on some aspect of Talmudic law; these days he usually comes closer to giving an Oscar-acceptance speech thanking his family while praying silently that his voice doesn't break. He then reads (in Hebrew or sometimes English) a passage from the holy books.

Befitting the sanctity of the occasion, the boy's father (or nearest male relative if the father is deceased) will present the boy with a *tallis* (prayer shawl). After the service there is a party that may go well into the night in honor of the bar mitzvah boy. Money, books, secular gifts, and, yes, fountain pens are appropriate gifts.

Usually the boy has come to bar mitzvah following religious instruction, which is augmented by special bar mitzvah lessons prior to the big day. The rabbi of the congregation can consult on all aspects of the event.

Bas Mitzvah. In recent decades Jewish girls have been welcomed into womanhood with a bas mitzvah at the age of twelve (the tradition being that girls mature sooner than boys). Although controversial among Orthodox sects, the bas mitzvah has become a social as well as religious occasion.

Late-in-Life Bar Mitzvah. As with late-in-life baptisms, one can always be welcomed into a new faith or deepen one's commitment to one's present faith. It is a joyous occasion that can inspire friends and family members to reaffirm their beliefs. Adults in a congregation wishing to attend tutorials together (to avoid having to go to Hebrew school with a bunch of twelve-year-olds) may make arrangements through their rabbi. Other late-in-life religious rituals (such as circumcisions) may involve matters that transcend etiquette.

Christian Religious Observances

Communion. Catholic precept embraces the eucharist (wafer and wine) as the actual body and blood of Christ through the doctrine of transubstantiation. Because of this, a child's first communion (i.e., receiving the host) is a unique moment in his or her life.

When a boy or girl turns seven, he or she begins a course of instruction at church in advance of making the first holy communion. Usually the entire class attends a special mass at which beaming parents and godparents will be present, and they receive the host as a group. Non-Catholics who are in attendance do not partake.

Girls usually wear white dresses and veils; boys are attired in suits. A luncheon will follow, frequently in the church's recreational facility, where the children are given gifts. The gifts may be anything, although those given by parents and godparents should be of a religious nature (bible, rosary, prayer book, etc.).

Confirmation. When a boy or girl swears to the baptismal vows that were made for him or her by his godparents, he or she is confirmed in the faith and becomes a member of the congregation. Catholics and Protestants confirm their children around ages twelve or fourteen, whereas Eastern Orthodox will confirm a child at the time of baptism. One can also be confirmed later in life, such as after changing one's faith.

After successfully passing a course of instruction, the confirmation class is presented to the congregation. For Protestants, this occurs during a regular Sunday service; for Catholics, it is at a service apart from the regular mass. The participants wear respectful attire: girls in white or light-colored dresses, boys in dark suits or subdued jackets and ties.

The post-confirmation party can be in the church recreational area, but it also can be held in a private home or restaurant. As with communions, proper gifts include religious objects.

FAMILY OCCASIONS

Dinner with the Family

The greatest cultural loss of our modern age is the family dinner hour. In far too many homes the tradition of everyone sitting down together for a meal has been replaced by eat-and-run to sports practice, ballet lessons, evening meetings, social commitments, and other activities that strengthen the individual but weaken the family unit.

Sociologists extol the dinner table as the primary means of acculturation. It is over dinner that mothers, fathers, sons, and daughters exchange the minutiae of their lives, pick up signals about each other's personalities, learn attitudes and behavior, and grow into productive members of society. Suffice it to say that the only thing that should distract a family during dinner is the telephone, and even that should be ignored.

Bringing Friends Home

As discussed in Chapter 2, the ritual of presenting one's dates to one's parents is as time-honored as it is uncomfortable. When the friend is just a friend and not a date, the dynamics may be different, but no less important.

Every parent worries whether his or her child is running around with "bad company." The danger of gangs and drugs in America today makes this concern legitimate. At the same time, no kid wants to be seen seeking parental approval. The solution is usually for parents to encourage their children to bring their friends over to the house to play or for lunch or dinner. The question, "Why don't we ever get to meet your friends?" is sometimes a difficult one to ask, but it's an important one.

Friends who spend time at one another's houses should be polite and respectful not only of those living there but also of the property itself. Ask permission to use the telephone or to have something from the kitchen. Asking permission to use the bathroom is not a rule, although an offhand "Where is your bathroom?" is a none-too-subtle hint.

Main Squeeze at the Table

It usually happens when a young person goes away to college: he or she brings back a "friend" for Thanksgiving. The friend may be just that, a friend too far from her home to commute, so she comes to yours. He or she also can be a lover.

COMPANIONS AND FRIENDS

An elderly or infirm relative who brings a companion, or a dating relative who brings a special friend to a family gathering is asking the rest of the family to welcome that person into the fold.

Paid companions or nurses should be accorded the respect shown any friend. They should be included in place settings (next to their charge) and given relief from duties while the rest of the family takes over for a while.

Friends and dates may be enfranchised more warmly. It is a nice gesture to have one or two generic, gender-neutral gifts on hand at holiday time to be able to provide a visitor with something to unwrap.

Conversely, visitors to somebody else's family must remember that they are guests and should take their behavioral cues from the person who brought them there. Drinking is to be discouraged unless everybody is doing it.

Holidays are a time to embrace people, not distance them. A guest should be welcomed warmly in acknowledgment of the trust placed in the family member who

WHO ARE THESE PEOPLE?

DEFINITION OF ONCE REMOVED

When two siblings and their spouses have children, those children are first cousins to each other. If those cousins have children, their children are second cousins to each other. But the child of one cousin and the grandchild of another cousin are "once removed" from each other. The "once removed" means that the relationship skips a generation. It does not mean that somebody got divorced and still hangs around.

FAMILY VALUES

Traditional families start with a mother and father and work along from there. A family tree can help orient one to who is related to whom, and how, and what to call someone. Here's how it goes:

Great-Grandparents
Grandparents
Parents
You/Your Siblings

Your Mother   Your Father
Mother's Brother (your uncle)   Father's Brother (your uncle)
Mother's Sister (your aunt)   Father's Sister (your aunt)

Aunt's or Uncle's Children (first cousins to each other,
first cousins once removed to you)
First Cousin's Children (second cousins to each other,
first cousins once removed to you)

Great-grandparents accrue as you add one "great" for each generation back. Great-aunts and Great-uncles likewise add a "great" for every generation back. Societal taboos (and, in most states, the law) forbid marriage between first cousins or closer.

WHO ARE THESE PEOPLE?

DEFINITION OF RELATIVES BY FRIENDSHIP

Within an extended family it is sometimes convenient for a child to refer to a good friend of the mother or father who is not related by blood or marriage as "Aunt" or "Uncle." This is a term of affection rather than an actual genealogical designation and is generally harmless . . . with one exception.

That one exception, however, can be a beaut. If a separated, divorced, or philandering parent is in a romantic liaison and doesn't know how to, or want to, explain it to a child, the child is sometimes encouraged to call the girlfriend or boyfriend "Aunt" or "Uncle." This is neither accurate nor proper. The crucial difference must be explained to the child as soon as he or she is old enough to grasp it.

STEPPARENTS

There are two extremes in the concept of stepparents: <u>The Brady Bunch</u> and <u>Cinderella.</u> What occurs between them is reality. When a person's mother or father remarries, either after divorce or death, the new spouse is the stepparent. It is a harsh-sounding term and, all too often, a harsh relationship for the child to accept.

Siblings that arrive from the stepparent's previous marriage are called stepbrothers and stepsisters; siblings that result from the new union are sometimes called half brothers and half sisters, although this is not a proper term. The proper name for them is "brother" or "sister."

invited him or her. Because family gatherings will remind the stranger of her distance from her own family, special attention should be made to make her feel at home—if not at hers, then at yours.

Orphans' Holidays

Despite the ease of travel in modern society, the crunch of short weekends, such as for Thanksgiving and Easter, means that it is often impossible for individuals to be with their families at meaningful times of the year. One of the most thoughtful things you can

do, therefore, is to invite these "orphaned" friends to your own home to share your food and company.

If they are invited to visit at a gift-giving occasion, they should be told that they are not expected to bring gifts. Nevertheless, it is a kind gesture for the visiting "orphan" to send a floral arrangement or centerpiece to the hostess ahead of time.

A visitor can feel like an interloper no matter how hard everybody works to enfranchise him. It is the responsibility of the person who invited him to pay special attention at these times and to offer the use of the family phone so that he can call his own family at whatever the distance.

Still other "orphans' holidays" (Thanksgiving, in particular) can be easily arranged among people who cannot, for various reasons, travel to their own families. Thus several friends can gather, share cooking duties, celebrate, and commiserate on their common predicament. Customary dinner party rules apply, although the emphasis should be on informality.

Ex-spouses at Family Events

Nothing makes a child's birthday, confirmation, graduation, or wedding more tense than deciding whether to invite an ex-spouse. The strain can be particularly rough when the child is clearly torn between loyalties or if there are friends, not to mention family, in common. It gets even rougher when the ex-spouse has remarried.

Unless there is a restraining order in place, the etiquette is consistent: invite the ex. The spouses divorced each other, not their child, and it is important for both of them to be present at his or her milepost. It is not necessary for them to mingle, but they should be there.

Single Older Relatives

Most large families have a middle-aged man or woman who hasn't married and who always attends family events alone. Even if the subject isn't discussed out loud, everybody probably wonders if he or she is gay.

Unless the man or woman has publicly acknowledged his or her homosexuality, it is impolite (not to mention potentially libelous) for anyone else to do so.

When asking an avowedly gay or lesbian couple to a family or friendly gathering, the address on the invitation lists them alphabetically by their last names.

Mr. John Best
Mr. Richard Crawford
The Ansonia
New York, NY 12345

Home for the Holidays

Holidays present a convenient occasion for families to gather at a time of joy. Unfortunately, it's also a chance for family enmities to bubble to the surface. Etiquette during this time applies equally to family and acquaintances, and resolutely suggests taking the high road by offering ways to avoid veering off onto the low.

The feast of Thanksgiving is America's only major national celebration that has neither patriotic nor religious significance. It commemorates the pilgrims' surviving their first year at Plymouth, Massachusetts, courtesy of the local Native American tribe. Thanksgiving is about family—and also pro football, food, and the beginning of the Christmas shopping season—but mostly family. Families also gather for other holidays, and, ceremonies of faith aside, the dynamics are remarkably consistent.

It is customary for the eldest capable members of a large family to have first choice of hosting the major family gathering per year, usually Christmas, Thanksgiving, Passover, or Easter (whichever applies). If a family is spread apart and travel is an issue, the hosting chore may be divided equitably.

Alas, sometimes families do not get along, and the playing field for their disputes is too often the dinner table during a holiday meal. Those who refuse to be caught dead in the presence of another family member may be cajoled or tolerated, but the most efficient way to deal with them is to say that the meal will go on as planned, so-and-so will be invited, and if you choose not to attend, the rest of us will miss you.

Family Reunions

If holiday gatherings don't offer sufficient opportunity for families to enjoy reunions, summer vacations do. Travel often is cheaper, the weather more convenient, and resorts can offer special group rates.

Large families love to make regular pilgrimages to an ancestral home (frequently that of their patriarch or matriarch). There they divide into time-honored teams: cooks, athletes, kids, croquet players, horseshoe tossers, and so on.

It's helpful for someone (or a couple) to assume the position of social director so that large families don't mill around aimlessly waiting for meals to be served or the hammocks to free up.

Pleasant activities can include showing slides, movies, or videos taken at previous reunions; mercilessly ribbing a cousin going through an awkward growth spurt; phoning absent members long distance; welcoming those who have been newly born; and paying homage to those who have departed.

The same holds true for inviting estranged family members to family events. Unless there are compelling reasons not to, do it. Some day the feud may be settled and all that will remain will be the sting of a social rebuff. Besides, sentimental holidays are a perfect time to mend fences.

THANK-YOUS

Families who see each other often—say, every week—may find that sending out the usual social thank-you letters is not only burdensome, but also ridiculous. For customary family visits, a simple "Thank you" spoken on departure or phoned the next day is enough to meet one's obligation, even to doting grandparents. Written family thank-yous are more commonly appropriate for birthday and holiday gifts or for the relative who has gone out of her way to extend a kindness (graduation gift, sleepovers, an annuity, etc.).

CHAPTER FOUR

MATING
RITUALS:

Engagements
and Weddings

Hollywood screenwriter was once having trouble with the plot of a romantic script. He explained his problem to a friend: once the boy met the girl at the beginning of the story it was hard coming up with twists that would keep them from going to bed together until the end of the film. The friend suggested that, in many communities, men and women waited until they were married to have sex.

"Say, that's a pretty nifty idea!" said the screenwriter.

The same might be said of some relationships in which marriage is seen more as an end than a beginning, like buying a warranty on a car you've already been driving. As originally designed (and that's what we're concerned with here), marriage is an important, even sacred, institution, the foundation on which all other human relationships are built, defining, as it does, the concept of family, home, and the very structure of civilization itself.

Nothing like putting a lot of pressure on the newlyweds, eh? But this explains

> *Of all actions of a man's life, his marriage does least concern other people; yet of all of our actions of our life, 'tis most meddled with by other people.*
>
> —John Seldon, *Table-Talk "Marriage"*

why there are so many formalities connected with the wedding ritual and why couples frequently try bending them. It's a delicate balance: every betrothed wants to enjoy all the time-honored traditions of the wedding ceremony and wants to imbue his and her wedding with something distinctive.

This chapter suggests ways of dealing with questions of etiquette that arise with weddings. It is not a checklist; readers wishing greater detail on preparation should consult *The Everything® Wedding Book* or *The Everything® Wedding Etiquette Book*.

There also are, of course, some pretty convincing arguments *against* marriage, but that's not what this chapter is about. Attention will be paid, however, to the etiquette involved in nontraditional living arrangements (where part of the allure is doubtlessly that they don't invoke the sanctity of marriage). For just as some married couples can be divorced in every way except the decree, so can some unmarried couples be joined together in every way except wedlock.

What follows are guidelines for wedding etiquette up to the point of saying, "I do." After that, either you do or you don't.

ENGAGEMENTS

The Proposal

A couple's public declaration of their intent to get married is the beginning of their engagement. The actual wedding date and all that accompanies it can be established later. Although, in days past, the man, and only the man, would propose marriage, often on a bent knee, the custom has become less formal. Today, he gets to sit on the couch. However it is done, the consent must be mutual. After that, each party refers to the other as "my fiancé."

Parental Consent

When children are above the age of consent (eighteen in some states, seventeen in most, lower in a couple, but check first), it is not a legal requirement for parents to give permission for their children to be married. Meeting the parents, however, is a courtesy that should be extended once the couple has agreed to become engaged. It is sad for a couple to brave the ocean of marriage in a skiff tossed by parental anger. Only after informing parents and step-parents may a couple's circle of friends and more distant relatives be notified. A phone call will do, but these people should also be included in the mailing of any formal written announcement.

Telling the Children

Singer Billie Holiday began her autobiography with a stunner: "Mom and Pop were just a couple of kids when they got married. He was 18, she was 16, I was three." If there are children, either by a previous marriage or who preceded the one about-to-be, they should be informed of the engagement. It is not essential that children of divorce give their consent (they probably won't at first), but compassion should be used in breaking the news, for they will very likely regard it as a repudiation of their other parent.

POPPING THE QUESTION

*S*hort of a coin toss, there are less traditional ways of asking for someone's hand in marriage than getting down on one knee and begging. In the last few years, media outlets have reported some lovers popping the question as imaginatively as possible, using such devices as:

Airplane banner
Billboard
Movie theater trailer
TV talk show
Announcement halftime
  at a football game
Live balloon delivery
Custom fortune cookie
Singing waiters
Request line on rock radio
Groom disguised as clown in
  circus

Ex-spouses

Where a divorce or annulment involved minimal rancor, it is a courtesy to tell an ex-spouse that one is about to become remarried. If the divorce was acrimonious, then tact must be observed, especially if there are child custody issues at stake.

In-laws

After meeting each other's parents, the couple should respond personally to their future in-laws. A young woman's thank-you note for the luncheon or a young man's pleasant acknowledgment of the get-acquainted dinner should follow immediately after the occasion. Thank-you notes are, and will continue to be, a mainstay of proper behavior. Each person writes his or her own.

Engagement Parties

The parents or mother of the bride hold a party at which the formal announcement is made and the groom is presented to the friends and family (who may already know him anyway, or should by now). That is where the mother makes the announcement.

The announcement is supposed to be a surprise, so no mention of it is made on the party invitation. Consequently, no gifts should be expected (although some will likely follow).

If the bride lives in a different city from her parents, the party may be held in her city so that more of her friends can be in attendance.

Engagement Announcements

A typed, formal engagement announcement may be sent to the society page of the local newspaper to appear the day after the engagement party. A photograph of the bride-to-be (but not the groom) may also be sent. Newspapers have varying policies regarding engagement announcements, and a call to the society editor or features editor will secure them.

Mr. and Mrs. Adam Claypool of Hillandale, Maryland, announce the engagement of their daughter, Miss Justine Claypool, to Mr. James Brendan Danielson of Dallas, Texas. Mr. Danielson is the son of Dr. and Mrs. Roger Wakefield Danielson, also of Dallas. A November wedding is planned.

Miss Claypool is a graduate of the University of Maryland and is a development executive for National Public Radio. Mr. Danielson is a graduate of the Rochester Institute of Technology and is a biochemist with the Naval Ordinance Laboratory.

The parents of the bride-to-be make the announcement of their daughter's engagement. If the parents are divorced, then the mother makes the announcement, but the father must be mentioned. If both parents are deceased, then a close relative makes the announcement. If the couple are older and have been on their own, they may make the announcement themselves. Engagement announcements are made only for the first wedding. Any subsequent marriages require only a wedding announcement.

"Congratulations"

When one hears from a female friend of her engagement, one does not say "Congratulations!" Contemporary custom holds that such an exclamation secretly means "I thought you'd never find a beau" and is therefore an insult. Go figure. Courteous and enthusiastic acknowledgments include "That's wonderful!," "You have my blessings," and "That's great news!"

Engagement Rings

Engagement rings often are more ornate than the wedding band, but outside of their show-and-tell value they are not a legal requirement of betrothal. Young couples of limited means should shop for an engagement ring together and purchase one that they can afford. It can be a charming anniversary gift, given in later, better times, to upgrade one's engagement ring.

A man wishing to "pop the question," but who does not want to risk buying a ring that his intended might not like, may proffer a toy ring "as a symbol of the one we'll choose together."

Prenuptial Agreements

In these cynical times, a prenuptial agreement is the marital equivalent of eating something before dinner in case you don't like what they're serving.

Prenuptial agreements insulate the assets of a husband, wife, or both, against attach-ment by the other in case the marriage fails. They are signed before the wedding and may be useful if there are estates, intellectual properties, or business assets that would ensnare third parties following a divorce. They are more properly the domain of lawyers than of manners.

Premarital Monogamy

Engaged couples should not date other people. No "last flings." It is still not proper for engaged couples to sleep in the same bed, to take overnight trips together, or to exhibit passionate shows of affection in public.

When asking an engaged couple to a social event, the invitation is addressed to the gentleman with his betrothed invited in the same letter, as in "Dear Mr. Smith, the honor of your company and that of Miss Jones will be appreciated."

Living Together

POSSLQ. This cute acronym is pro-nounced "possle-cue" and stands for "Person of Opposite Sex Sharing Living Quarters." In other words, this is a hetero-sexual couple living together without benefit of clergy. There is no corresponding acronym for a homosexual couple living together.

An unmarried couple's cohabitation raises the issue of how one party intro-duces another socially. "My friend" is too vague and "my lover" is too specific. "My significant other," "my cohabitant," "my sin-mate," and "my co-item" also fall into etiquette limbo. If it's anybody's business, one may introduce the other matter-of-factly with "This is Amanda Newman; we live together."

When a cohabitating couple becomes engaged, the wedding should be soon, inasmuch as they have presumably already gotten to know each other and should be pretty far along in assembling their home.

Broken Engagements

If an engagement is called off, any gifts received by the no-longer-a-couple must be returned. The accompanying note should reiterate the thanks, but say that the engagement has been called off. No elaboration is required.

A simple statement about the abrogation should be sent to any newspapers who initially reported the engagement.

If the man dies before the wedding, the woman is entitled to keep the engagement ring and any gifts. If the woman predeceases the man, the gifts should be returned and the ring may be returned to the jewelry store for credit.

"Say Hi to What's-Their-Name": Addressing the In-Laws

A future son-in-law or daughter-in-law is not the same as the real thing. Until they are part of the same family, the engaged couple should continue to call each other's

parents "Mr." or "Mrs.," unless, that is, the parents suggest something more informal. As a rule, children-in-law shouldn't be more familiar with a spouse's parents than the spouse is; in other words, no first names. "Mother" and "Father" are appropriate in-law vocatives.

Dowries

In some cultures a woman's dowry—an endowment her family is prepared to give to the man who marries her—is a matter of intense importance and great social rank (see Chapter 6). The practice does not officially exist in America, although informal instances of it may survive.

Engagements Following Divorce

A divorce must be final before one partner announces his or her engagement to someone else.

PLANNING THE WEDDING

Location

The bride has first call on the location of her wedding. It may be where her family resides, if a different city from where she is living, although it also can be the town where she and her fiancé met and are planning to dwell when married.

TROUSSEAU

*T*he word <u>trousseau</u> is a nostalgic one that bespeaks a time when brides brought their own "things" with them into their new home: doilies, fine linens, lingerie, and other such personal items.

The days of exquisite, homemade needlepoint and lace may be passed, but the need for a new bride to begin her marriage with a "hope chest" has not. Although in olden times the bride and her mother were responsible for the hope chest, modernity has spread the duty to include family and friends. The idea is to help the couple start building a home by providing them with the things they will likely need during their first year. Here is what a bride and groom need:

- Bed linen (at least three sets for the master bedroom and two for the guest room)

  > Fitted sheets
  > Flat sheets
  > Pillowcases
  > Pillows
  > Blankets
  > Mattress pad or cover
  > Bedspread or comforter

- Table linen

  > Napkins for eight
  > Large formal tablecloth
  > Napkins and plastic mats for informal use
  > Cotton or pad liner for tablecloth
  > Smaller tablecloths and napkins for "children's table"

- Bath linen

  > Four large bath towels
  > Matching hand towels
  > Matching face cloths
  > Mid-size "hair towels" for women's hair
  > Bath mat
  > Shower curtain
  > Small guest towels

- Cookware

  > Frying pan
  > Covered saucepans (large and small)
  > Tea kettle
  > Utensil set
  > Baking pans

TROUSSEAU

- China (formal service for eight, sometimes twelve, plus everyday service for eight)

  Dinner plates
  Salad plates
  Cups and saucers
  Creamer and sugar bowl
  Salt and pepper shakers
  Soup bowls
  Bread and butter plates
  Dessert plates
  Serving platters
  Glassware/crystal
  Water goblets
  Wine glasses
  Cocktail glasses
  Champagne glasses

- Silverware (formal service for eight, sometimes twelve, plus everyday service for eight)

  Knives
  Dinner forks
  Salad forks
  Soup spoons
  Teaspoons

- Silverware (additions to formal service)

  Butter knife
  Fish knife
  Dessert fork
  Shrimp fork
  Iced tea spoon
  Steak knife
  Specialized serving utensils
    (carving knife, slotted
    spoon, pie server, gravy boat
    and spoon, chafing dish)

Any bridal registry will be only too happy to provide an exhaustive list of gift items. The understanding in assembling a trousseau is that couples just starting out their lives together may not need to do formal entertaining and that everyday service will do for the first year or at least until they become more established.

"I DO" . . . WHERE?!?

*E*veryone wants a memorable wedding, but some have made the news because they were held in places nobody could forget, such as:

Underwater
Hot air balloon
Roller coaster
Bowling alley (partially closed
*   for the occasion)*
Mountaintop
Private subway car
Dirigible
Skydiving
Flatbed truck on freeway
Middle of traffic in rush hour
Skiing down slope
Carousel

Guest Lists

Guest lists are prepared by the bride, the groom, and their respective families. The number of guests should be limited to what finances will bear. When names appear on two or more lists, all is well. Here are some simple rules:

1. Each side invites 50 percent of all guests (if they are old friends, there will be duplication).

2. In theory, everybody who is invited should be considered a probable attendee.

3. There should be an "A" list and a "B" list. This is just pragmatism. When people from the "A" list send regrets, those from the "B" list may be invited (this is why invitations go out so early).

4. Finally, harmony is important. In a close call, weight should be given to the bride's side, as the bride's family is footing the bill.

Religious and Civil Ceremonies

A church, chapel, synagogue, or mosque wedding includes religious recognition, active clergy, and a heritage of spiritual tradition.

A civil ceremony involves a judge or justice of the peace and a somewhat less ornate ritual. Under some circumstances (such as when a religious official, for whatever reason, is not empowered by law to perform a marriage ceremony), a judge or justice of the peace also must be present to officiate. These weddings are held in hotels, private clubs, restaurants, and catering facilities. They also may be given—often with touching intimacy—in private homes.

Where one or both partners are in military service, the wedding may be held at a chapel on the military post. When reserving facilities, remember that the institution may have its own wedding protocol. Religious institutions and military bases tend to be traditional, but there is some leeway. The boundaries, however, must be determined in advance.

Strangers in a Strange Land

Guests of one religious denomination invited to attend a wedding (or any other service) of another denomination must respect the beliefs of their host. But this does not mean that they are expected to participate in them. However, if one's religion calls for one to kneel in prayer where another religion dictates that its followers stand, it doesn't hurt to go along with the majority.

Military Weddings

Commissioned officers (male and female) may enjoy military weddings on the base or may wear their uniform to civilian weddings off the base. The base marriage itself is performed as any other; and if all the ushers are in military service, they may form a line and have the newlyweds pass beneath an arch of raised, crossed swords as they leave the chapel. If not all the ushers are in military service, nonuniformed ushers stand in place between the uniformed soldiers.

Roman Catholic Weddings

The rite of marriage can be lengthy and includes a mass as well as the individual wedding ceremony. Roman Catholic marriages must be planned sufficiently far in advance to allow the *bann*, or notice, to be proclaimed publicly three times before the date. Most churches prefer that the best man and maid of honor both be Catholic; some allow that only one need be; the other atten-

dants can be of any religion. Catholics may marry during Advent and Lent, but not with a nuptial blessing. Special permission must be obtained for an evening ceremony.

Guest attire is becoming less formal, and veils and hats for women are now considered optional except for weddings performed at noon High Mass. Men should wear suits.

Prayer may be conducted kneeling with genuflection. Guests (especially non-Catholic members of the wedding party) may follow at their discretion. Only Catholics may accept communion if it is offered.

Brides do not receive visitors before the ceremony.

Protestant Weddings

Unlike Roman Catholic weddings, Protestant ceremonies may take place in the evening. They are less formal and more brief. The wedding party can be of any faith. Marriages are not held during Lent or on Sundays. Brides do not receive visitors before the ceremony.

Jewish Weddings

Jews are not married on their Sabbath, which runs from sundown Friday to sundown Saturday, or on specified Jewish holidays. All men entering a synagogue should cover their heads. For those who are not already wearing hats, there is always an arrangement of skullcaps near the entrance. Women often cover their heads with scarves or hats. Some temples in the Reform sect have abandoned head coverings. Inside, the immediate family stands beneath a canopy, or *chuppah*, for the service. Prayers are recited by the congregation from a sitting or standing position.

One of the favorite moments in the Jewish ceremony is when the groom crushes a glass (usually after a lengthy explanation of the ritual from the rabbi). The entire congregation then says "Mazel tov" (good luck). Brides may receive callers (not including the groom) before the ceremony.

Christian Science Weddings

A Christian Science wedding ceremony is similar to a Protestant one, except that the marriage must be performed by an ordained minister of the gospel or other proper legal authority. No alcohol is served at the reception.

Quaker Weddings

Given that the Quaker ethic is to reject worldly display, Quaker weddings are more spartan than those of other faiths. A notice of intent to wed is read at least a month beforehand at a meeting of the Society of Friends. The ceremony itself may involve a procession, at the end of which the bride and groom take seats facing the congregation. They exchange vows and sign a marriage certificate.

Eastern Orthodox Weddings

Unlike the Roman Catholic ceremony, the Eastern Orthodox Church marriage is celebrated without a mass. Services are usually in the afternoon or the evening.

Although traditions are changing, the hour-long service takes place not at the altar but at a special table at the front of the church. The bride and groom hold lighted candles. Great importance is placed on the number three: three recitations, three revolutions of bride and groom together, the exchange of three rings.

Mormon Weddings

Only members of the Church of Jesus Christ of Latter-Day Saints who have received a Temple Recommend may attend a Mormon wedding ceremony. Non-Mormon friends of the bride and groom are invited to wait on the grounds of the temple and may join the newlyweds after the service.

Muslim Weddings

Marriage is a contract, a covenant, under the Qur'an, and mutual assent, or affirmation, is required to make it binding. Under Islam, the bride's father presents the groom with a dowry, or *mahr*, commensurate with his means. It is paid half on the new wife's demand and the rest on the death of either party or the dissolution of the marriage, should that happen.

The marriage is publicly declared during Islamic services through a sermon or other announcement. After the ceremony there is a feast (*walimah*) celebrating the union.

Hindu Weddings

Marriage (*vivaha*) is permitted between cousins, but not between castes. It is an essential practice for those who have not renounced the world.

The marriage of daughters is an expensive affair in which the bride's family gives gifts to the groom's family as part of her dowry. The father of the bride gives his gift to the father of the groom, and together they make an offering into a fire.

For the ceremony itself, the bride's wrist is tied with a small ribbon and she steps three times around a grinding stone belonging to the groom's family. The couple then takes seven steps around a sacred fire into which the groom makes an offering.

The ceremony and celebration may continue for several days before the bride begins to dwell in the groom's home.

Interfaith Weddings

Many, but not all, religions demand that the bride and groom share the same faith before the marriage can be consecrated under their clerical purview. They also may not recognize the validity of a civil ceremony. Couples who have questions should check beforehand.

Wedding Invitations

The formality of a wedding (even informal ones!) starts with the wedding invitation, the wording of which can be as complicated as contract negotiations for a corporate merger—which, in a way, a marriage is. Wedding consultants and printers/engravers can also advise on the fine points.

Inviting an Unmarried, Cohabitating Couple. An invitation to a couple whose relationship is publicly acknowledged is addressed to both partners alphabetically by their last names.

If a guest is known not to be in a relationship, or if his or her partnership status is unknown, the invitation may be extended either to him or her ". . . and guest."

All guests should be invited in pairs, and it is their responsibility to inform the host otherwise. The R.S.V.P. must provide the name of the guest.

The honour of your presence is requested at the marriage of
Miss Beth Elaine Parker
and
Mr. Justin James Clark
Saturday, the third of August
at two o'clock
Center Street Baptist Church
Fairview, Pennsylvania

Inviting a Recent Widow or Widower. Just because someone is in mourning is no reason to exclude her or him from a wedding. Where a woman or man has recently lost a partner, she or he may be sent an invitation with a hand-written addendum saying, "We hope you can attend our wedding," and leave the question of escort or guest until acceptance.

R.S.V.P.

The initials *R.S.V.P.* (or R.s.v.p.) stand for *Respondez s'il vous plait,* which translates to "respond, if you please." It is the height of rudeness for an invited guest not to inform the host of his or her intention to attend or decline a wedding invitation.

The response must be made immediately upon receipt of the invitation, which is traditionally sent six to eight weeks in advance of the wedding date. To encourage a quick response, hosts enclose self-stamped response cards.

After having accepted an invitation, one is obligated to attend the wedding. One may not attend a wedding to which one has not been invited or to which one has previously declined to attend.

Mr. and Mrs. Adam Claypool of Hillandale, Maryland, announce the marriage of their daughter, Justine, to Mr. James Brendan Danielson of Dallas, Texas. Mr. Danielson is the son of Dr. and Mrs. Roger Wakefield Danielson, also of Dallas.

The bride, who will retain her last name of Claypool, is a graduate of the University of Maryland and is a development executive for National Public Radio. The groom was graduated from the Rochester Institute of Technology and is a biochemist with the Naval Ordinance Laboratory.

The couple will reside in Bethesda, Maryland.

Please respond on or before
June 9, 1997

M _____
____ *persons will attend*

Newspaper Announcements

Newspapers print wedding announcements the day after the wedding, but the copy should be submitted two to four weeks in advance. As with engagement announcements, check with the society editor. Some newspapers have begun charging for this service or print the announcements only if they have room.

The wording for the announcement may be terse or verbose. Regardless, this is an opportunity for the bride to go on record by announcing whether she will retain her own last name. If this is not indicated, it should be assumed that she is taking her husband's surname.

Who Pays for the Wedding?

Tradition dictates that the bride's family pay for and host the wedding and reception, and that the groom's family host the rehearsal dinner. Where finances are a concern, both families may share, although the bride's family will still be the host. If the bride's parents are deceased, a close relative may host. Couples holding their own weddings (for reasons of deceased parents, second marriage, etc.) must, of course, bear their own costs.

No bride and groom should be pressured into giving a wedding they cannot afford. If funds are limited, it may be a more loving gesture to dedicate them to establishing the home than to financing the nuptials. In such cases a small, private, at-home union might be planned. Often, these are more personal and meaningful than an ornate cathedral service.

Clergy

Clergy have witnessed more weddings than the participants and are therefore the best suited to advise on the ceremony, if necessary.

If the bride, first, or groom, second, have a favorite clergyman or clergywoman whom they would like to have perform their wedding, then he or she should be asked far enough in advance to secure his or her services. The officiating fee can be discussed matter-of-factly. It is paid by a check made out to the cleric, not the church.

If the cleric is being asked to perform the ceremony at another cleric's church, the host cleric's permission also should be secured. In such a situation, only the officiating cleric need be invited to the rehearsal dinner and wedding reception, although it is a courtesy to invite the other, too. (Neither should be invited to the bachelor party!)

The presence of clerics of two different faiths is not unusual when one partner wishes his or her favorite clergyman to perform a joint service. This is frequently the case with interfaith marriages.

The Bridal Registry

Better department and specialty stores offer a free bridal registry service and a staff consultant who will advise the bride and groom on what items they might need to start a home. The registry keeps a list, advises inquirers about what's on it and how much it costs, and keeps the bride posted on progress.

The custom is based on the belief that friends and family want to give something but don't always know exactly what or may not want to duplicate gifts. The dilemma is how to tell people without sounding crass.

Well, tell them. Not on the invitation (that *would* be tacky), but when they call to ask what you need. The belief is that wedding guests expect, even want, to give gifts, and what better object to give than something the bride and groom have declared they could actually use?

Brides whose guests have a wide range of incomes may register at two or more stores (upscale, moderate, utilitarian, etc.). (Note: retailers count on wedding consumers shopping one step above their financial class.)

No Gifts, Please

Some couples, aware that certain guests may not be able to afford presents, consider printing "No gifts, please" on their wedding invitations. Similarly, couples entering into a second marriage, who have all the furnishings they need, may also ask that no gifts be given.

WEDDING GIFTS

In the 1988 movie Bull Durham, actor-comedian Robert Wuhl happened to suggest that candlesticks would make a nice wedding gift, thereby causing a run on the item at department stores. Newlyweds appreciate other gifts, however, as the bridal registry can attest. Other items (bought individually or by friends who team up for the big ones) can include:

Videocassette recorder
Camcorder
Laser disc player
Microwave oven
Food processor
CD-ROM drive for computer
Fine cutlery
High-end cookware
Place settings (china, silver, crystal)
Garage door opener
Computer software
Closet storage/shelving
Carpeting (gift certificate), or fine rugs
Floor or table lamp
Clock radio
Coffee maker

Neither request is proper on the invitation. A handwritten note to specific guests will do the job: "We look forward to seeing you at our wedding, and we are asking our friends not to bring gifts. Your presence in itself will be as fine a gift as we can imagine."

Choosing the Wedding Ring

Although the engagement ring can be a showpiece of great import, the wedding ring is a more private matter. Once the couple selects the ring and the bride-to-be has her finger measured by the jeweler, she will not see the actual ring again until the groom puts it on her finger during the ceremony.

A bride's wedding ring is customarily plainer than her engagement ring; the groom's is not adorned at all. Tradition allows the groom to engrave the couple's initials and wedding date on the inside of the band. Both bride and groom wear their bands on the same fingers. It is subsequently permissible for both parties to temporarily remove their wedding bands for athletics, chores, radiology, and so on.

Formal, Semiformal, and Informal Dress

These three key words dictate the style of the wedding, and all decisions flow from the choice. A church wedding may be formal, a club wedding semiformal, and a home wedding informal. Other factors are time of day, season of the year, and, finally, the expense, not just for the immediate wedding party, but also for the guests.

Formal

Bride: Long white dress and train
Groom: Cutaway or tails
Female Attendants: One maid/matron of honor plus four to ten bridesmaids, also in long matching gowns; flower girl
Male Attendants: Best man plus one usher for each bridesmaid, also in matching cutaway or tails
Guest attire: Formal or evening wear
Reception: Club, hotel, garden
Service: Catered
Meal: Full sit-down, hot meal; full bar

Semiformal

Bride: Long white dress
Groom: Tuxedo or sack coat
Female Attendants: One maid/matron of honor plus two to six bridesmaids in fashionable matching gowns; flower girl
Male Attendants: Best man plus one usher for each bridesmaid, also in matching tuxes
Guest attire: Evening or business dress
Reception: Club, garden, restaurant, home
Service: Catered or restaurant
Meal: Buffet; bar

Informal

Bride: Simple gown, suit, or dress
Groom: Dark business suit
Female Attendants: One maid/matron of honor plus flower girl or ring-bearer
Male Attendants: Best man plus one usher, also in business attire

Guest attire: Business dress
Reception: Church parlor, restaurant, home
Service: Catered or friends
Meal: Light buffet; bar

The maid of honor and bridesmaids are expected to purchase their own ensembles, but the best man and the groomsmen get away with renting theirs.

DRAMATIS PERSONAE

Best Man

As the groom's legal witness, the best man should help the groom in any way possible. Where the bride has her entire family to support her, it is the best man who looks out for his friend, the groom.

Big brothers and close friends are usually chosen as best men, although this can vary depending on age and experience. The best man's foremost job is to get the groom to his wedding on time and, ahem, sober.

At the reception the best man mingles. He is not part of the receiving line.

Other duties may include:

- Driving the groom to the wedding and making sure he has the wherewithal (wallet, tickets, keys) to make his departure
- Buying the groom a gift from himself and the ushers, and collecting the money from them to finance it

- Signing the wedding certificate as witness
- Getting the wedding ring from the groom before the ceremony, holding it until it is called for, or securing it to the ring-bearer's cushion, whichever applies
- Making sure the groom is dressed correctly
- Taking the groom's change of clothes to the reception so he can change later
- Paying the clergyman (usually done before the ceremony or after the recessional)
- Making the first toast to the bride and groom
- Conspiring to throw the groom's bachelor party, in which case he also may become known as "bad company," but that's another story

Maid or Matron of Honor

The maid of honor (or, if married, matron of honor) is the bride's legal witness and personal assistant throughout the wedding process. She exists, foremost, to help the bride.

It is she who precedes the bride down the aisle, holds the groom's ring (in a double-ring ceremony), and adjusts the bride's train. In the receiving line she stands at the groom's left and later sits to his left at the reception. Afterward, she helps the bride change into getaway clothes. She may also host the wedding shower and collect money from the other bridesmaids to choose their gift to the bride.

Groomsmen/Ushers

Ushers seat the invited guests in the church, synagogue, or hall. Ideally there is one usher for every four dozen guests, so they can rotate. Ushers chip in for a gift for the groom and may be asked to sit at the bridal table in formal weddings.

The head usher may be accorded the privilege of escorting the bride's mother to her seat. Other ushers may unroll the aisle runner before the procession.

Bridesmaids

Unlike groomsmen, bridesmaids are accorded little attention at the wedding ceremony. They may assist in throwing the bridal shower, will pool money to buy the bride a gift (after they have already laid out money for their dresses), and are excluded from the receiving line.

Flower Girls/Ring-bearers

Young family members often are chosen as flower girl or ring-bearer (the distinction is no longer gender-specific). The flower child walks down the aisle ahead of the bride and scatters flower petals at her feet. The ring-bearer carries a velvet cushion or silver tray on which the wedding bands are held until needed. Both duties earn "oohs" and "aahs" from the guests.

At the reception, just when they thought all the attention was for them, they get stuck at the children's table and ignored. It's a jungle out there, kid.

Out-of-Town Guests

Travel, hostelry, attire, and gift pose four daunting expenses for any guest attending an out-of-town wedding. The costs can sometimes be prohibitive. If a large private house is available for the occasion, it softens the financial burden. Failing that:

- The groom pays for the travel and accommodations of his out-of-town groomsmen if they are unable to bear the cost themselves; likewise, the bride (or her family) spring for the bridesmaids.
- The bride or groom may make reservations on behalf of out-of-town guests at local hotels but the guests are expected to pick up their own expenses.

Burdensome Guests

Nothing is more difficult than the guest for whom travel is difficult (age, infirmity) but whom the bride and groom very much want to attend. Should they provide door-to-door livery, hire attendants to help them, and spend more time on them than other guests?

A potentially burdensome guest should realize that he or she requires service that may be beyond the time and ability of the bride and groom to provide, and should accept or decline the invitation accordingly.

Other ways to handle this touchy circumstance are for the bride and groom to promise to make a special trip to see the favored friend or relative "should you not be able to attend the wedding" (this provides a face-saving out). Another is to ask, "We would like to contribute to your coming; let us know what arrangements you make and we will help" (this presumes that the guest must make some effort, too).

The bottom line: if the bride and groom truly want the guest to attend, they make the arrangements.

PREWEDDING PARTIES

Bridal Showers

Two to three weeks before the wedding, the bride's friends hold a party in her honor at which they "shower" her with gifts. This is a party for those close to the bride, but is not typically hosted by her immediate family (although they will attend). Showers also may be jointly hosted. They are usually held at midday lunch or on a weekend day in a private home or separate dining room of a restaurant.

An invitation to a shower implies that a gift is expected. (Shower gifts are separate from wedding gifts.) As such, the honoree is asked to make up a guest list. Showers are generally small affairs and should not overshadow the wedding reception. Should the marriage later be called off, shower gifts must be returned.

THANK-YOUS

There is no more certain way to curse a marriage than to fail to write thank-you notes for wedding gifts. If there has been a lapse of courtesy in writing thanks in general, the absence of a handwritten appreciation for a wedding gift is unforgivable.

- *It must not be phoned.*
- *It must not be spoken in person only.*
- *It must not be printed in a newspaper.*
- *It must not be left on an answering machine.*
- *It must not be a form letter or computer mail merge.*

- *It must be custom written, by hand, on stationery, and include thanks, a notation of how much the bride and groom appreciate the specific gift, and how happy they were to see the guest at the wedding, or how much they missed seeing the guest who could not attend, and so forth.*

Even if you hated the gift or got the same thing from someone else, the note must sound spontaneous, even though the bride and groom have been writing twenty of them a day, all week. And, yes, the groom is now expected to do his share of the letter writing.

If the wedding gift has not arrived, but the registry has promised one, then the thank-you note may be delayed until the gift appears. Even guests who attended the wedding but failed to send a gift should be thanked for coming. All thank-yous must be sent within three months of the wedding, if not earlier.

Bachelor Parties

From Paddy Chayefsky's 1955 television drama *The Bachelor Party* to Lerner and Loewe's *My Fair Lady* ("Get Me to the Church on Time"), and certainly before, there has been a tradition in our popular culture of "one last fling" for the groom-to-be.

According to legend, this can turn into a stag party replete with drinking, reminiscing, and half-clad women jumping out of unbaked cakes. There is no etiquette for such an affair, but a wide selection of municipal statutes may apply.

In practice, it is best to schedule bachelor parties several days prior to the wedding so that the groom can recover. The party is thrown in a private dining room by the best man or sometimes by the groom's father if his father also is best man.

Bachelorette Parties

Prior to the wedding, the maid of honor and bridesmaids may fête the bride at a bachelorette luncheon or tea (once again, the bridesmaids get the raw end of the deal).

Fortunately, modern practice has been evolving (or is it devolving?) the bachelorette party to the same status as bachelor party. Reconfigured as a "girls' night out," such affairs include drinking, reminiscing, and whatever it is that half-clad males look good popping out of.

An even more modern technique is for the friends of the bride and groom to throw them a joint last fling.

THE CEREMONY

Former Spouses

Ex-wives and ex-husbands should not be invited to their former spouse's re-marriage. However, divorced spouses are expected to participate when their children get married. This can be tense, but warring exes should call a truce for the good of their kids.

Usually the parent who has had custody of the child will host the wedding; if so, only that parent's name will appear on the wedding invitation. The other parent will, of course, be invited.

Where the mother and father, though divorced and remarried, are still friendly, both of them may host the wedding and share the invitation. In such cases the father gives away the

bride *or* stands with the groom, whichever is appropriate, then sits behind the immediate family while his (new) wife sits farther back in the audience. If the father is hosting the wedding, then the mother sits behind while her (new) husband sits farther back. *Two divorced and remarried couples should not be expected to sit together as a foursome!*

Seating the Guests

Invited guests should arrive at a wedding fifteen to twenty minutes early. Once there, they must wait until they are seated by an usher. If the guest does not say so on his own, the usher will ask, "Friend of the bride or groom?" and lead the guest to a seat on whichever side of the hall is appropriate. Guests should not seat themselves.

When couples are seated, tradition has the usher squire the woman on his right arm while her husband or escort follows. A more egalitarian method would be to have the usher say, "This way, please," and have the couple follow him. When they get to the row or pew, the usher turns to face the guest, indicating to enter. They do not walk past him.

Babies at Weddings

Unless they are getting married, babies do not belong at wedding ceremonies. After all, the day belongs to the bride and groom, not an infant who may suddenly demand attention. It is not the responsibility of the marital couple to provide day care either. Guests should not attend if they cannot make baby-sitting arrangements (this should be settled before they R.S.V.P.), and the bride and groom have the perfect right to specify "no children, please" on their invitations. They may welcome children if they wish, but the choice is theirs.

Marriage . . . with Children

An exception to a "no children" policy is where the bride and groom have children from previous marriages, or where they have a child of their own. In such a case they may want to welcome additional children to keep their own occupied.

Vows

Certain wedding requirements are prescribed by law. They include statements by witnesses, and a declaration by the couple that they are marrying of their own free will, that nobody protests their union, and that the person marrying them is, in fact, permitted to do so.

The bride and groom pledge each other their troth either by repeating the vows as prompted by the official or by reciting vows they have written themselves. These can be either touching or tacky, depending on how meaningful the words are and how nervous the bride and groom may be about reading them out loud.

Pregnant Brides

A bride who is pregnant or has delivered a child out of wedlock faces a number of hurdles if she pursues a traditional wedding. It will go a long way toward mollifying the tongue-clickers if the bride's parents send out the wedding announcements.

From the standpoint of etiquette it would be inappropriate for the bride to wear a white dress or a veil, both of which signify virginity. As the veil is not used so much anymore, it may not be missed, but it would be inappropriate for a mother-to-be to wear a white gown. An ivory gown, or one with color trim or highlights, would still be attractive and yet not out of place.

Some clergy may decline to perform the marriage under the circumstances, but those who place a higher value on love and commitment will consent.

Above all, this should be a happy and positive occasion for the bride, and anyone who feels otherwise should stay home on her special day.

Gay Weddings

Despite what the state of Hawaii says (and the matter is in bombastic flux as this is being written), same-sex marriages are neither the custom nor the law in America. This is ironic, given that one of society's chief criticisms of gay relationships is that they are transitory, yet gay people are denied the one sanction that would accord them permanence.

Be that as it may, gay and lesbian partners often seek to declare their union before friends and family. Doing so before the law is another matter, and one not within the reach of etiquette.

Guests Departing

Guests do not leave a wedding ceremony before the bride and groom do unless it is an emergency (no beepers or cell phones!). Once the wedding party exits, the rows empty in an orderly manner from the front to the rear of the hall.

THE RECEPTION

Formal Bridal Table

Whether set up in a horseshoe or one long dais, the head table dominates the reception even as the bride and groom dominate the table. Their parents and close family are seated at another table.

Looking toward the bride and groom, the seating order is as follows, left-to-right: usher, bridesmaid, usher, bridesmaid, best man, bride, groom, maid of honor, usher, bridesmaid, usher, bridesmaid.

Children's Table at Reception

This is, of course, a trick question, as children should attend wedding receptions only when they are old enough to sit with their parents.

Toasts

Once all the reception guests are seated, the best man offers the first toast. Next, the groom rises to toast his new wife. After that, toasting should be kept to a minimum, or at least to those seated at the head table and parents' tables.

Throwing the Bridal Bouquet

When the bride and groom decide to leave the wedding reception, the bride signals her bridesmaids, who gather at the foot of a staircase. Other guests follow. The bride ascends the staircase and, halfway up, turns her back on everyone and throws her wedding bouquet over her turned shoulder; superstition says that the bridesmaid who catches it is to be the next married.

Snapping the Bridal Garter

There is a parallel custom to throwing the bridal bouquet in which a groom removes his new bride's garter (especially installed for this purpose) and snaps it over his turned shoulder so that his groomsmen may playfully fight over it. This event has no place in a formal wedding reception.

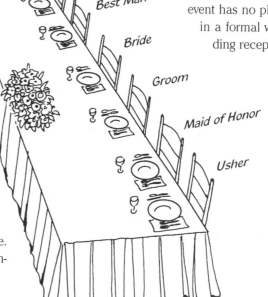

Bridesmaid

Best Man

Bride

Groom

Maid of Honor

Usher

Decorating the Departure Car

Newlyweds who plan on leaving their reception in their own car run the risk of having the groom's friends decorate it. Such decorations can include a "Just Married" sign and ribbons, tin cans, old shoes, inflated balloons, or even condoms tied to the bumper.

This is why many couples hire a limousine to make their getaway (limousine drivers fiercely protect their property). A "Just Married" sign affixed with medical tape (other adhesives and shaving cream can ruin a car's finish) and a few tin cans tied to the bumper are enough of a signal for strangers to honk their congratulations.

Throwing Rice

Guests toss rice at departing newlyweds as a symbol of fertility, but environmentalists rightly point out that birds may die after eating the scattered grains, which expand in their stomachs.

As a compromise, many ceremonies provide birdseed to be tossed (not lobbed) at the departing couple. Some wedding venues, particularly those that don't want to attract birds, forbid the tossing of any grain altogether.

When to Leave the Reception

Unless there is an emergency, a wedding guest should stay at the reception at least until the bridal couple has cut the cake. Even then, a discreet departure is expected.

WEDDING GIFTS

Gifts may be sent to the couple up to one year after the wedding, although practice is to send them to the bride ahead of time. Gifts should not be brought to the reception, not only for the sake of security, but also because the bride and groom will be leaving on their honeymoon and will therefore be unable to look after them properly. If for some reason it is necessary to bring a gift to the reception rather than send it ahead to the bride, or timed to arrive after the honeymoon, it may be left on a small table erected for that contingency.

Money in Lieu of Gifts

Some cultures approve of giving wedding gifts in the form of cash, whereas others dictate otherwise. It is improper for the bride and groom to specify "no gifts" or "cash in lieu of gifts," or anything else, for that matter, on their wedding invitations. People who attend weddings expect to give gifts, the precise manner of which is up to their ability and discretion.

The newlyweds always have the option of returning gifts to the store for cash or credit, or of giving them away. In any event, a proper "thank you" must be extended first.

Gifts to Attendants

Considering the amount of money that ushers and bridesmaids must expend when they participate in a wedding ceremony, the bride and groom should present each of them with a personal gift before the ceremony.

THE RECEIVING LINE

*G*uests are welcomed into the reception by the wedding party according to protocol. Here is the order of appearance from the door:

Mother of the bride
Father of the bride
Mother of the groom
Father of the groom
Bride
Groom
Maid of honor
Bridesmaid
Bridesmaid (etc.)

Notice that the best man and ushers do not stand in the receiving line.

In the case of divorced parents, the parent hosting the wedding stands in line, and the father or mother is invited as a guest. If the father and stepmother are hosting, they stand in line, and the bride's mother is invited as a guest. One bump: if the father is paying for the wedding but has not remarried, he does not host; instead, the bride's godmother or close relative stands beside the father to host. If the groom's parents are divorced, only his mother is in the receiving line.

None of the guests will be seated, or begin eating, until they pass through the receiving line. For this reason it is helpful to move everybody along (and to have waiters offer beverages to those still waiting). A simple "hello" or "thank you for coming" is sufficient greeting (the wedding party will mingle in the course of the reception anyway). Brides are always "lovely" and "beautiful" and given "blessings," but are never congratulated per se. As the bride and groom are standing together, each should prompt the other with the name of who is coming next.

RICE

These may be monogrammed. Gifts to best man and maid of honor should be of slightly greater value.

Groomsmen gifts include fine pen/pencil sets, cufflinks, wallet (empty), belt buckle, or business card case. Bridesmaid gifts include bracelet, compact, brooch, hair comb, charm, earrings.

GLITCHES

Cancelled Weddings

It happens. If a wedding is called off after the invitations have been sent out, then follow-up notes must be sent to the guests informing them of the change. No further explanation need be provided.

If the cancellation occurs so close to the wedding that gifts have already been sent, they must be returned immediately. Guests who purchased nonrefundable airline tickets or bridesmaids who spent money on gowns should be reimbursed by the couple for whatever expenses they cannot otherwise recover. After all, they wouldn't have gone to the expense were it not for the wedding.

Postponed Weddings

When a canceled wedding is rescheduled, all of the original guests are notified of the new date with an added note referring to the former date so there is no confusion.

Intra-family Snits

Every family has its disagreements, some petty, some cataclysmic; none belongs at a wedding. Boycotts, coarse behavior, and other *petit gestes* are bound to hurt the feelings of the celebrating couple and create deeper animosities, or animosities where none existed. They will have little of their

intended effect, which is presumably to make a statement about family relationships.

Common Law Marriages

In most states a man and woman who have lived together for a number of years (often seven) acquire the obligations, but not necessarily the legal protection, of marriage.

The status is called *common law marriage* in that it derives not from legislation but from past decisions rendered by judges. That should provide a hint that common law marriages wind up in court often enough to suggest making it legal.

Shotgun Weddings

If the bride-to-be also is a mother-to-be, a long engagement may be out of the question. If a full wedding is planned, it should he handled as if there was no pregnancy.

Some expectant couples find it advisable to have a private civil wedding immediately and have a full formal wedding later on. Whether it can be a church wedding depends on the church involved. As with all questions concerning weddings, what is important is the future, not the past.

Elopements

Since elopement is, by its very definition, the denial of the wedding ritual, there is no etiquette for it. If a private civil ceremony is performed, close friends or family may be invited to a party after the fact. No gifts should be expected, as no invitations were extended.

CHAPTER FIVE

PDE:
Public Displays
of Etiquette

The eponymous Bolshevik official in the 1939 film *Ninotchka* may have been trying to score a point for equality, but it was the train porter who won the laugh in the scene. What Ninotchka (played by Greta Garbo) was fighting was the concept of *noblesse oblige*—literally, the responsibility that the ruling classes owe those beneath them. America's egalitarian ethic would seem to argue against such class consciousness. But when many workers today are excluded from minimum wage coverage, either by redefining what they do or being forced to survive on tips, courtesy and position loom more crucial than ever—on everyone.

Europeans have a different attitude toward those who attend them. There, in restaurants, hotels, and spas, serving is not something one does while looking for a better job, it is a profession. As such, it is regarded by the customers as being worthy not only of remuneration, but also of equally professional behavior on the part of those being served.

In America, though, the myth of equality has eroded the distinction between servant and master. Here masters are more concerned about being liked than obeyed, and servants have lost all pride and interest in what they are hired to do. The problem, according to at least one business consultant, is at crisis level: many top-notch hotels and restaurants cannot find employees who will train in formal service and remain long enough to uphold the house tradition.

And it isn't only in the area of food and valet service. How often have you seen a department store salesperson deflect a merchandise question by pointing, "It's over there—ask her." Or haven't you ever called a government office, waited on hold for twenty minutes, and then got a clerk who had no idea how to answer your question and didn't offer to find someone who could?

For their part, consumers, too, have dropped the ball. How many of us have waited at the post office while a customer filled out forms that he should have completed before he got in line? Do restaurant customers realize that their job is to decide what they want before calling the waiter to the table?

It's all part of being a responsible consumer, as well as a polite human being. People send signals to each other beyond

> *Ninotchka: Why should you carry other people's bags?*
> *Porter: Well, that's my business, Madam.*
> *Ninotchka: That's no business. That's social injustice!*
> *Porter: That depends on the tip.*
>
> —Charles Brackett, Billy Wilder, and Walter Reisch, *Ninotchka*

what can be codified into what we call etiquette. Living together requires codes of conduct, and how we act in public is a good place to start. In other words, noblesse oblige is as much about oblige as it is about noblesse.

THE HELP

It is the job of a servant to serve, not to be a friend. A waiter shouldn't introduce himself with, "Hi, I'm Sean." In fact, he shouldn't introduce himself at all. Excessive familiarity is unseemly in an employer–employee relationship and gets in the way of doing the job. People hired to cook, clean, serve as butler, drive, serve hors d'oeuvres, or wait tables should know precisely what their duties are. By the way, sitting down at the table with the employer is not one of them.

House Servants

When visiting homes that employ domestic help, it is important to be aware of their function.

Butlers supervise the house staff. Theirs is a highly skilled and honorable profession. They are addressed by their last name only, with no prefix; in other words, a butler named Wilfred Smythe is referred to as "Smythe" with no "Mr." preceding it. The butler answers the door and collects guests' coats, thereafter announcing their arrival to the hostess or host.

Housekeepers or maids are responsible for the cleanliness of the house and, in

smaller homes, performing light kitchen duties. How they are addressed must be established when they are hired: "Would you prefer to be called Gladys or Mrs. Phibbs?" Children of the house should use "Mrs. Phibbs."

Cooks do precisely that—cook—as well as serve the meal and clean up afterward. It is their choice how they are addressed.

Chauffeurs maintain and drive the family car designated solely for that purpose. They, too, may be addressed as they wish.

Gardeners and groundspeople tend to the flora, clear leaves and snow, and maintain the grounds. They may specify their form of address as well.

The employer's social title, "Mr.," "Mrs.," "Miss," "Ms.," or "Dr." is always used by hired help. Servants should address the family children by their first names until they reach eighteen. Family children and children of servants may use each other's first names.

Managing the Help

Salary, duties, house rules, and days off must be established when a servant is hired. Employment contracts are not necessary, but proper tax and Social Security forms must be completed.

People in service are not lesser life forms who may be abused at will or whim; they are people whose job is to attend to the needs of their employers. They are not invisible and may only coincidentally be deaf or mute, so they should not be ignored, but allowed to go about their business.

Days off, once established, must be respected. They may also be discussed if both parties are willing, such as if their holiday travel and your holiday entertaining conflict.

It is important to check the references of someone whom you seek to employ, particularly inside your home. Do not be bashful about asking why the applicant left his or her last position, and by all means phone the last employer to confirm the information.

Salaries for servants vary widely according to the duties required, number of hours, amenities provided, community, and experience. The value of room and board is accounted for in setting the wages of live-in servants, and experienced live-out or part-time servants will probably have a rate already established. Amounts vary by community; consult an employment agency.

Letters of Recommendation

What a servant's letter of recommendation doesn't say may be as important as what it does say.

A perfunctory letter from a previous employer may indicate an uncomfortable parting or unsatisfactory service, but nothing actionable. An effusive letter, on the other hand, may oversell the applicant. Only a phone call will determine what is actually the case.

RESTAURANT DOS AND DON'TS

Making Restaurant Reservations

In most cases one may phone a restaurant on the day a reservation is desired.

Give them the number of people who will be attending, the name in which the reservation will be held, and ask any necessary questions: Do they take credit cards? Is there wheelchair access? Do they admit families with children? Can they accommodate someone in your party who has special dietary requirement? And so forth.

Fine restaurants, such as hotel main dining rooms, book tables weeks in advance, especially around the holidays. Phone well ahead of time. Some trendy restaurants think they are so special that they refuse to accept reservations. Go somewhere else.

Canceling Restaurant Reservations

If you find that you are not going to be able to keep your restaurant reservation, call them to release your table. Even if you remember at the exact moment you were due at the restaurant, call anyway.

Restaurants plan on a certain amount of overbooking, to be sure, but that is no excuse to forget your obligation. After all, because you held a table, another patron was turned away. The next time it could be you. (Some restaurants now require a credit card number for a reservation and apply a cancellation fee to no-shows. They are to be avoided—two wrongs don't make a right.)

Arriving at the Restaurant

If you have made a reservation, arrive on time and report to the host or hostess at the door. He or she will check off your name and either show you to your table (if it is ready) or suggest how long you may have to wait. Any wait longer than fifteen minutes in an established restaurant is a hint that something is wrong.

The maitre d' may suggest that you have a drink at the bar until your table is ready; the restaurant should buy it if the delay is their fault. (Even if you are "comped" for the drink, you should leave a cash tip for the bartender of 15 to 20 percent of the drink's value).

Proceeding to the Table

Some restaurants will not seat parties that are not complete; this is a needless inconvenience. The maitre d' will lead the diners to their table. The lady walks behind the maitre d', followed by her escort. At the table, the maitre d' seats the lady and offers the other chair to the man. He may also proffer the menu or summon the captain to take a drink order.

If It's a Lousy Table

Not all restaurant tables are created equal. Those near the bathroom, kitchen, piano, or busing stations are less desirable than those in quiet corners, or near the window, or with a view.

If you are unsatisfied with your table as you are led to it, ask for a better one—but only if you really want it, not just to show off. Look around to see whether there even *are* any others. If so, are they already reserved? Be prepared to wait if you change because others are in line. Tipping the

maitre d' seldom helps you get a better table if there are none available.

Addressing Waiters

Vernacular has begun calling waiters and waitresses *servers*, *waitpersons*, and *waitrons*, all of which are incorrect. Waiters are properly called "waiter," and waitresses are properly called "Miss." Waiters are not called "sir." That's just the way it is. They should never be called *garçon*, which is an insult in America (it means "boy"). The customer also should pay attention to the waiter's face to distinguish him from another table's waiter.

In America, one does not wave or snap one's fingers to get a waiter's attention; it is the waiter's job to notice his tables. If he doesn't, a patron may ask a passing waiter to "please ask our waiter to come over."

Finally, customers who purposely belittle a waiter actually belittle themselves. The proper way to complain about a waiter is to summon the maitre d' and inquire about what the problem is (if there is one, he needs to know about it for everybody's sake).

Disturbances in Restaurants

Patrons who shout, sing, laugh loudly, or toss objects—in other words, who think they're at home—disturb others and ruin the dining experience (unless the restaurant is known for its party atmosphere). If the restaurant manager receives a request from other patrons, it is his or her job to get the noisy party to be quiet.

Children in Restaurants

It is important for parents to expose children to good restaurants so that they may grow up accustomed to enjoying fine food and practicing good manners in public. If the parents cannot get them to behave, they are not welcome.

Parents have every right to bring pouty toddlers and crying babies to "family" restaurants. Customers who wish to avoid children should dine elsewhere or request a seat away from them. A parent whose child misbehaves in a restaurant should leave the room with the child until he or she calms down.

Deciphering the Menu

Menus in restaurants serving international cuisine often are written in the native language of that cuisine. The customer in America has every right to expect an English translation. The waiter can explain anything that the menu does not.

Ordering the Meal

Years ago (and even today in some restaurants) the gentlemen was handed the menu with the prices on it, while the lady's menu had none.

Today there is a counterpart: the waiter recites the day's unlisted specials, usually omitting the price. You should not hesitate to ask the prices if it is a concern. The waiter will then take drink orders, bring them, and leave.

CODE WORDS

*W*hen you see these words on menus, here's what they mean:

- A la carte ("ala CART"): all items are sold individually.
- Au poivre ("Aw PWAV"): with pepper, such as steak au poivre, crusted in pepper and cooked. This actually reduces the hotness . . . but not entirely!
- Au jus ("aw-JOO"): served with natural juices.
- Blanquette ("blahn-KET"): stew cooked in wine or stock and finished with cream.
- Bonne femme ("bohn FAHM"): served with butter.
- Flambé ("flahm-BAY"): a dish doused with brandy or liqueur and set afire, usually at tableside.
- Paillard ("Pa-YARD"): a boned, joined double breast of a fowl, usually chicken.
- Prix fixe ("pree fix"): a meal sold at a single price, which includes selections of a limited range of items. Often this is a convenience for pretheater meals or diners in a hurry.
- Table d'hôte ("tayb-dote"): a public dining area in a hotel.

The waiter should not be summoned back to the table until each guest is ready to order; when all guests have closed their menus, the waiter knows to approach. Questions about the menu may be asked at this time, as well as inquiries about ingredients, preparation, and so forth. A waiter should be completely knowledgeable about what his kitchen is serving or must offer to find out. Ladies order first. Historically, this has been so that they are not pressured by the gentleman to have what he is having or to have something in the same price range.

Wine

The wine steward, or *sommelier*, can help you choose a wine that is within your price range and that suits the meal. To be sure, some are more diplomatic at it than others.

Generally speaking, you should match the color of the wine to the color of the food: red for meats, white for fish. When in doubt, match a sturdy food with a sturdy wine: chicken and white wine, duck and red wine, and so on. Above all else, though, the wine you like is the wine that's right, and vice versa.

The *sommelier* will present the chosen wine bottle to the person who ordered it. The routine is as follows: you will examine the label to confirm that it is correct. The *sommelier* will then open it and place the cork in front of you. The innermost end of the cork should be moist, which suggests that the wine has been properly stored on its side and no air has gotten in to spoil it.

TOASTING

The ritual of toasting a guest of honor is as old as the spirits chosen with which to make it. The host offers the first toast. If there is talking, he may quiet the room and gain attention by tapping carefully on the edge of a wine glass (don't try this on fine crystal!).

A toast should be to the point. The person making it stands and raises his wine glass toward the honoree. Other guests merely raise their glasses. When the toast has been made, each guest takes a sip of wine.

Nondrinking guests may raise their empty wine glass, or a glass of whatever else they may be drinking, except water. Raising the water glass, or not raising a glass at all, may be construed by some as disapproving the toast. Children may raise their milk glasses. The recipient of the toast sits and does not drink to himself. He may respond with his own toast. In large dining functions where there is a dais, only those people on the dais may propose toasts.

A small amount of wine will then be poured into your glass. This serves two purposes. One, obviously, is to allow you to taste it. The other is to prevent guests from getting any small bits of cork that may have fallen in when the bottle was opened.

Examine and admire the color and bouquet of the wine. Then taste it (first cleanse your palate with a sip of water or piece of white bread). Don't slurp the wine, just taste it. If it is satisfactory, nod, thank the *sommelier*, and direct him to fill the other glasses. If the wine has spoiled, you may send the bottle back without obligation and request another.

In fine restaurants the *sommelier* will sometimes taste the wine first with a silver cup hanging around his neck. This means that he will catch the cork bits, but, more important, that he will ensure that the wine hasn't spoiled in shipping or storage (it sometimes does). In such restaurants it is customary for the waiter to refill the glasses.

Refusing Wine. If one does not want wine, one covers one's glass with one's hand when it is offered, or simply says, "No, thank you," when asked. The old custom of turning over one's wine glass so that it cannot be filled is ostentatious and clumsy.

When the Meal Is Served

The host does not begin eating until all other guests are served. The kitchen is supposed to time their preparation so that all meals for a table are ready at the same time. The waiter is supposed to monitor this.

If there has been a major delay with one meal, the waiter may offer to bring out the others with apologies to the stranded diner. If the delay is to be more than a few minutes, everybody else should begin.

Complaints about the Food

Waiters in better restaurants never ask, "Is everything all right?" because, if the food wasn't all right, it should never have been brought to the table in the first place. If a patron has a complaint about the meal, he should stop eating and the host should summon the waiter. Others at the table are not required to stop eating. The waiter should remove the offending meal to the kitchen for adjustment or replacement, no questions asked.

Clearing the Place

Because people eat at different speeds, some will finish before others. No plate should be cleared until all diners have finished their meal.

The signal for a finished meal is to leave the knife and fork on the upper-right-hand edge of the plate, in the "10 and 2 (o'clock)" position. Regardless, many restaurants today insist on clearing the table before all parties have finished ("Let me just get these out of your way"). Perhaps they are short of dishes. Perhaps they want to rush you out the door. More likely, they just have bad manners. It also is rude for one patron to ask to have his place cleared ahead of the others in his party.

Discrimination

Historically, some restaurants have given poor service to pairs of women on the assumption that they take too long to order and to finish, and then undertip. Doctors also are frequently disdained by waiters; they have a reputation as bad tippers. College-age diners also may suffer discrimination on the assumption that they are newly independent and have not been taught how to tip. Celebrities are reputed to be eclectic tippers—they leave too much or too little, depending on how much they value their reputations.

Doggie Bags

There is nothing wrong with requesting the waiter to wrap an uneaten portion of a meal to take home. After all, you paid for it (at fancier restaurants, the bag is presented to the departing guest at the door).

Reaching for the Tab

The person who asks the waiter to bring the bill is the one who will be expected to pay it, and the waiter should set it before him or her. A waiter who brings the bill without being asked to do so is subtly hinting that he wants you to leave the restaurant. He will usually place it in the center of the table, equidistant from the diners.

The host of a meal should reach for the bill when the waiter brings it, check the addition, and leave payment. Cash or credit card are the usual means of payment, although personal checks and travelers

checks are accepted (inquire when making the reservation). Patrons using coupons should inform the waiter at the time they are first seated.

The waiter will return with the credit card slip or cash change, usually with enough small bills to make tipping convenient. Waiters earn the bulk of their income from tips, despite having to report the income to the IRS. Some patrons will charge the meal, but leave the tip in cash, which is a very kind gesture.

Fighting over the Tab

The person who asks others to dine is the one who pays the restaurant tab and should make this clear at the time the invitation is extended. There is no need for the guest to make a grand gesture of reaching for it or to ask to leave the tip. An offer to reciprocate is always welcome. When a woman invites others to dine, she may have to stress specifically that she does, in fact, expect to pay the bill.

In some communities (particularly Hollywood), people are known to go to extraordinary lengths to pick up a restaurant tab, probably as a tactic to obligate others. Techniques include arriving early and asking the headwaiter to imprint one's credit card; excusing oneself to the rest room and secretly settling at the register; and signing the tab to one's private restaurant account. Legend has it that Marlon Brando once won a check-grabbing contest by threatening his guest, "If you don't let me pay, one of us is going to leave this restaurant naked." It is rude to deprive a host of the privilege of paying for the meal.

Tipping at Restaurants

For table service, a tip of 15 percent of the pre-tax total is an accepted tip for adequate table service; 20% is fast becoming the norm, however. It all depends on the level of service. For groups many restaurants automatically add a 16 to 18 percent gratuity for parties of eight or more (the additional points are meant both to reflect the need for more service and to counteract the 3 to 6 percent credit card surcharge the restaurant must pay).

For counter service, 15 percent is adequate (but never less than 25¢). No tip is expected in a self-service restaurant or cafeteria except where someone refills coffee cups or iced tea glasses, carries your tray to the table, or provides personal service, in which case 10 percent left on the table is adequate. Busboys are not tipped (they are tipped by waiters).

Bartenders get 15 to 20 percent. If you have ordered a drink while waiting for a table, you may settle the tab before you leave the bar. If the bartender rolls your tab over into your dinner bill, you should nevertheless tip the bartender before you take your table.

At catered affairs the servers' tip (15 percent) is covered by the contractor, but patrons may leave $1 for a bartender over the course of the evening (not per drink).

A wine steward receives 15 to 20 percent of the cost of the bottle if he has helped you choose the wine, has not tried to force a more expensive one than you

wanted, and has seen that your glass was never empty. The tip is paid to him directly in cash as you leave the restaurant. If he has merely taken your order and left you to refill your own glasses, 10 to 15 percent is adequate, paid the same way.

The maitre d' (host) is not tipped each time, although $5 to $20 (depending on the restaurant) slipped to him once in a while is appropriate if you are a regular customer and he gets you an especially good table. Otherwise, a $5 bill is sufficient.

The captain depends on tips for his livelihood. If he has been helpful in taking your order, worked hand-in-hand with the waiter, and then seen to your additional needs, he must be tipped. Take whatever tip you would give for service (say 20 percent) and give one-quarter of it to the captain and three-quarters of it to the waiter. Charge slips used by finer restaurants have a special line for this split.

Restaurant musicians get tipped $1 for a special request, and it is perfectly all right to keep eating while it is played, as long as you don't talk through it. Some restaurants have strolling musicians who expect a tip of $1 just to go away. Funny thing is, if you don't pay them a dollar, they still go away.

Coat check is $1 per item, regardless of how many hangers they use. Many checkrooms require advance payment, which is insulting and does little to speed up retrieval.

Parking valet: If there is not a service charge posted at the door ($2 to $5 in most cities), $1 to $2 upon delivery is adequate. Valets are not paid when the car is dropped off (tips are usually pooled). Flamboyant people with expensive cars have been known to tip $20 in advance and ask the valet to use two parking spaces to prevent accidental scratching.

At the Dinner Table

Dinner is the synthesis of all human endeavor. It is the combined product of hunting, science, and industry—not only because of the process itself but also because it comes at the end of the work day after people have engaged in those activities. People become vulnerable at the dinner table (just as animals, prey and predators alike, declare a truce at the watering hole) in the greater interest of exchanging knowledge and extending their relationships.

People can tell more about each other's character by their behavior at dinner than by anything else they do. This is where etiquette levels the playing field.

The Dinner Invitation

A formal dinner invitation (see Chapter 11) is typically extended between two and four weeks before the scheduled event. It will include date, time, address, and the name of the host or hostess. It also may include mode of dress and will most likely request an R.S.V.P.

Replying to a Formal Invitation

One must reply immediately, by telephone if the number is given, or in writing if it is not, to a formal invitation. Failing to do so is unforgivable.

The response must be "yes" or "no" (or, in more formal terms, *accepts* or *regrets*). If you're not sure about whether you can go, then you should say no. The whole purpose of requesting an R.S.V.P. is to allow the hostess to order food and arrange seating, so a "maybe" is never acceptable.

If you want to go but are otherwise committed that evening, you may not break the previous commitment to attend the "better" one. There is no such thing as "I'll come over for coffee and dessert" in formal entertaining. When responding in writing, one should repeat the date, time, and address as it appears on the invitation.

Special Diets

Whether for aesthetic, health, or allergenic reasons, some people must bring their special diets out with them. If one is on a particular eating regimen, one should discuss it with the hostess when accepting a dinner invitation. If she can accommodate the diet, fine; if not, she has no obligation to tailor her entire menu to suit one guest (unless he or she is the guest of honor). It is important for guests suffering from life-threatening allergies (such as MSG or shellfish) to disclose this to the hostess, who may avoid these substances or alert the guest to skip certain courses.

If a guest does not like what is being served, he should accept only a small portion and then ignore it. Vegetarians and those who may be offended by something that is served need not partake of it. One may explain one's reasons to the hostess privately, but should not make a political speech at the table. Guests with even more esoteric eating requirements either should not accept the dinner invitation in the first place or should eat on their own beforehand.

When to Arrive

If the dinner is scheduled for 8:30, guests should arrive at 8:30. In some areas of the country, people arrive fifteen to thirty minutes later than the specified time. If hosts write "eightish" on the invitation, it means to arrive up to 8:30. Because it would be bad to arrive at 9:00 for a dinner that was timed for 8:30, the only way to pin it down is to ask the host when you R.S.V.P.

Changing Your Mind

Once you have accepted an invitation, you may not back out at the last minute for any reason short of death or sudden illness. On the other hand, if a compelling out-of-town trip arises, you should notify your hostess as soon as you learn of the conflict and apologize for your impending absence. (Note: there really has to be such a trip.)

Conversely, if you find that you are suddenly available after having sent regrets, you may be out of luck. If it's a large reception, you may be able to call and ask the hostess if you can still come if she has room. For a small gathering with place cards, however, you should resign yourself to staying at home with a good book.

The Extra Man

Single men whom the hostess knows to be unaffiliated should not automatically assume that a dinner invitation issued to them includes a female guest. "Extra men" are socially valuable as such. A hostess may be planning on pairing him (for the evening, but, hey, who knows?) with a similarly single woman. There is an important distinction between an "extra man" and a gigolo: an extra man's duty ends after dinner.

B.Y.O.B., B.Y.O.F., and Pot Luck Dinners

"Bring Your Own Bottle," "Bring Your Own Food," and "Pot Luck Dinner" parties are always thrown among friends. They are wonderfully informal gatherings to which each person brings whatever he or she desires to consume and share.

The notations "B.Y.O.B.," "B.Y.O.F.," and "Pot Luck" have no place in formal entertaining. The hostess or host is expected to provide everything.

Bringing Wine

One does not bring anything to a formal dinner; the hostess will have planned everything and will require nothing beyond your presence. It can, however, be a thoughtful contribution to a dinner among friends to bring the hostess a bottle of wine. Some bring dessert instead. It is not incumbent upon the hostess to serve the gift if it does not complement the meal she has already planned. It is perfectly proper for the hostess to thank the guest and save the gift for a more appropriate time, e.g., "What a wonderful gift, but I've already opened a bottle, so why don't we enjoy this another time."

TO CLINK OR NOT TO CLINK

Large groups do not clink their glasses during toasts. Individuals (particularly lovers, but anybody toasting a special occasion) may touch their wine glasses together if they wish. Superstition suggests that the glasses be "clinked" at unequal height, never at the same level. If those raising their glasses in a toast are seated too far apart to touch them, the raising itself is sufficient.

Keeping Kosher

Observant Jews and Moslems may restrict their food to that which is kosher or what their religious teachings decree to be "clean." This diet goes beyond prohibitions on pork and shellfish and can extend to types of beverage, to mixing meat and dairy, and even to what kind of dishes are used.

Unless a host already maintains a kosher home, he is under no obligation to change his habits to accommodate others who do. Such guests may either eat ahead of time or refrain from eating at the table.

They also may bring their own food, plates, and utensils to informal gatherings, although it is improper to usurp a host's arrangements on formal occasions.

Seating Arrangements

The hostess decides who will sit where at a dinner party. If she does not lay out place cards, she may direct people where to sit. Thoughtful hostesses will write the guest's name on both sides of the place cards so that persons sitting across from each other can read them.

A gentleman will steady a lady's chair while she sits. No gentleman should be seated until all ladies are seated, with the exception of the hostess (if she is serving), who may stand and advise her guests, "Please be seated." Guests must sit where directed.

If the first course is a cold course (such as melon), it will already be on the table. If it is a hot course (such as soup), the hostess should tell her guests, "Please be seated while I get the first course." Guests need not ask if the hostess needs help. If she does, it is her duty to request it ahead of time or make arrangements for it.

Serving and Removing Plates

Serve from the left and take from the right.

Beginning the Meal

Upon being seated, place the napkin on your lap. Napkins do not belong tucked into collars. Remove the napkin completely from the napkin ring if one is used. Only when the hostess or host picks up her or his fork may the other guests pick up theirs.

Buffet Dining

Buffets, or serve-yourself meals, are popular for feeding large, informal groups. Hosts choosing a buffet should provide food that can be easily served, cut, and eaten, preferably on small tables, but usually balanced on laps.

Guests should not fill their plates to overflowing and should be careful not to mix foods or serving utensils on the buffet table. They should also not sneeze on, cough over, or taste selections until they are eating from their own plates.

Seconds

Guests are not offered additional helpings at formal dinners, although individuals may help themselves if platters are passed. A hostess at an informal dinner will not ask, "Does anyone want seconds?" per se, but may offer them spontaneously. If only one person takes some, the hostess should take some more, too. Buffets, of course, are fair game as long as the food lasts. Friends gathered around the table after dessert may continue to pick at the remains. That's what friendship is all about.

Eating Habits

The old joke goes, "Is it proper to eat olives with the fingers?" "No, the fingers must be eaten separately." In truth, some foods *may* be eaten using fingers, others are best savored with forks, and even with sticks.

Despite popular belief, it is *not* automatically permitted to pick up food with bones (such as lamb chops, chicken, or ribs) unless the food is either served at a picnic, in a rib joint, or at some other place where that eating style is encouraged, *or* if the chop has paper wrapped around a trimmed end bone (the "panty"). There are exceptions, however.

Right-Hand-Only Eating

Some Eastern cultures insist that eating be performed only with the right hand. Using the left hand would be an insult, a tradition harkening back to the days when the left hand was devoted to matters of personal cleanliness.

Ethiopian food, for example—a mound of a spicy, succulent stew served in the middle of a large, round bread presented to the group on a platter—is eaten with the right hand. One tears off a small piece of bread, pinches an amount of the food with it, and carries it to the mouth.

Asian Dining

In Chinese, Japanese, Korean, and other Asian cultures, people eat with chopsticks. One should not attempt to use chopsticks unless one is reasonably skilled with them. Chinese dishes are brought from the kitchen when they are ready, and all at the table share them, carrying a serving to their own rice bowls and eating individually from the bowl. It is rude to jam your personal chopsticks into a common dish. You should use the serving spoon or chopsticks provided.

Your own chopsticks may be left on the edge of your rice bowl while you are still eating, or rested on the edge of your individual serving bowl or plate when you are finished.

Asian noodle dishes are brought to the mouth with chopsticks. When you bite off the excess, you should be careful not to splash. Larger objects, such as wontons, pot stickers, and dumplings, are brought to the mouth with chopsticks, and a bite is taken from them. Slurping is a sign of appreciation, but don't get carried away.

Sushi (raw or cooked fish on rice cakes) may be eaten by hand or chopsticks, but sashimi (sliced fish alone) is eaten with chopsticks only.

The European Knife and Fork

The custom in America is to hold the fork in the left hand while the right hand, holding the knife, does the cutting. One then lays down the knife, switches the fork from the left hand to the right, spears the food, and carries it to the mouth. One also uses the fork to scoop up peas, corn kernels, and other elusive objects.

The European custom is to keep the fork in the left hand, use the knife to push food onto it, and bring the fork to the mouth. In Great Britain, peas, corn, and other small objects are eaten by squashing them onto the fork for delivery to the mouth. Each version has its advantages. Using one style when the majority uses the other has become entirely appropriate.

The One Exception

It is improper to hold the fork in one's fist and stab the meat with it. The fork is held with the left hand, tines down, left index finger extended along the bridge to steady it.

Cutting Up Food

A diner cuts up his food as it is eaten, not all at once, unless he is doing so for a small child.

Eating from Another's Plate

It is impolite to take food from someone else's plate. If one desires to sample or share food, a small portion may be offered on the bread-and-butter plate.

How Much to Take

When a serving dish is passed around the table instead of the meal being individually plated, one may take what one wishes to eat. Some items are clearly portion-controlled (a breast of chicken, a chop, a baked potato, a fish fillet, etc.), in which case the diner accepts a single one unless the hostess suggests otherwise.

For vegetables or less precise foods (shrimp, stews, etc.), try to see what others are taking. When in doubt, take what appears to be a 6-ounce serving (this is standard for restaurants and may be applied to the home). Platters are passed around a table counterclockwise, by the way.

Licking Fingers, Smacking Lips

Food, once it goes into the mouth, should not be seen or heard from again by anybody but the person eating it. Chew with your mouth closed, without talking. If the meal is "picnic style" one may lick one's fingers.

Messy Foods

Ideally, dinner parties feature food that can be eaten with a minimum of fuss. In a perfect world, grapefruit is served already sectioned; shrimp is already peeled; cornish hens are pre-boned; nobody serves chili dogs; and so forth.

In reality, however, if you find you cannot chew something, place it discretely on the side of your plate with your fingers where it won't be noticed.

If you catch a morsel of food between your teeth and cannot dislodge it with your tongue, do not pick at the table, but excuse yourself to the rest room. Should you drip something on your tie, blouse, or pants, you may ask your hostess (or a servant) for assistance. If the splash goes on the table-cloth, say "excuse me" and ask for help (see Chapter 12).

Clearing One's Place

It is the job of the host or servant to remove spent plates from the guests. Guests may not push their own plates out of the way. It is improper to clear the table by stacking or passing; each place must be cleared individually. No plate should be heard touching another plate.

Elbows

Yes, it's true, elbows do not belong on the table at a formal dinner. On informal occasions, however, it is perfectly alright to lean forward and relax (once the plates are cleared, of course).

Smoking

No ashtrays means no smoking.

DETAILS, DETAILS

Place Settings

Nothing intimidates dinner guests more than coming face to face with an array of glistening implements, many apparently duplicating each other. This shouldn't happen. No more than three of any kind of implement should be on the table at the same time. And silverware is placed in order of its use. Always remember: *use silverware from the outside in. If in doubt, watch the hostess.*

The exception is when a piece of silverware is in the wrong place. Discreetly use the correct one. Should the guest of honor use the incorrect implement, however, other guests should do the same, as embarrassment is to be avoided, even at the awkwardness of eating prime rib with a shell-fish fork.

A basic formal dinner place setting includes, left to right (see illustration; see also Chapter 11): fish fork, meat fork, salad fork; plate; salad knife, meat knife, fish knife; soup or fruit spoon. If there is a shellfish fork it goes to the right of the spoon. *Notice that the cutting edges of all knives face inward, or to the left. The most frequent mistake people make in setting a table is putting the knives on the left of the plate or facing them the wrong way. A helpful rule: place knives so they can be picked up and used as is.*

The butter knife is placed on the bread-and-butter plate between 10 and 2. As coffee

and dessert are served after the main course, teaspoons and dessert spoons or forks will not be presented until they are brought with the dessert. The tablecloth in front of the guest must never be exposed. It is set with a large service plate on to which the first course will be placed. The napkin is placed to the left of the forks if the first course is placed on the service plate or on the center of the service plate if the first course will be served hot.

Unlike formal meals, informal meals do not include all the courses, wines, and conventions. Salad and meat forks, a single knife, and a soup spoon usually are adequate. A water glass and single wine glass

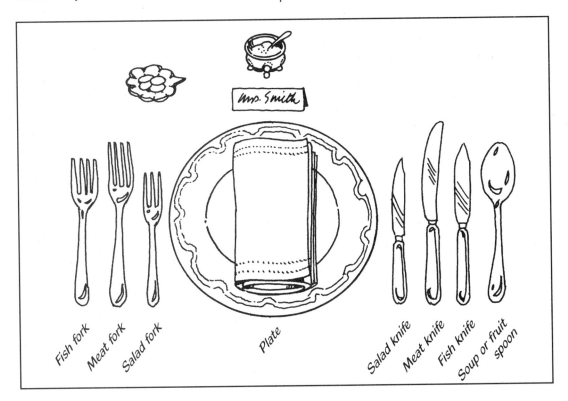

will also do the job. The napkin is placed to the left.

Glasses

Unlike silverware, drinking glasses are placed in order of height and are used as they are filled, according to the meal: water goblet, white wine glass, red wine glass, sherry glass.

Champagne

Water goblet *White wine* *Red wine* *Sherry*

Wine Glasses. Oenophiles differ on the appropriate shape for a basic wine glass, but if there is one all-purpose glass it is one with a tulip-shaped bowl. There is, however, a good reason for having such an assortment of other shapes: tall, narrow, rounded, tapered, small opening, large opening, or fluted. Because the human tongue can receive different sensations (salt, sweet, sour, bitter) at different points on its surface, wine glasses are shaped to deliver a particular

wine to the specific area of the tongue that can best taste it.

Wine is poured from the right, and the glass is never filled more than halfway. It is raised to the mouth by its stem, not the bowl, to keep the hand from warming the contents.

Red wine, which may contain sediment, can be cradled at an angle in a wine basket and poured that way; either red or white wine may be placed upright in a special collar to prevent drips from staining the tablecloth.

Centerpieces

Nothing is worse than a floral centerpiece so tall that guests opposite each other at the table cannot see past it. However, if a guest has been so kind as to send the centerpiece ahead, it would be an insult not to display it. An unwieldy centerpiece can be displayed, acknowledged, and adored, and then removed gallantly to a sideboard prior to a formal meal service.

Formal Table Service

Professional servers are trained in French service in which portions are lifted from the serving platter, which is balanced on one hand, with the serving fork and spoon held in the other hand. Service is almost always from the guest's left; plates are cleared from the guest's right. As previously mentioned, at no time should the bare tablecloth be exposed before the guest; a plate should always cover it. Replacement silverware is brought as needed.

Informal Table Service

Dinner guests who serve themselves from passed bowls or platters should take a reasonable portion and finish it. Platters are all passed counterclockwise at a table.

SPECIALTY SILVERWARE

*O*ver the years, specialty silverware has been developed for particular needs:

- *Shrimp or oyster fork*
- *Olive spoon*
- *Iced tea spoon*
- *Combined dessert spoon and fork*
- *Escargot holder*
- *Pickle fork*

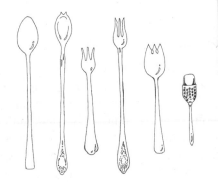

Can you tell which is for what?

Holding on to Silverware

The utensils used for one course are removed with the spent dishes for that course. One does not carry utensils from one course to the next. If a guest has mistakenly used the wrong fork or knife, it is cleared without comment along with those that should have been used and replaced with the appropriate clean one(s) for the next course.

Lemons

If lemons are not already wrapped in cheesecloth to prevent seeds and squirts from escaping, one may insert the tines of one's fork into the lemon wedge and squeeze it over the food. This should prevent accidental squirting.

Salt and Pepper

One does not add salt or pepper to food until one has tasted it. Salt and pepper are shaken directly on to the food, not into the palm of one's hand first. The shaker with lots of holes contains salt, and the other the pepper.

Hors D'oeuvres

Crudités (raw vegetables), canapés (food on crustless bread), and hors d'oeuvres (everything else) are finger foods served before the meal to whet one's appetite, absorb alcohol, and encourage conviviality. They are eaten while standing, mingling, or in any case prior to entering the dining room for the formal meal.

If one serves hors d'oeuvres, a waste plate should be conspicuously placed (and replaced) to allow guests to discard shells, toothpicks, and uneaten food.

Bread and Butter

A small plate, placed to the upper left of the dinner plate, is for bread and butter. The small, rounded butter knife will rest on its upper edge at 10 to 2.

One takes a roll or slice of bread from the basket as it is passed and places it on the bread-and-butter plate. One slices a pat of butter from the butter dish with one's butter knife and transfers the pat onto the edge of the bread-and-butter plate. Thereafter, one tears the bread into small pieces and butters each as needed from the small mound on the plate.

Do not butter an entire roll or slice of bread at once, or take butter directly from the common butter plate to the bread.

Soup

The soup spoon is pushed away from you in the bowl, touched briefly to the side of the bowl to deposit excess drops, and then lifted parallel to the mouth. Only if the spoon is small enough may it be placed into the mouth; otherwise, it is emptied silently into the mouth from its side. The last spoonfuls of soup may be savored by tipping the soup bowl away from you and spooning it as before.

Soup bowls should always be served on a plate so that the soiled spoon may be

placed on the edge of the plate and not left in the bowl.

Consommé and Bouillon. These are clear soups, sometimes served cold or jellied, and are eaten with soup spoons. If the soup is specifically served in a bouillon cup with handles on the sides, it may be lifted to the mouth and drunk in that manner, when cooled. A spoon may, of course, also be used.

Salad

Salads may be served before the main course (American style) or after the main course and before the dessert (European style). Either way, they should be prepared with the lettuce torn into bite-size pieces. Salads of asparagus, heart of palm, whole leaves, lettuce wedges, or other items that require cutting by the guest should be accompanied by separate salad knives and forks (see formal place settings).

Caesar Salad. Usually, Caesar salads are dressed and tossed before they are presented on a salad plate. One form of Caesar is presented with whole (or halved lengthwise) leaves of Romaine lettuce, which the guest then holds by the stalk end to scoop up the tangy dressing. It may also be cut with salad fork and knife.

Asparagus

Plain chilled asparagus may properly be eaten with the fingers by holding the bottom of the stalk and dipping, where provided, into dressing. Where the stalks are presented already dressed, a knife and fork are appropriate.

Artichokes

Artichokes are members of the thistle family. They have a tender heart surrounded by a bristle "choke" and outer leaves, the inner tips of which are edible.

An artichoke is eaten by tearing off individual leaves, dipping the inside end into a sauce or dressing, and scraping the tender flesh off with one's teeth. The "heart" is savored last by scooping out the bristles with the knife. Some chefs will thoughtfully remove the choke prior to serving and may also fill the center with the dip. Scraped leaves are discarded neatly on the edge of the serving plate.

Melon

If a slice of melon is not already cut into chunks, then one uses a spoon to scoop out bite-size pieces with one hand while steadying the wedge with the other. Sometimes a wedge of lime or lemon may accompany the melon. It may be squeezed onto the melon if desired.

Bacon

If bacon is crisp enough to shatter when cut, it may be eaten with the fingers, but if it is soft-cooked it is eaten with a knife and fork.

Small Fowl

Legs of squab, quail, pheasant, and Cornish game hens may be eaten with the fingers after the rest of the meat has been removed with a knife and fork.

Peas

Only the Three Stooges eat peas with a knife. Peas should be scooped or speared with a fork.

Other Veggies

Celery, olives, carrots, jicama, and other vegetables presented as crudités on a relish tray may be eaten with the fingers. Vegetables served dressed or within a salad should be eaten with a fork.

Corn on the Cob

Suitable for informal dining, corn on the cob is grasped with the fingertips of both hands. It is buttered, salted, and peppered only a few rows at a time, with the butter pat first brought to the plate from the butter dish, as with bread and butter.

Pizza

If it's soft and runny, use a knife and fork to cut it into bite-size pieces until the remainder of the slice is small enough to pick up by the edge crust. Or you can just say, "Hey, it's pizza," and go for it; etiquette, schmetiquette.

Chips and Dip

Whatever is to be dipped into salsa, dressing, guacamole, and so on should be dipped in only once. It is inappropriate (and unsanitary) to put something back into a common dip that has been in one's mouth.

Finger Bowls

Following a meal, guests may be presented with a small dish of liquid, frequently with a slice of lemon or a flower floating in it. This is a finger bowl. One does not drink this liquid. One dips the edges of one's fingers into it, one hand at a time, then wipes them dry on the napkin. One may also touch the lips with the liquid to cleanse them.

The finger bowl may signal the end of the meal, although it may also precede the dessert. Watch the hostess to see whether she moves her finger bowl aside (making way for dessert) or keeps it in front her (that's all, folks!).

Demitasse

A demitasse is half a cup of coffee served in a half-cup-size coffee cup. It is served with a small spoon.

How to Hold a Teacup

It is the Western custom to grasp a teacup by slipping the index finger through the looped handle and placing the thumb on the top of the loop to steady it. One does not wrap one's hand around the cup or lift it with both hands, as in Eastern cultures, unless one is in the East at the time, of course.

Bread-and-Butter Notes

The day following the dinner, guests should send a thank-you note to the host or hostess. The colloquial term for this is a *bread-and-butter note*. It should say how much you enjoyed dinner, what a scintillating evening it was, and how much you would like to invite your hosts over to your house soon.

Returning the Favor

A reciprocal dinner date should be made within three or four months of the initial evening if both parties are agreeable. If it is not possible to return the favor at home, invite the other party to a good restaurant as your guest. There is less of an obligation to reciprocate if you declined the original invitation, although you may still wish to show your gratitude for the initial thoughtfulness.

TIPPING

There are so many people who perform so many services that it is difficult to decide who gets a tip and who doesn't, and how much or how often. This is exacerbated by the myth that America is a classless society, yet tips signify class difference.

Well, think again. As America moved from a manufacturing economy to a service economy, more and more Americans began depending on tips for their income. This is because service workers tend not to be protected by unions or covered by the same level of minimum wages as production workers. As a result, tips are no longer the icing on an employee's cake. Too often, they can be the cake itself.

European Tipping

It is the custom in most European countries to include the tip, or gratuity, usually 15 percent, in the restaurant bill before it is presented. In America the customer is required to compute it himself. This can lead to embarrassment and even antagonism. When they hear customers speaking with an accent, some American waiters may take it upon themselves to remind Europeans that the tip is not included.

Restaurants with a European clientele will often print a discreet notice on the menu to remind travelers of the distinction. Detailed information on international tipping will be found in Chapter 6.

When Your Host Undertips

Not everybody tips at the same level, but sometimes an obvious mistake can be made. If you notice that your host has grossly undertipped—and if this is a restaurant where you are known or to which you are apt to return—you may *discreetly* leave more money on the table as you leave.

Tipping Servants

The employer, of course, pays a salary and so has no need to tip his or her household help. Guests need not tip a friend's

house staff unless they have been particularly helpful over the course of several days' stay. In such case, $10 to $20 would be appreciated, handed discreetly.

Limousine drivers usually have their tip (17 to 20 percent) added to the overall cost of hiring a chauffeured car. Inquire at the time you make the reservation. Remember to make allowances for your driver to take meal breaks when you do (some hotels and restaurants make special provisions).

Tipping the Boss

As much as proprietors of barber shops, beauty salons, flower shops, garages, and other businesses grumble about it, customers do not need to tip them as they would employees. Regular customers may give the owner a holiday gift, however.

Tipping Golf Caddies

At a club or public course, a caddie is tipped 15 to 20 percent of the worth of the green fee.

Barbers and Hairdressers

A tip of 15 to 20 percent, and in no case less than $1, is adequate for a barber or hairdresser. Separate services performed by manicurists and shampooists should also be tipped another $2, more for unusually good or detailed service.

Skycaps

Uniformed airline personnel who check luggage curbside are colloquially called skycaps. They earn their salary from tips. A skycap should be tipped at least $1 per checked bag, paid at the time he hands over the claim checks.

Delivery Persons

Florists, supermarket delivery people (whether to the door of the house or trunk of the car), the pizza guy, fruit basket people and telegram messengers get $1 to $3 depending on the number of or weight of the items.

Federal Express, DHL, UPS, and U.S. Post Office delivery people are not usually tipped, but a $10 to $20 Christmas tip for regular service is appreciated.

Apartment Staff

Apartment complexes and condominium associations usually have a "Christmas pool" into which residents contribute a given amount that is split among the workers who have been attending them all year. Other apartment buildings may have a checklist that they will happily provide to residents for individual seasonal gratuities.

If a building employee has been consistently or especially helpful (rehanging curtains, running out for a quart of milk, parking the car, being discreet in certain manners, etc.), a specific gratuity is called for. Cash always is more appreciated than presents—and is certainly better than booze. The following applies:

- *Repairmen.* If you tip them each time they do work, then $5 to $10 at year-end is fine; if you do not, then $20 is more suitable.
- *Building superintendent.* A resident super is a blessing, and if he has performed work for you throughout the year, $50 to $75 is not too much to bestow.
- *Doormen.* A tip of $25 to $50 is appropriate. The high end applies if he's called taxis, carried baggage, walked your pet, or shepherded your kids.
- *Front desk.* A tip of $25 to $40 is appropriate for the day clerk who sorts your mail and $10 to $20 for the night clerk who rings you when your cab arrives.
- *Others* (delivery person, cleaner, paper boy, etc.): A tip of $5 to $10 per person is appropriate in a large building, $10 to $20 in a smaller building. If you are in a pinch, the building management can make suggestions.

Nursing Home Attendants

As with apartment and condo staffs, the year-round service by nursing home personnel may be rewarded at Christmas by a single donation to a staff fund. Individuals who have a particularly close relationship with a resident may be given a present, but not liquor.

CHAPTER SIX

A LITTLE
TRAVELING
MUSIC:

*Getting Around
the World*

Mad Magazine (ever the arbiter of popular taste) once flouted plane geometry by noting, "The shortest distance between two points is a taxi." Obviously, that doesn't apply to modern city driving.

America's streets—and, increasingly, its highways—are no longer the simple means of conveyance for which they were built. Now they are concrete gauntlets through which motorists must pass while other motorists play out their psychodramas, often with deadly results. Freeway shootings, high-speed chases, overpass assaults, and drive-by killings have become hazards of modern commuting. The collective term for it is *road rage.*

Against the harsh reality of road rage, the notion of etiquette seems trivial. Yet the way people treat each other while traveling (whether they do the driving themselves or leave it to professionals) is a symbol of how people should behave in general. Car culture is only the most pervasive example.

A line from the 1984 movie *Repo Man* said it all: "The more you drive, the less intelligent you become." As Americans spend more time in their cars, they lose respect for the tangibility of other people. Human exchange has changed to the point that people communicate mostly through fax,

> *The vagabond, when rich, is called a tourist.*
>
> —Paul Richard,
> *The Scourge of Christ*

phone, e-mail, answering machines, telephone computer directory, and rumor. Social scientists actually worry that young people are being raised without the ability to have reasoned face-to-face interactions with strangers: the risk is that, when they encounter a point of view different from theirs, the only way they will know to oppose it will be with violence rather than discourse. Yet this is happening at a time when Americans are able to travel more widely and easily than ever before, so that meeting new people has become inevitable.

Airline deregulation has lowered fares to the point where the skies are no longer the domain of the rich, but of people who, ten years ago, would have taken the bus. This egalitarianism has created a culture clash: travelers bring their local customs with them, but those customs may be at odds with those found at their destination. Given the way Americans have of insisting they are always right, this cannot help but breed some annoying breaches of etiquette.

This does not happen only when New Yorkers visit Iowa; the ultimate culture clash is, of course, with other actual cultures—that is, the rest of the world. Legends of the "ugly American" are neither new nor false, and although U.S. dollars are prized around the world, U.S. attitude is not.

The situation reverses itself when international visitors—of whatever visa status—

arrive in the United States. Americans who behaved themselves while abroad (remembering the admonition, "When in Rome, do as the Romans do") now bridle when they see immigrants rejecting American traditions in favor of those they supposedly abandoned in coming here. Today no election is complete without at least one xenophobic initiative. So "travel etiquette" covers a wide range, and it begins in the driveway.

DRIVING

Car Alarms

There is some evidence that the car alarm has replaced "The Star-Spangled Banner" as the national anthem. Maybe a car alarm does drive off a car thief now and then, but more often it is simply a sleep-shattering annoyance. Most alarms are adjusted to go off at the slightest provocation: when a truck drives past, a motorcycle revs up, an old person steadies herself on the fender, or another car taps the bumper while it is being parked. Car alarm owners themselves are often unable to disable their own device before opening the door!

As a result, communities are enacting laws permitting police to tow a car whose alarm has sounded for more than fifteen minutes. When even that doesn't satisfy vigilantes, it is common for alarm fanciers to have their tires slashed by neighbors who are tired of being awakened at 3 A.M. Bad manners cost money.

Hogging Two Parking Spaces

There are laws against parking in red zones, in airport terminals, in blue wheelchair spaces, in front of driveways, and close to fire hydrants, but apparently nothing to prevent anyone from hogging two parking places. What the law forgets, courtesy should remember.

Turn Signals

Beyond the law's designation to signal fifty yards or five seconds before a turn (the length varies by state), it simply makes sense to let other drivers know what you're doing. Some people regard turn signals not as direction indicators but, rather, as invisible hands that nudge other cars out of the way. Needless to say, a warned driver is a safer driver.

The "Finger"

Aggressive driving is an American trait, and nothing is more aggressive than flipping the bird (a.k.a. one's middle finger) at another driver. Everybody knows what it means, and nobody likes to be on the receiving end. Needless to say, it is bad manners to flip anybody off at any time, and in heavy traffic it can be deadly if the flippee is armed.

Cruising

The 1973 movie *American Graffiti* showed the rest of the world a social driving activity known as "cruising." Cruising is driving slowly on a public street so as to be noticed in one's car, to notice people in other cars, and to notice people watching from the sidewalk. Cruising used to be peculiar to small towns, and usually only on weekend nights. It has since spread to major cities (police actually close streets in Los Angeles to curtail it).

The practice has its adherents, which do not include drivers who want to get anyplace fast, and social mores: who gets to ride with whom, whose car is cooler, and whose radio is louder.

A more specific form of cruising takes place in urban areas. This involves drivers who stop in the middle of the street to talk with their friends, who may be on foot or in their own cars, and mindlessly allow traffic to back up behind them. It is considered being sociable.

In other contexts, *cruising* is a term applied to the solicitation of prostitutes. Neither form of cruising is considered to be good manners.

Horn Blowing

Rather than pull into a nearby parking place, a driver picking up a friend will idle his or her car outside the friend's house and honk the horn until the friend appears. This practice disturbs neighbors and cheapens the reputation of the person being called for.

Headlight Customs

The law may say when and how headlights are to be used, but over the years drivers have developed their own informal rules that are mysteriously passed down from parents to children rather than from legislature

to constabulary. (Note: these are presented here for reference only.)

1. If you want to pass a slow car in front of you, flash your brights (high beams).
2. If a semi signals to pull in front of you, turn your lights on and off twice to let him know when there's room (likewise, accord a semi a wide berth on downgrades; no jackrabbit passing).
3. If one or more oncoming motorists flash their lights on and off at you, it means that there is a police speed trap ahead.
4. If somebody calls out "Lights!" it means that you are driving with your headlights off when they should be on.
5. If an oncoming car flashes his brights at you, it means that your brights are on (and shouldn't be).
6. Flashing headlights sometimes indicates a traffic accident or other disturbance ahead.

Alas, there is no informal symbol for "Hey, stupid, your turn signal has been flashing for the last three miles!"

Traffic Cops

Next to domestic disturbances, routine traffic stops expose police officers to the greatest dangers. As a result, they can be extremely tense when pulling drivers over for presumed driving violations. Don't push their buttons—remember Rodney King.

If stopped by a police officer, pull off the road, kill your engine, and wait with your hands in full view for the officer to approach. Do not get out of the car. There may be a delay while the officer runs your license plate through the computer for other violations.

When he or she approaches, slowly roll down your window. If you have a legal weapon in the car, this is the time to tell the officer and wait for specific instructions. (If you have an illegal weapon, why are you reading an etiquette book?)

The officer will tell you why you were pulled over. If he does not, then he may have another agenda, in which case be very careful indeed. He will ask to see your license and registration. If your registration is in the glove compartment, tell the officer, "It's in the glove compartment" before reaching for it slowly. If your license is in your wallet or purse, likewise retrieve it slowly. Hand only the license to the officer; he doesn't want to be accused later of removing cash (or anything else) from your wallet.

Don't argue with the officer, even if you are right; it won't do any good, and he might even be baiting you. Save it for court if you choose to fight the citation. If you are a passenger in a car whose driver is pulled over, keep your hands in sight as well and sit quietly.

PUBLIC TRANSPORTATION

The problem with public transportation is that the general public uses it. When people ride together in a single means of conveyance (bus, subway, train, trolley, elevator, etc.), the wrongful assumption is that nobody violates anybody else's personal space, whether by body odor, bad breath, radios, whistling, self-talking, stretching, or standing too close. Legislation is written to protect all people, even if it is selectively enforced. Etiquette demands no less.

Seating

People who board a bus or subway early enough to get a seat may sit wherever and however they want. Should the car fill to the point of crowding, then persons taking up two seats should shift to occupy only one. Younger people should yield their seats to the elderly or persons with disabilities; if they don't want it, they should politely decline. A gentleman should offer his seat to a lady, even a younger one.

One offers a person a seat by rising and graciously asking, "Excuse me, would you like to sit down?" It sounds begrudging to say, "Hey, I'm getting off at the next stop anyway, so why doncha park it here?"

Parents with Children

Parents should watch their children to keep them from bothering other passengers. If a child is young enough to get onto a bus or train for free, the child should occupy the parent's lap, not a seat, if the car is crowded.

Annoying Passengers

Disturbances on public transportation are best handled by the transit police, who unfortunately are seldom there when the trouble occurs. It may be dangerous for passengers to attempt to intervene, and, as behavioral scientists too often report, people generally ignore others in trouble rather than assist them. Therefore, the drunk, disturbed, obnoxious, smelly, feverish, or perverted passenger should be cut a wide swathe rather than be confronted. That may not say a lot for human kindness, but it does strike a sad blow for pragmatism.

Spitting, Smoking, and the Like

Despite rules against it (both legal and hygienic), people insist on smoking on buses and subways. As posted signs and common knowledge make it clear that smoking is not allowed, it's reasonable to assume that people who ignore them do so on purpose. Nevertheless, one should first politely ask the smoker to extinguish his or her cigarette, cigar, pipe, or joint. As the reply will very likely be some version (verbal or nonverbal) of "no," one should summon the bus or subway conductor.

This probably won't do much good, so the next step is just to change seats. Sad to say, the cretins in our society get what they want more often than respectful people do.

Elevator Etiquette

Elevators are microcosms of society. While using them, people generally stand close together, face forward, watch the floors change, mind their own business, and wonder what the person standing behind them is thinking.

If wearing hats, men should remove them when ladies or elders enter. The person standing nearest the control panel should press the "door open" and floor buttons if people call them out—adding "please," of course.

Women should be allowed to enter and exit ahead of men, unless it would be obviously awkward for everybody in the car to shuffle. In that case, a man may exit first and say, "Excuse me."

People who have eaten beans and garlic are reminded to control themselves while inside elevators.

Every now and then, somebody gets the bright idea of making a sunny, inoffensive comment in a crowded elevator. This usually causes everybody to chuckle, smile, and look around pleasantly at each other. It has even been known to brighten people's day—just a thought.

PASSENGER TRAINS

Gone are the days (er, nights) when the Twentieth Century Limited would depart New York with a pomp and circumstance reserved for coronations and arrive in Chicago the next evening to a gaggle of reporters straining to hear the illustrious passengers' every utterance. Now Amtrak has taken over and, snazzy as they try to be, it's all Congress can do every year just to appropriate enough money to keep the engines stoked.

Many people prefer rail travel, and not just those who hate flying. It's a fine way to see the country and meet people. Too bad that trains can't treat their passengers as well as their passengers treat them. It's hard to get reservations on the few sleepers that still run, and the food in the dining car is apt to be microwaved. Smoking is still allowed in the club cars, and there aren't always enough porters (redcaps) to go around.

Train travelers with sleeper reservations report to the sleeping car within half an hour of departure and present themselves to the conductor, who shows them to their assigned compartment. The redcap stows their baggage (tip: $1 per bag or as posted; the conductor is not tipped).

The pullman porter can hang clothing in the compartment, arrange for dining car reservations, take shoes to be shined overnight, set up bedding, and provide wake-up calls (tip: $3 per passenger per day for turning down the bed; more with increase of service provided, paid on leaving; be sure to ask if the porter changes shifts so you can tip him before he goes). Club car bartenders and dining car waiters are tipped the customary 15 to 20 percent.

Diners traveling alone may be seated in the dining car with a stranger. This is proper and traditional. Each party pays for his or her own meal. In olden days the waiter would introduce the two diners, who would then have permission to talk—for the meal only. These days, chat is at the diner's own discretion.

Passengers not traveling in sleepers may book first-class club seats or travel unre-served coach, in which case they must sleep sitting upright.

One should be careful not to roll one's head onto a fellow passenger's shoulder while asleep, or drool on his lapel. Aisle passengers who recline in their seats should allow window passengers to pass for whatever reason. In the absence of porters or conductors, younger or more able people should help older or less able passengers stow their luggage in overhead racks.

As with airplanes, people who use the lavatories should go about their business quickly and tidy up after themselves.

Parents traveling with small children should prevent them from making noise or racing up and down the aisles, as other passengers usually try to work or sleep. Finally, it is perfectly all right to bring food back to one's seat and consume it beside a stranger.

CRUISE SHIPS

Whether you are on a transatlantic crossing or a sightseeing "cruise to nowhere," luxury liners remain a popular and glamorous means of travel. Since they harken back to a more gracious time, most cruise ships try to preserve the elegance of the golden age of ocean voyages.

Arriving

Departing passengers should arrive at the dock an hour or more ahead of time. The dock porter (stevedore) will carry baggage on to the ship for placement by the cabin steward. Get his number from his ID tag in case you have to follow up. He will expect a tip of several dollars ($2 per bag, minimum $10 to $15).

Stateroom farewell parties may be held, but only by prior arrangement. Bring your own liquor, as ships are not usually licensed to sell alcohol while in port. All guests must leave the ship when informed "all ashore that's going ashore."

Problems en Route

Ship's facilities are booked well in advance and are difficult to alter. If you are housed next to noisy passengers, or if your deck chair puts you in the midst of people whose habits do not complement your own, ask the purser if you can change. Just be aware that it might not always be possible.

Children at Sea

Children must be told in absolute terms that they must obey the rules of the crew, as they involve their personal safety. They should not be allowed to run freely and disturb other passengers. As with resort hotels, cruises are where people go to unwind, not unravel.

Shipboard Dining

When passage is confirmed, you should immediately book a dining room table with the purser. There usually are two seatings: early and late. Families with kids should arrange to take the first seating. Unaccompanied men and women may

CRUISE SHIP TIPPING

Ship personnel should be tipped at the end of each week for longer voyages; if yours is a short-term cruise (say, a long weekend), tip each helpful person separately as you leave. The total allotted to tips should be 15 percent of the fare (the cruise line will happily send a breakdown list):

- Officers: Officers are never tipped (a big no-no).
- Stevedore: Tip $2 per bag, minimum $10 to $15.
- Cabin steward: Tip $25 to $30 per week.
- Dining room steward: Tip $25 per week (or more, per service).
- Dining room chief steward: Tip $20 per week.
- Busboy: Tip $7 to $10 per week (on ships, busboys are tipped).

Other ship's staff, such as bartenders, hairdressers, masseurs/masseuses, may be tipped at the time they render service.

On "high concept" cruises, such as sports fan voyages or movie buff trips, the celebrities are not tipped.

request a "miscellaneous" table to meet people, at which the dining room steward will make introductions if the guests themselves do not.

The Captain's Table

An invitation to dine at the captain's table is a compliment that may be extended but not requested. The captain is addressed by his surname, as in "Captain Sherwin."

Dress

Some cruises insist on formal dress on the first and last night out to sea or the night before putting into port. This custom has relaxed a great deal, but one should inquire before packing.

Men are expected to dress in black tie, but women may wear evening dresses (not gowns) and, on subsequent nights, suits. Dinner garb such as white jackets for men and evening suits for women also are expected.

Luncheon in the dining room usually requires jackets and ties for men, and dresses for women. Desktop dining, such as a buffet, may be casual.

Seasickness

The ship's doctor can treat what a passenger's own doctor may have missed. Over-the-counter motion sickness medications are usually effective in addressing *mal de mer,* but remember that *they work only if taken prior to sailing.* A great deal of sensitivity should be accorded those who suffer from

seasickness. It is never proper to dwell on, or exacerbate, somebody's seasickness. Just tell them that you hope they feel better and try to stand back in case they don't.

AIRPLANES

People can behave strangely in airplanes. Either they are very friendly because they're all crammed in the same tight space or they are diffident—because they're all crammed in the same tight space. Because of this cramming, it is imperative that airline passengers respect each other more than in any other mode of public transport.

Air passengers should refrain from wearing strong perfume or spraying scented water. Passengers should also bathe and avoid garlic before a flight and should control their children just as they would, say, in church. We've all heard the joke about the kid who made so much racket on board a plane that the flight attendant sent him outside to play.

Flight Attendants

Even though they function primarily as waiters and waitresses, flight attendants are highly trained in everything from first aid and sea rescue to pillow fluffing and diplomacy. Some can even make a mean Long Island iced tea. Flight attendants should be accorded respect and cooperation, particularly where the safety of the plane and its passengers may be concerned.

BUSES

Long-distance bus trips are the most accessible of travel arrangements and are favored by those making medium-length jaunts between areas where air travel is either too costly or unavailable.

Passengers checking bags may do so with the driver (who is not tipped) or through a redcap at the bus terminal (who is tipped at $1 per bag).

In recent years, bus companies have tried to cleanse their reputations as havens for reprobates. Deportment aboard a tour bus should be as proper as on any other means of travel. The driver should be called upon to handle any problems with passengers who are drunk, ill, or otherwise indisposed.

Generally speaking, people snooze toward the front of the bus and party toward the back (where the rest rooms are). Strangers should respect their neighbor's wishes not to engage in conversation.

Travelers may plan to bring along food (nothing too aromatic) that can be eaten neatly on board. Long-distance buses will also pull into rest stops every few hours for dining and stretching.

TAXICABS

It seems that getting a job driving a cab is the first thing an immigrant does after he lands in this country—ahead of learning English or directions. Cab service in major American cities is so appalling that municipal governments and taxi companies have joined forces to ensure that drivers are clean, polite, honest, and—most important—know where they're going. It's still a struggle.

Cab drivers are tipped 15 to 20 percent of the fare shown on the meter, plus $1 per bag if they load it into the trunk themselves. If several passengers share a cab, such as from the airport or during blizzards, there will be a payment formula posted in the cab.

Always look for a city medallion and picture ID of the driver. It is not advised to take so-called "gypsy" (unlicensed) cabs or cabs whose drivers actively solicit passengers on the street.

When the passenger gets into a cab, she should tell the driver exactly where she wants to go and make sure the driver knows how to get there. If the driver does not know, he should consult a guide book (every cab carries one) or radio the dispatcher for directions.

It is sad, but true, that some drivers will try to take advantage of women, minorities, tourists, and non-English-speaking passengers. It also is true that police hackney divisions have no patience with drivers who do such things, and a customer complaint (with medallion number, license plate, or driver's name) will usually bring swift justice.

If you want to frustrate a nasty driver, lock both passenger doors when you get out.

HOTELS

Making Reservations

Some hotel procedures are guided by tradition, others by efficiency, and still others by law.

Reservations may be phoned, written, or made through a travel agent. If one plans to stay in a first-class hotel, reservations are essential. Rates can vary widely according to season, day of week (some hotels offer reduced weekend rates), position of room or suite, and corporate versus personal account. With a few lucky exceptions, rates correspond to quality and service.

When phoning for a room reservation, ask for "reservations." Know in advance the days you plan to arrive and depart. Check-in time is usually after 2 P.M. and check out time is generally noon, so a late check-in or check-out must be arranged in advance. You may also "guarantee" the room with your credit card number (especially important if you expect a late check-in); this also means that you are obligated to pay even if you fail to show up. Cancellations must usually be made twenty-four hours in advance to avoid charges.

This is also the time to pin down specific rates, ask for smoking or nonsmoking rooms, inquire about day care (if you are traveling with children), and—sometimes helpful—inquire about any large conventions that may be booked in the hotel at the same time.

Arrival at the Hotel

The doorman will open your car door, unload your luggage, and see that it gets safely into the hotel lobby near the registration desk. For this he should be tipped no less than $1 and more if there was a lot of luggage. If you have a car, the doorman will either have a valet drive it to the parking garage or direct you to a temporary parking place.

Registration

Introduce yourself to the desk clerk by giving the name under which the room reservation was made. The desk clerk will offer a registration form on which to write your name and address (business or personal), how many nights, and the method of payment.

The hotel may require your credit card impression even if you plan to settle your account with cash. If you do not use credit cards, you should make arrangements when you place your reservation. Some hotels and motels may require your car license plate number. If you are traveling with others, you may register for them unless they have their own reservations or payment obligations.

After you have registered, the desk clerk will then direct a bellman to show you to your room and fetch your bags. Even if you brought only one bag, allow the bellman to take it. The desk clerk is not tipped. The bellman is tipped $2 for the first piece of luggage and $1 for each additional one.

HOTEL TIPPING

A hotel is home—at least for a couple of nights—and the people who work there are like household servants. There is at least one major difference, however. In a hotel you are expected to pay tips, not salaries, for services rendered, so it helps to travel with a wad of $1 bills. Since motels usually offer reduced service, use the lower end of the fee range:

- Bellman. Tip $2 for the first bag, $1 for each additional bag, per bellman.
- Concierge. For nominal help, such as driving directions, they receive no tip. For making reservations, tip $5. If they get you tickets for a prized show, figure on $10 or more.
- Desk clerk. No tip is necessary.
- Dining room. See restaurant tipping sidebar.
- Doorman. Tip $1 to $2 if he helps you in or out with your bags, $2 to $5 if he gets you a cab (higher if it's raining), and an additional $2 to $5 upon departure if he has held the door for you numerous times along the way.
- Elevator operator. Tip $1 per day, as you leave.
- Housekeeping. You may never see the maid who makes your bed, but she could use $3/night left in an envelope on the dresser (or at

the front desk if you leave on a weekend and the maid won't be back till Monday).
- Newsstand. No tip is necessary.
- Room service. Tip $2 for ice versus 15 percent of the food bill, which will be on top of the room service fee tacked on by the kitchen.
- Shoe shine. Tip $1 plus the cost of shine (if done while you sit).
- Spa attendant. Tip $2 if he or she provides towels or services.
- Valet. The charges for the valet service will appear on the room bill, but $1 in cash (more if you have more items delivered) is a good in-person tip.
- Washroom attendant. Tip $1 or 50¢, depending on swankiness, for the attendant who hands you a towel or brushes off your clothing.
- Innkeeper of bed & breakfast. No tip is necessary.

Showing the Room

The bellman will open your room door with the key. More hotels are adding key cards and access codes to make access safer, if trickier. The guest enters ahead of the bellman.

The bellman will show the room, unload baggage, recommend the hotel restaurants, point out the room mini-bar, and hang suit-paks in the closet. The bellman can answer questions about the hotel or the city, with one important exception: guiding a guest toward illicit activity.

Examining the Room

Once the bellman has departed, it is important to explore the area surrounding the room because it will be unfamiliar should you be awakened by an emergency during the night. Check for the nearest light switch, telephone, exit, and fire escape. Make sure that the room clock or clock radio is set correctly. If you need more bathroom linens or phone books, call the front desk to have them sent up.

Room Service

Room service menus are usually in the room. Allow thirty to forty-five minutes for delivery; the restaurant can advise any delay when ordering. Ice (if the hotel doesn't have a guest-accessible machine), liquor, corkscrews, setups, and other services also are available through room service.

The Concierge

At a separate desk in the lobby is the concierge, a well-connected man or woman who can obtain restaurant reservations, tour information, or theater tickets and give directions. The concierge is a key to the human side of a city.

Messages

A hotel that cannot take accurate messages might as well close. To alleviate the problem, some hotels have instituted voice mail. This is not a solution, it is an admission that they cannot handle basic duties.

After checking into a room it may be necessary to call the front desk to ask that outside service be switched on. This done, there is usually a red light that flashes when a message has been received. Finer hotels slip a written message under the guest's door and use the phone light as a backup. Still others leave the message folded in the guest's mail slot at the front desk.

Going In and Out

The custom in America is for the guests to keep the room key with them when they temporarily leave the hotel. In Europe it is to deposit it with the desk clerk. On returning, one may inquire at the desk whether there have been any messages.

Guests and Assignations

For security reasons, many hotels will not give out a guest's room number, but will direct a visitor to the house phones so he can ring the guest's room. This certainly is true in hotels that cater to celebrities.

Regrettably, some hotels will act suspicious toward a single woman, no matter how well dressed, who arrives at the hotel after dark and inquires after a guest. Frankly, they may think she is a call girl. A lady who feels she is being treated in this way should ask to speak to the manager immediately.

Checking Out

Check-out time usually is posted on a list of house rules behind the front door of each room. It is generally between noon and 1 P.M. A guest may phone the front desk to prepare his charges and send up a bellman; he may summon a bellman and alert the front desk when he gets there; or, in some hotels, he may check out using a two-way television system. Some hotels even slip the bill under a guest's door as a reminder that it's time to leave (tacky, but efficient).

Accounts should be squared at the front desk. If there are any questions, they are best settled now rather than later, before credit card charges go through. Hotels in some cities append a startling number of additional charges: city room tax, sales tax, hotel tax, phone surcharges, and so on.

This also is the time to explain any irregularities with the mini-bar, such as a previous guest who drained the dark-tinted bottles and put the empties back in the rack.

The bellman should again be tipped, as should the doorman who fetches a cab and loads the bags in its trunk. If one has parked one's car in the hotel lot, the valet should be tipped.

Room Damage

Unless you are a rock group (and even then it's frowned upon), leave the hotel room in the condition in which you found it. This includes all ashtrays, towels, bathrobes, furniture, and silverware, but not the cute little shampoos. If you have hosted an unscheduled overnight guest, you may be billed an additional charge if the second bed was used.

Treatment of Employees

As a rule, hotel employees are discreet. After a while, they have seen it all and could not care less.

On the other hand, a bellman, maid, or night clerk should never be forced into an untenable position (such as witnessing open drug use, guests running around naked, or a prostitute being brought in) that may compel him or her to summon security.

ALL-INCLUSIVE RESORTS

Resorts such as Club Med have their own, highly informal rules that are designed less to preserve their clients' privacy than to encourage them to share it. It may be fun, but it's not proper etiquette.

HOTEL SLIP-UPS

Sometimes hotels lose reservations. Sometimes room service is really, really late. Sometimes a wake-up call comes at the wrong time. Sometimes the switchboard puts a caller through to an empty room and leaves the phone ringing.

Guests should never lose their temper or create a disturbance; all it does is calcify the hotel's position. Instead (as with many conflicts, by the way), you should realize that the hotel probably has a fair way of settling discreetly posed disputes, to wit:

"Perhaps you can find me a day room until mine is ready, and then I can move."

"Isn't there some way of revising my room rate as, after all, the neighbors' party did keep me up all night."

"Funny, here's your confirmation number for my reservation. Why don't I wait in the cocktail lounge while you find me a room at a comparable hotel. Of course, I will appreciate your forwarding all my messages there, since I told everybody I was staying here."

In other words, hotel managers can be magicians if they are accorded the respect their post deserves, rather than being treated like an employee who screwed up.

TRAVELING ABROAD

It is not only helpful to research local customs when traveling abroad, it is essential. Although American commerce is prized, the international community no longer feels that it must yield to American people at the expense of their own integrity. As the passport office may suggest, every American traveling abroad becomes an ambassador for the United States.

There are an increasing number of books giving detailed descriptions of customs, both business and personal, in various countries, and the reader should consult them if closer contact is anticipated.

Something else is worth remembering: when you are in another country, you are subject to its laws. If you take along prescription drugs (of any variety), bring them in the original container and have a doctor's certificate authorizing you to possess them.

Smoking

Although Americans have cut down on smoking and banned it from many public buildings, be aware that this is the world exception, not the rule. Europeans and Asians are known by the smoke they trail in public, in private, and in transit, so tourists with sensitivity to tobacco must steel themselves.

Languages

English may be a useful language internationally, but it is not the only language, and traveling Americans would do well to acquaint themselves with some basic phrases. Hotels and landmarks that attract American tourists usually have bilingual employees. However, there are some helpful phrases to memorize or write phonetically on paper:

1. Where is the bathroom?
2. How much?
3. How do I get to (fill in name)?
4. Check, please!
5. Which way to the American Embassy?
6. Yes, no, please, thank you, hello, goodbye.
7. I don't understand.

As a matter of practicality, it is best not to try to speak too much in a language that you don't know, even if you have inherited the Sid Caesar gene and can double-talk in what sounds like a foreign tongue.

Cameras

People in some cultures believe that when you take their picture you are stealing their soul. Others believe that when you take their picture *for free* you are stealing their income. Either way, you must ask permission to take a picture of a person (unless they're in the distance in a landscape). The people of other countries aren't on exhibit for you; they live there.

One important note: do not photograph military or government buildings without official permission. It may be construed as an intelligence-gathering act.

Attire

The best dress is inconspicuous; avoid the flowered Polynesian sport shirts that advertise "tourist." Although students can get away with greater informality than business travelers, it is better to dress at the level of local attire, without presuming to wear native garb.

Hotels

Major cities have fine hotels that are very similar to those in American cities; in fact, some may be part of the same chain. Seasoned travelers, however, may prefer to sample more intimate, less standardized lodgings. A good travel agent or the recommendation of friends can secure the names of such places. Reservations may be made in writing, by phone, or, increasingly, via the Internet.

It is especially important to confirm the method of hotel payment when you make your reservations to avoid problems with currency exchange or credit.

Passports

An American passport is one of the most valuable documents in the world. Nevertheless, guests in hotels abroad may be asked to deposit their passports with the hotel as a security measure. In such cases, it is perfectly legal to carry around a photocopy of your passport in addition to the original and to surrender only the copy. One should also carry a photocopy in public while locking the original in a safe place in case of robbery.

As a rule, it is very difficult to replace one's passport while traveling abroad. If this becomes necessary, contact the local American embassy or consulate immediately.

National Anthems

When a host country's national anthem is played before a sporting or theatrical event, the visiting American should show respect by standing. Please note that, unlike ours, the last two words of other peoples' national anthems are not "play ball."

Dining Tips: China

Chinese eating is communal, and all parties dig into the same large serving dish with their chopsticks. When not being used, chopsticks belong on a chopstick rest, parallel across the top of a bowl, and are never left crossed. Each person has a rice bowl that may be lifted to the mouth and its contents cleanly brought in with the chopsticks. Soup is eaten with a spoon. Noodles are lifted to the mouth and bitten off at convenient lengths, being careful not to splatter.

Dining Tips: Japan

In traditional Japanese restaurants and homes, shoes are removed on entering and are replaced with slippers, so always wear good socks.

A moist warmed cloth will be offered before the meal. It is for the hands only, never the face. After use, the towel should be placed neatly aside.

Where food is served on a central platter, one takes portions by reversing the chopsticks and lifting the food with the "clean" end that hasn't been in the mouth.

Chopsticks, when not used, are placed together on a chopstick rest or parallel to the diner's edge of the table. Sushi and rice rolls are eaten with chopsticks by biting off that which can be chewed. Some fish (such as squid) may not bite well, so a little deftness may be required. Sashimi is eaten whole with chopsticks. As with Chinese meals, noodles are brought to the lips and bitten off.

Soup is eaten by bringing the individual bowl to the mouth, with food morsels eaten with chopsticks if they cannot be swallowed whole.

Finally, the meal may be assisted by unusually helpful Japanese women (geishas in geisha houses, waitresses in restaurants).

Nothing other than politeness may be inferred from their attentions.

Doing Business

Schedule meetings to account for jet lag. (Remember what happened to President Bush!) Business conducted abroad must hew to the procedures and ethics of that country. In Japan, for example, strict formalities are observed in the manner in which offers are made, discussed, considered, and countered. Silence during a conversation is not to be considered indecisive; it reflects contemplation and should not be interrupted. The group supersedes the individual, and a cordial distance is always observed in interactions. Meetings and celebration can continue after business hours. Above all, the Japanese word *hai*, which means "yes," does not mean "agreement," it means "I hear you"—a crucial distinction.

In England one may plan on conducting business in the morning, then sealing the deal at a pub or at the club. By the same token, in Italy, businesses virtually close down at midday while locals enjoy a long lunch. In Sweden, behavior is very formal, and people may loosen up only with regimented drinking; likewise in Germany, where manners are effusive to a point that Americans would regard as obsequious. At the same time, calling another by his or her first name is *verboten* unless the two of you are close friends.

Business Cards

More so in Japan, but also around the world, one presents a business card as a means of introduction. The business card (see Chapter 2) must contain not only one's name and company but also one's position at that company. When given someone's card, do not put it in your pocket; keep it in front of you at the conference table and refer to it.

Note that business cards and calling cards are different items and are not interchangeable.

East–West Manners

Nowhere are cultural differences from the West more profound than in Japan. Although the Japanese may be tolerant of Westerners (*patronizing* might be more accurate), it behooves Westerners to make an effort to blend in.

Bowing (not handshakes) is a form of respect upon meeting someone. Your degree of respect dictates the depth of the bow: the young bow more deeply to the elderly, labor bows more deeply to management, and so on. For Americans, a slight bow or nod of the head usually suffices.

Entertaining is rarely done in the home. Restaurant and club visits (which can become quite raucous) are more the rule, and inviting a Westerner into one's home is a tremendous honor. In such an event, a visitor should bring a small gift.

Tipping

Customs can differ widely, so it is best to consult travel guides or your travel agent for specifics. In the meantime, here are a few.

Italy. Restaurants include 15 percent in the tab, but an additional 5 to 10 percent is appropriate for better service. A 500-lire tip is proper for table service in a city café, and a 300-lire tip for a provincial café. Hotel bartenders expect 1,000- to 1,200-lire tips. Taxi drivers should be given 10 percent of the fare on the meter.

France. The French have a word for it, all right: *more. L'addition* at restaurants and bars include gratuity, but an additional few francs are *de rigueur.* Hotel chambermaids should be left 10 francs per night if you stay more than one day; porters are paid 10 francs per bag; and other hotel personnel are tipped 5 to 10 francs (room service, washroom attendants). If you don't see a sign reading *Pourboire interdit* (which means "tipping prohibited"), you may see one that suggests how much.

Mexico. Tourism supports much of Mexico, but only barely, and travelers will note a disturbing chasm between conditions at resorts and the nearby shantytowns where the workers live. Waiters get 15 percent of the bill if the gratuity is not already added in (it varies). Hotel porters are paid NP$4 to NP$8 (new pesos) per bag, depending on the hotel. Maids get NP$3 per night at hotels. Taxi drivers are not usually tipped, but may be given NP$4 to NP$6 for helping with bags. Note that American dollars are accepted nearly everywhere in Mexico, but don't let the "$" sign make you confuse dollars and new pesos!

Great Britain. George Bernard Shaw noted that the English and the Americans are two peoples separated by a common language. With gratuities, however, no translation is needed. Hotels and restaurants add 10 to 15 percent to the bill to cover tipping. Pubs are different: one does not tip the bartender, or *publican*, but one may buy him a drink. Tipping barmen and barmaids 10 to 15 percent is permitted. A £1 coin given to a doorman who fetches you a cab is more than generous; a bellman may accept 50 p per bag with a £1 minimum. Taxi drivers (and they are the best you will ever encounter) get 15 percent of the metered fare.

Greece. Restaurant and café gratuities are not always included in the tab. A 15 percent tip for the waiter is left on the tray, and an additional 5 to 10 percent tip for the busboy is left on the table (waiters and busboys don't share tips). Taxi drivers get 10 to 15 percent of the metered fare (they will let you know!), and hotels usually add gratuities into the final bill, but check with the desk clerk or manager to see what the individual hotel's policy is.

Scandinavia. Waiters and hotel employees get 15 percent of the total, included in the tab. If you have paid in cash, leave a few coins on the change tray at restaurants.

Japan. Generally, there is no tipping, although porters, taxi drivers, and other employees who have rendered exemplary service may be tipped discretely (porters: ¥200–300 per bag; hotel assistance: ¥2,000–3,000; taxi drivers: ¥500).

Russia. Tipping, which signifies social class, used to be outlawed under Communism. It isn't any more. A 10 to 15 percent tip is expected in restaurants in par-

BRITISH TEA SERVICE

To half the world, tea is a drink made from boiled leaves. To the other half (the former British Empire), it is a symbol of civilization itself, a spiritual enterprise, and a procedure bordering on the religious. To Westerners, the most well-known form of tea is English, and it refers not only to the drink itself, but also the manner (emphasize <u>manner</u>) in which it is served.

In brief, tea is served at 4 P.M. as a refresher between lunch and dinner. Invitations are extended by telephone. Loose leaves (not tea bags) are placed into a previously warmed pot to which boiling water is added. The leaves steep 3 to 5 minutes. The tea is then poured through a fine strainer into teacups and passed to the guests. The pouring is performed by <u>anyone other than the hostess</u> because the hostess must be free to address her guests' other needs. The person who pours is called "mother," as in "I'll be mother today."

In addition to the liquid tea, other food items are served, such as thin, crustless sandwiches of cucumber and butter, smoked salmon and butter, watercress and butter, or cream cheese and olive. Scones with jam and clotted cream (<u>crème fraiche</u> can substitute), little pastries, cakes, and shortbread also are served.

Once the first servings of tea are made, more boiling water is added to the pot, which may be covered with a padded teapot cozy to keep it warm.

Tea can be served with lemon and sugar, but traditionalists will assert that only tea with milk (not cream) is "proper British tea." Moreover, they will go on for hours if asked whether one adds the milk to the tea or the tea to the milk. Go ahead. Try it.

ticular—but remember to have it in cash to the waiter; don't charge it.

American Slang Abroad

American English is a minefield of idioms that when taken literally by people not accustomed to colloquial speech, will always create problems. For example, in England *fag* is slang for a cigarette; in America it is a derogatory term for a male homosexual. In America, *bum* is slang for a vagrant; in England it is a vulgarism for a person's rear end. Thus, although it may be charitable in the States to hand a cigarette to a vagrant, in England it can be awkward to give a fag to a bum.

International Dos and Don'ts

Here are some guidelines that can help the hapless traveler:

Portugal. Do not make the "okay" sign by touching the ends of thumb and index finger into a circle. It is an insult here (and in Brazil).

Thailand. Most Thais smile upon introduction. This is not a come-on; it is a courtesy and a way of masking uncertainty. The nation's Buddhist religion is not subject to comment by outsiders. Never touch a Thai person on the top of his or her head or let him or her see the bottom of your shoe; both are deep insults to the spirit.

Japan. Never compliment an individual; Japanese culture is collective and teamwork is extolled. Never express affection in public, point, sniffle, or look anybody in the eye for more than an instant. Bow and smile when greeting others; handshakes are very rare.

China. The Asian concept of "face" is inviolate. Modesty, group effort, and consistency are prized. Never embarrass anyone or pick one person for comment, even if for praise. Silences are frequent and do not signify social stalemate. Unlike in Western cultures, eating noises are considered a compliment. Luck and joy are associated with the color red, and green means growth. Do not show impatience, which is considered deceitful; likewise, candor is rude, and one must accept the Chinese trait of circumlocution.

England. Avoid using such normal American words as *stuffed* (sex), *napkin* (diapers), *bloody* (damn), and *sharp* (devious), and be prepared to misunderstand such typically English expressions as *knock me up* (awaken me), *pecker* (chin), *rubber* (eraser), and *spotted dick* (raisin custard). Physical contact is minimal. Handshaking is allowed, but seldom kissing or hugging, except by old friends; ask no personal questions in casual conversations, and use last names unless otherwise permitted.

Canada. There are really two Canadas: English-speaking and French-speaking. Signs reflect the country's bilingual tradition, except in Quebec, where they are generally in French. So don't make the mistake of thinking of Canada as "England lite."

Germany. Avoid personal questions, including ones about sex, religion, and what a person's family was doing between 1933 and 1945. Stick to last names and small talk until you know someone better. Sports, the economy, and national accomplishments are safe topics for discussion.

Italy. Food, opera, and art are good topics for discussion. Males may be demonstrative toward each other (peck both cheeks). Use hands when talking. These days women may be smiled at but not, as legend had it, pinched. If introduced to someone with a professional title (such as Doctor), continue to use it in conversation. Likewise, do not use the vocative *signore* for a man without also using his surname, as in *Signore Boccato* (without it, it just means "sir").

France. Don't speak French unless you know how to do it well, and then be prepared for extended conversation, which is more important than the American habit of heading straight for the point. Hold off discussing business until the end of dinner. Politeness is a must, as is an operating awareness of a specific bathroom appliance called a *bidet*. Hand-shaking is an important courtesy, and cheek-kissing (actually brushing) is expected when friends meet.

Russia. Introductions are made with three names: Yuri Andreyovich Zhivago. Unless you know him well, you should address him as "Yuri Andreyovich." Handshakes are traditional greetings; cheek-kissing is only done by good friends. There may be remnants of reticence to discuss the Russian government, so don't press politics; yet it is safe to discuss America when asked (although you might find yourself straining to explain crime, mores, freedom of the press, and Michael Jackson). Visits to private homes are an honor, as are the extensive vodka toasts accompanying them. Formal dinners (don't ask, just eat) will go on for hours.

Mexico. Slow down. Don't get angry when you are given incorrect driving directions. If you plan to drive in Mexico, you must buy Mexican insurance and have notarized papers that prove you are the car's owner, renter, or borrower.

CHAPTER SEVEN

R-E-S-P-E-C-T:
Meeting and Greeting

America is a friendly country, sometimes too friendly. Whose business is it if somebody has had an affair or takes an extra Sweet 'n Low packet from a restaurant? In fact, how come there are so many people who don't want so many other people to be allowed to do so much stuff? Maybe all they really need is to have a little respect.

What *is* respect?

Respect is honoring other people and their feelings. "I try to be aware of my neighbors," says a lady who lives in a large, impersonal apartment complex in a big city. "For example, whenever I see elderly persons in the hall, I always smile and say hello to them. It seems minor, but so many old people live alone that I may be the only person all day who says anything to them." *That's* respect.

It's also allowing people to live their own lives, and living one's own life so as to not infringe on the lives of others. It's the belief that, "My right to swing my fist ends where your nose begins." Finally, it's people having enough faith in their own way of living that another person's way of living doesn't threaten them. Etiquette shows us how to reach this level.

> *Spilling your guts is just exactly as charming as it sounds.*
>
> —Fran Lebowitz

FORMS OF ADDRESS

Unless a formal title of royal, political, or religious office dictates otherwise, ordinary men and women are referred to in the following ways in conversation and correspondence:

- *Master.* Boys under twelve; between twelve and eighteen they are addressed by their name only.
- *Mr.* Men over the age of eighteen.
- *Messrs.* Two or more brothers with the same last name. This designation is not used for father, son, or people with different last names, such as law firm partners.
- *Miss.* Unmarried women in years past were addressed this way, but "Ms." (pronounced "Miz") has come to be accepted in formal matters. "Miss" is still appropriate for girls under sixteen, if only because "Ms." sounds silly. The older/oldest sister in a household is referred to with only her last name, such as "Miss Sloan." Her younger sisters are called "Miss Susan Sloan," "Miss Edna Sloan," and so forth.
- *Mrs.* A married woman uses her husband's name, as in "Mrs. Elmer Davies," not "Mrs. Gertrude Davies."

- *Ms.* Can be used for any woman, either by her request or when her marital status is not known.
- *Esq. or Esquire.* Custom reserves this term solely for a gentleman. It is widely reserved for lawyers, although in strict practice it is still not used for female lawyers. Perhaps, it should be. If "Esquire" is used, the "Mr." or "Ms." is not used.

Younger people still should call older people "Sir" or "Ma'am." If the older person wants to be called otherwise, he or she will say so. On the other hand, an older person calling a younger person "Sir" or "Ma'am" is awkward and, depending on vocal inflection, can be an insult.

It is never insulting, however, for two people to refer to each other as "Mr. Smith" or "Mrs. Jones." Even an older teacher, who is always "Mr. Smith," may properly address his younger student as "Miss Jones" or "Ms. Jones." Only people of the same age, or whose relationship has become informal, may, with mutual consent only, properly use each other's first names.

Addressing Professionals

Nothing is more disconcerting than a patient calling her physician "Dr. Miller" while he calls her "Judy." Imagine if she then said, "How ya doin', Steve?"

While the doctor–patient bond is almost that of a parent and child, children don't pay their parents a professional fee, and lines of conduct are not governed by licenses and ethics, as is the case with doctors.

It is inappropriate for a doctor to call his or her patient by a first name unless the patient permits it. Likewise, it should always be "Dr. Miller" from the patient unless, of course, there is a friendship that predates the professional relationship. These rules apply to all other professional relationships.

Married Name Versus Unmarried Name

Although the term *maiden name* is becoming obsolete, the question remains whether a newly married woman will continue to be addressed by her former name or will acquire her husband's.

Whichever she chooses, it is her obligation to make her choice known, either through a line in the formal wedding announcement ("The bride will continue to use her unmarried name of Sloan"), on her business card, or, more rarely, on her calling card. She should also reintroduce herself by her chosen name to those who knew her before her nuptials. If she does not do so, others are correct in believing she has assumed her husband's last name.

Children's Last Names

Any teacher who reads a class roster has had to deal with the extraordinary assortment of hyphenated and nonmatching names brought about by family change. Divorced mothers may resume using their maiden names whereas their children retain the mother's married name (Scott Gross, son of

Susan Fricke and James Gross). Second husbands may adopt the children of their new wife's first marriage (Tracy Blum, daughter of Sarah Cohen and Al Blum). Parents may hyphenate their last names and give them to their child (Justin Smith-Menz, son of Edie Smith and Thomas Menz).

However, a child living with her remarried mother may not assume her stepfather's last name unless she has been formally adopted by him (Meagan Meadows, daughter of Sam and Shirley [*née* Graham] Peterson). The designation *née* means "born as" and is used to indicate a married woman's former, unmarried (*née*: maiden) name.

Addressing the Clergy

Addressing prestigious personages is more noticeable when it is done improperly than when it is carried out according to etiquette.

The Pope
   Official title: His Holiness, the Pope
   Written salutation: Your Holiness
   Spoken: Your Holiness
Cardinal
   Official title: His Eminence, William Cardinal Smith, Archbishop of
   Written salutation: Dear Cardinal Smith or Your Eminence
   Spoken: Your Eminence
Bishop
   Official title: The Most Reverend William Smith, Bishop of
   Written salutation: Dear Bishop or Your Excellency
   Spoken: Your Excellency

Archbishop
   Official title: The Most Reverend William Smith, Archbishop of
   Written salutation: Dear Archbishop or Your Excellency
   Spoken: Your Excellency
Monsignor
   Official title: The Reverend Monsignor William Smith
   Written salutation: Reverend Monsignor
   Spoken: Monsignor
Priest
   Official title: The Reverend William Smith
   Written salutation: Dear Father Smith
   Spoken: Father Smith
Nun
   Official title: Sister Agnes Luke
   Written salutation: Dear Sister Luke
   Spoken: Sister
Brother
   Official title: Brother Francis Paul
   Written salutation: Dear Brother Paul
   Spoken: Brother
Protestant clergy
   Official title: The Reverend Gary Smith
   Written salutation: Dear Dr. (or Mr. or Ms.) Smith
   Spoken: Dr. (or Mr. or Ms.) Smith
Episcopal bishop
   Official title: The Right Reverend Gary Smith, Bishop of
   Written salutation: Dear Bishop Smith
   Spoken: Bishop Smith
Rabbi
   Official title: Rabbi Edgar Magnin
   Written salutation: Dear Rabbi Magnin
   Spoken: Rabbi Magnin

Addressing Public Officials

President of the United States
  Official title: The President
  Written salutation: Dear Mr. (or
    Madam) President
  Spoken: Mr. (or Madam) President
First lady of the United States
  Official title: The First Lady
  Written salutation: Dear Mrs. (last name)
  Spoken: Mrs. (last name)
Ex-president
  Official title: The Honorable James
    Earl Carter
  Written salutation: Dear Mr. Carter
  Spoken: Mr. Carter
Vice president
  Official title: The Vice President
  Written salutation: Dear Mr. (or
    Madam) Vice President
  Spoken: Mr. (or Madam) Vice
    President
Ex-vice president*
  Official title: The Honorable J.
    Danforth Quayle
  Written salutation: Dear Mr. Quayle
  Spoken: Mr. Quayle

  * Ex-presidents and ex-vice presidents
    sometimes revert to a military title
    they held prior to their election,
    such as "General Eisenhower."
    Because there can only be one pres-
    ident of the United States, even ex-
    presidents are called "Mr."

Cabinet members
  Official title: The Honorable Blanche
    Harlon

Written salutation: Dear Madam (or
  Mr.) Secretary
Spoken: Madam (or) Mr. Secretary
Chief justice of the U.S. Supreme Court
  Official title: The Chief Justice
  Written salutation: Dear Mr. (or
    Madam) Chief Justice
  Spoken: Mr. (or Madam) Chief Justice
Associate justice
  Official title: Madam (or Mr.) Justice Hill
  Written salutation: Dear Madam (or
    Mr.) Justice
  Spoken: Madam (or Mr.) Justice Hill
U.S. senator
  Official title: The Honorable Jerry
    Jones
  Written salutation: Dear Senator Jones
  Spoken: Senator Jones
Ex-U.S. senator
  Official title: The Honorable George
    McGovern
  Written salutation: Dear Mr. McGovern
  Spoken: Mr. McGovern
Speaker of the House
  Official title: The Honorable Jerry Jones
  Written salutation: Dear Mr. (or
    Madam) Speaker
  Spoken: Mr. (or Madam) Speaker
Congressman or congresswoman
  Official title: The Honorable Jerry Jones
  Written salutation: Dear Mr. (or Ms.) Jones
  Spoken: Mr. (or Ms.) Jones
Governor
  Official title: The Honorable Michael
    Miller
  Written salutation: Your Excellency or
    Dear Governor Miller
  Spoken: Governor Miller

State legislator
  Official title: The Honorable Susan
    Hayden
  Written salutation: Dear Ms. (or Mr.)
    Hayden
  Spoken: Ms. (or Mr.) Hayden
Mayor
  Official title: The Honorable Mayor
    Dan McGinty
  Written salutation: Dear Mayor McGinty
  Spoken: Mayor McGinty or Your Honor

Addressing the Nobility

Letters are sent to reigning monarchs through their private secretaries, never to the monarch directly. There is strict decorum when one is presented to a monarch, and members of the public so privileged will be briefed beforehand by a protocol representative. In general, one does not speak to royalty unless first spoken to, and must not offer one's hand unless the monarch's is offered first.

King or queen
  Official title: His Majesty the King/Her
    Majesty the Queen
  Written salutation: Your Majesty
  Spoken: Your Majesty (first time);
    Ma'am (or Sir) thereafter
Prince or princess
  Official title: His Royal Highness, the
    Prince/Her Royal Highness, the
    Princess
  Written salutation: Your Royal Highness
  Spoken: Your Highness (first time); Sir
    (or Ma'am) thereafter

POLITICAL CORRECTNESS

It's the Kryptonite of the nineties, the Rush Limbaugh of social topics—political correctness.
  Not that long ago, political correctness was called "The Golden Rule: Do unto others as you would have them do unto you." Nowadays it's a way of forcing people to respect others, with the understandable result that nobody respects anybody who forces them to do something.
  Good manners were here before political correctness and will survive it. All good manners say is, "Don't intentionally hurt other people." Whatever differs from that is not good manners.

Duke or duchess
  Official title: His Grace, the Duke
    of/Her Grace, the Duchess of
  Written salutation: My Lord Duke/Dear
    Duchess
  Spoken: Your Grace
Marquess or Marchioness
  Official title: The Most Honourable
    Marquess of/the Marchioness of
  Written salutation: My Lord/Lady
    Blankfort
  Spoken: Lord/Lady Blankfort

Earl or countess
  Official title: the Right Honourable
    Earl/Countess of Clemmence
  Written salutation: My Dear Lord/My
    Dear Lady
  Spoken: Lord Clemmence/Lady
    Clemmence
Viscount or viscountess
  Official title: The Right Honourable
    Viscount/Viscountess of
  Written salutation: My Lord/Lady
  Spoken: Lord/Lady Clemmence
Baron or Baroness
  Official title: The Right Honourable
    Lord/Lady Blankfort
  Written salutation: My Lord/Lady
    Blankfort
  Spoken: Lord/Lady Blankfort
Knight
  Official title: Sir Albert Hall or Sir
    Albert and Larry Hall
  Written salutation: Dear Sir Albert
  Spoken: Sir Albert

Addressing the Military

Only members of the military need salute, but it is a matter of courtesy to address serving members by their rank, when they are in uniform, or if so requested after their retirement. Here is how to identify military rank (Note: in America the rank of "lieutenant" is pronounced "loo-TEN-ent".)

Army
General of the army: five silver stars
General: four silver stars
Lieutenant General: three silver stars

Major general: two silver stars
Brigadier general: one silver star
Colonel: silver eagle
Lieutenant colonel: silver oak leaf
Major: gold oak leaf
Captain: two silver bars
First lieutenant: one silver bar
Second lieutenant: one gold bar
Chief warrant officer: one gold bar,
  brown enamel top, gold up and
  down along center
Warrant officer, junior grade: same as
  above except gold is side to side
  along center

Navy: In blue uniforms, gold stripes on sleeves indicate rank; in white or dress khaki, a sailor's rank is indicated by shoulder boards.
Fleet admiral: five silver stars, one 2-inch
  stripe, and four half-inch sleeve
  stripes with star of line officer
Admiral: four silver stars, one 2-inch stripe
  and three half-inch sleeve stripes with
  star of line officer or corps device
Vice admiral: three silver stars, one 2-
  inch stripe, and two half-inch sleeve
  stripes, star of line officer or corps
  device
Rear admiral: two silver stars, one 2-inch
  stripe, and one half-inch sleeve stripe,
  star of line officer or corps device
Commodore: one silver star, one 2-inch
  sleeve stripe, star of line officer or
  corps device (wartime service only)
Captain: silver spread eagle, four half-
  inch stripes, star of line officer or
  corps device

Commander: silver oak leaf, three half-inch stripes, star of line officer or corps device

Lieutenant commander: gold oak leaf, two half-inch stripes with one quarter-inch stripe between them, star of line officer or corps device

Lieutenant: two silver bars, two half-inch stripes, star of line officer or corps device

Lieutenant, junior grade (also called Lieutenant [j.g.]): one silver bar, one half-inch stripe with one-quarter-inch stripe above it, star of line officer or corps device

Ensign: one gold bar, one half-inch gold stripe, star of line officer or corps device

Chief warrant officer: one-quarter-inch broken gold stripe and specialty device

Warrant officer: one-quarter-inch broken gold stripe and specialty device

Marine Corps: General is the top Marine Corps rank bearing four stars. Other insignia are the same as for the Army.

Air Force: Top rank is general. Other insignia are the same as in the Army.

Coast Guard: Top rank is general. Other insignia are same as in the Navy.

Commissioned officers (sergeant and above) are called by their rank, as in "Major Major" or "General Ripper."

Noncommissioned officers (ranks below sergeant) are called by their title, as in: "Sergeant Ruttledge." A formal letter to a non-com may be addressed to Mr., Mrs., Ms., or Miss, followed by his or her first and last name. Never call a sergeant "Sir."

Medical officers are always called "Doctor" unless they are above the rank of admiral or general, in which case the rank is used; if the doctor is head of the base hospital, the rank is always used.

The naval officer in command of a ship is always called "Captain" regardless of his or her actual rank.

If two officers marry and the wife outranks her husband, she is addressed first, even if she assumes her husband's name, as in "Colonel Elizabeth O'Neill, U.S.A.F., and Lieutenant James O'Neill, U.S.A.F."

Chaplains are called by their military rank; informally they may be addressed as "Rabbi," "Father," and so on.

Female officers may properly be called "Ma'am." Another way is to refer to rank only, as in, "Excuse me, Captain, would the captain like more coffee?"

Addressing Ph.D.s

The degree of doctor of philosophy is one whose holder deserves respect and usually asks for it by appending the term *Doctor* to his or her name, as in "Dr. Pretorius." One who holds an honorary doctorate may still be called doctor.

VISITING

Sleepovers

When staying as a guest in someone else's house, you are expected to respect the moral beliefs of the host. This means that sleeping arrangements should be determined in advance of the visit or at least well before retiring on the first evening. It usually comes from parents when their living-away kids bring home a current squeeze, *to wit*, "I don't care what you do when you're on your own, but while you're under my roof you'll sleep in separate rooms!"

Unmarried guests should not put their host in the position of making a moral judgment. If the host directs unmarried guests to separate bedrooms, this is more than a hint but less than a command. Where host and guest are good friends, of course, such questions have long since been settled.

Couples (married or unmarried) involved in a physical relationship may enjoy having sex in new places. If that place happens to be somebody else's house, they should be discreet about it. It is also improper for a hostess to inquire after her guests' sex life.

Gifts for a Hostess or Host

Overnight guests enjoying the hospitality of a friend or relative should bring a house gift with them for the host or hostess. This can be anything from a bottle of good wine to a coffee table book. Toys for young children or remembrances for older children or other relatives living in the house will likewise be well regarded.

An additional way to show appreciation is for guests to take their host family out to dinner at least once during the stay.

Lagniappe

It's a Southern tradition for the host to present departing guests with a small gift, or *lagniappe* (LAN-yap, of French derivation). This can be anything from pastries "for the road" to a book of poetry or a handicraft that can serve as a treasured souvenir of a delightful few days' stay.

Guest of Honor

If a house guest is to be fêted by his host, the guest of honor should send flowers or a centerpiece to the home, timed to arrive before the party.

Guest Towels

Guests, when using the host's lavatory, should not use the host's personal bath towels. They should use—and the host must provide—separate cloth guest towels. A roll of paper towels will not do. If there has been any splashing in the lavatory, the guest should restore the cleanliness of the room before leaving it.

Smokers in a Nonsmoking Home

Smoking guests should refrain absolutely from smoking in a nonsmoking home.

If (when) smokers must light up, they should do so outdoors, preferably far enough from the house that their breath and clothing can air out before they step back inside.

TEN COMMANDMENTS OF HOUSE GUESTS

His

Guests enjoying overnight hospitality with friends incur certain obligations toward their host. In general, the tenet of good guest behavior is, "Except when they see you, you're never there."

1. Guests should neatly maintain their accommodations (whether a pull-out sofa bed in the living room or a full private bungalow) and not scatter their belongings all over the house.

2. Unless there is maid service (yeah, right), guests should make their own beds every morning until the morning they depart.

3. Remove personal toiletries from the bathroom after each use (unless it's your private bathroom).

4. Make sure the seat of the john is always down.

5. Don't use the phone without asking permission, and then don't tie it up. Use your own long-distance account, not your host's.

6. Treat the host's children, pets, friends, and property with respect.

7. Conform to the host's schedule; don't ask them to cancel their plans or eat an hour earlier or later.

8. Always ask whether the host needs help in the kitchen, in cleaning up, in repairing anything, in sharing driving, and so on.

9. If you break something, tell the host right away, and then deal with it.

10. Have firm arrival and, more important, departure times; remember Benjamin Franklin's exhortation that fish and house guests begin to smell after three days.

Most nonsmokers are offended by the lingering aroma of tobacco, even a friend's.

Nonsmokers in a Smoker's Home

Smokers may, out of courtesy, refrain from smoking when nonsmokers are guests in their house. It hardly matters, anyway, because their curtains, rugs, and upholstery already smell of smoke.

This can pose a family problem when out-of-town relatives refuse to remain under a smoker's roof. If this happens, the guest may explain exactly why he is staying in a hotel: "It's not you, it's your smoking."

Serving Alcohol

The heightened awareness of alcoholism and other substance abuse has made the general public more sensitive, in some cases overly so, about serving alcohol at social gatherings. A host or hostess is responsible for the safety of his or her guests, and this includes allowing them to overindulge. The wise host knows his own limits and stays sober to monitor the limits of others. If a guest appears to be losing control, the host should take all steps to cut him off from the bar or to take him aside and insist that he refrain, sleep it off, or leave in a taxi.

Alcoholics

Anyone who has acknowledged his or her dependency on alcohol and has joined Alcoholics Anonymous (or another program) should be respected. Too often, though, other people will assume that they may not drink, or even mention alcohol, around a friend who is a recovering alcoholic. It then becomes a burden on the part of the AA member to put everybody else at ease.

It is perfectly all right to serve alcohol at a gathering where one or more members may be in a program, provided, of course, that you provide nonalcoholic alternatives.

A person who does not care to drink *for whatever reason* should simply say, "No thank you, I don't want a drink." No one has the right to ask, or assume, why.

Let Sleeping Guests Lie

It is courteous to allow out-of-town guests to "sleep in" if they are visiting on vacation. This does not mean, however, that the host must reschedule his life around that of the person using the spare bedroom. Establish schedules in advance. For example, if four people have to use the bathroom in the morning, the guest may want to catch half an hour of extra z's.

Guest Safety

Hosts are obliged to indicate to their guests the nearest exit, where the first aid kit and fire extinguisher are, and what number to call for a doctor. Hosts in earthquake-prone areas might also advise guests on what to do if the earth moves (such as to keep shoes nearby, stand under the door frame, and use the flashlight that's kept under the bed).

Tipping Servants

If you are staying in a home that has them, the servants should be compensated for the extra effort they have had to expend to accommodate your visit as well as their regular duties. Inform the hostess that you wish to tip the help. A $10 to $20 cash tip handed privately and with thanks to a maid, cook, or butler after a stay of a few days is a gracious gesture.

Unannounced Guests

A host is under no obligation to see guests who drop in without calling ahead, or who phone from the car and announce that they happen to be in the neighborhood. Depending upon whether the host wants to receive the callers, he can stretch dinner portions, delay his own plans, or make new and inclusive ones. It is grossly rude to expect to be welcomed into a home that is not expecting you.

Residential Phone Etiquette

The telephone is a convenience that is often used inconveniently. In general, a ringing telephone should be answered, but there is nothing wrong with telling the caller that you haven't got time for an extended conversation now and asking him or her to call back later. Remember that the phone is an invention, not an excuse.

Unless you are familiar with someone's sleep habits, it is best to restrict residential phone calls to between 8 A.M. and 10 P.M. on weeknights, 10 A.M. and 10 P.M. on Saturdays, and noon and 10 P.M. on Sundays. Some people, particularly those who have known recent tragedy, come to regard wee-hours phone calls as harbingers of bad news.

An awareness of television programming and sports events is also helpful; phoning during *The X Files* or "sudden death" in NBA playoffs may be actionable in some social circles!

Never make phone calls when intoxicated. The slang name for this is "having the dialies." If you receive a call from a friend who is obviously in an altered state, first ascertain if there is a legitimate problem and, if there isn't, request that he or she

phone back during normal hours. Any conversation conducted under such circumstances is likely to be embarrassing the next morning for one or both parties.

NEIGHBORS

In *Mending Wall*, Robert Frost wrote that "Good fences make good neighbors." In today's more crowded world, the poet's observation seems downright prescient.

When it comes to fences, the law specifies that, regardless of whether an apple tree is rooted in a neighbor's yard, any apples that hang over your yard become yours. The same case law is not supposed to apply to pets, kids, party noise, drainage, snow, leaves, or the myriad other sore points that can put neighbors at odds with each other. That's where etiquette should be exhausted before the law is summoned.

NEIGHBORLINESS

New Neighbors

It's been decades since local merchants dispatched a "welcome wagon" to greet arrivals to a residential neighborhood.

Nowadays the salutation seems to be, "Hey, buddy, how long are you gonna park your damn U-Haul here?" Although the American credo seems to be "avoid thy neighbor," in fact a lot of potential conflicts could be forestalled or eliminated entirely by simply saying hello to the people who live nearby. Neighborhoods change, no doubt about it. Long-time residents pine for the days when families lived where students now dwell. Much of what passes for malice is just ignorance: new neighbors not knowing the values of the block they're moving into. Suburban kids who migrate to city apartments may not be aware that they can't play the stereo loud any more; that the local custom is to safeguard parking spaces; that trash collection isn't free and they can't just chuck stuff into anybody's garbage can; and so forth.

Housewarming Gifts. Despite these cynical times, new neighbors may appreciate token gifts when they move in. Something as simple as a few bottles of chilled spring water on moving day, or a list of nearby merchants (supermarket, laundromat, drug store, hardware store, service station, dry cleaner, and so forth) can be enormously helpful.

Pets

A dog that barks incessantly or a cat in heat next door can be annoying. Too often, a pet owner has no idea of the noise his animal makes when he's gone, even though the rest of the neighborhood

HOUSEWARMING GIFTS

*F*riends invited to housewarming parties can help by bringing household items, but it would be improper to throw a housewarming party in lieu of making a trip to the hardware store. Since most people usually require new kitchenware after they move, some possible gifts are:

Canister set
Coffee or tea
Dish drainer
Doormat
Kitchen gadgets (peeler, grater, etc.)
Kitchen towels
Place mats and napkins
Plants
Spice rack
Sponges and cleaning supplies
Strainer, colander
Wine glasses (everyday)

does. Pet owners should monitor their animals (a cassette recorder with a "voice-activated" feature can help) to make sure that they are not creating a neighborhood disturbance.

If a dog is disturbing you regularly, asking, "Is there anything you can do about your pet? His barking is keeping me up" is a safe place to start. If the problem continues, you may have to phone the overworked animal control officer at your local police department. If there is a question of an animal being mistreated, call the American Humane Association or the Society for the Prevention of Cruelty to Animals.

Most communities have leash laws, and, even if they don't, no community sanctions pet owners whose animals relieve themselves on a neighbor's lawn.

Loud Parties

People living in crowded residential areas who are planning large parties have a special responsibility not to let the celebration get out of hand. Most communities forbid noises after 10 P.M. or before 7 A.M.

In cities, student areas, and condominium complexes where proximity makes the noise problem worse, some precautions may be taken:

1. Keep the party indoors.
2. Hire security guards.
3. Invite your immediate neighbors to the party. Even if they decline, they will feel more involved and will be less apt to complain.
4. Set a clear end time, and let the neighbors know what it's going to be. Let your guests know it, too, and enforce it.
5. Invite no more people than you can handle.

If this seems too restrictive, then perhaps the party should take place in a more suitable venue.

Car Alarms

As discussed in Chapter 6, spontaneous car alarms pose a constant annoyance. The owner of a car with an alarm is responsible for seeing that it goes off only when the car is being stolen and at no other time.

Family Noises

Noisy kids, domestic "disagreements," and cataclysmic passion should stay within the home of the family having them. The sounds from those and other activities, however, sometimes stray from house to house or, more commonly, from apartment to apartment. Curiosity may have killed the cat, but it can give a neighbor some wrong ideas.

Parking Easements

The shared alley space between two adjacent houses is called an "easement," and it should remain clear and easily navigable, both as a courtesy and for fire vehicle access. Those who do not honor their neighbor's right-of-way not only are thoughtless but also may be violating the law.

Garbage

Neighbors have a responsibility to maintain securely locking garbage containers that leak neither odor nor contents.

RELIGIOUS CAVEATS

Visiting a Church as the Guest of a Parishioner

Religion is one of three subjects that divide people (the other two being politics and, as we discovered, etiquette). Yet if one attends services of a faith different from one's own, one is expected to respond with courtesy.

Some religions, notably Mormon, do not permit nonmembers to attend sacred services. Outsiders also may be excluded from certain Islamic observances. Still other religions forbid their own members to attend services of competing faiths.

As has been stated elsewhere, guests are not expected to participate in religious activities that run contrary to their beliefs. Respectful silence is the best behavior.

Discussions of One's Religion

Until very recently, one's religion was considered a private affair, not out of any sense of shame but because of the intimacy of the one-to-One relationship. History is rife with examples of people who were persecuted because of their religious beliefs. Indeed, the rise of religious fundamentalism, and the sometimes deadly fanaticism it inspires has become a divisive, rather than a uniting, worldwide trend.

Etiquette has a unique position on religion: *none*. Just as it is not proper to inquire after someone's religion, so it is not proper to force one's religion on someone else. Some sects believe that the proselytizing of their beliefs is not only sanctioned by Scripture but also divinely blessed. They should understand that others do not share their beliefs and, in fact, often resent them.

As etiquette seeks to avoid conflict rather than arbitrate it, the best response to someone who tries to impose his religion on you is to say, "No, thank you." Just as society considers it repulsive for someone to eat with his hands, tell vulgar jokes, or have bad hygiene, so does society disapprove of people who force their idea of God upon those who do not wish to share it. Such people also usually feel that God instructs them to supersede human laws in spreading His. In America this is a question best settled by the Constitution, not etiquette.

POLITICAL STANDS

As one of the Big Three divisive subjects, politics are out of place in an otherwise nonpartisan social gathering. There are reasons why lapel pins are not considered part of formal attire; neither are armbands, sashes, or AIDS ribbons, no matter how valid the cause. Historically, politics were discussed after dinner in the library over brandy and cigars—and by men only. While mores have changed, human sensitivity over politics has not.

Classroom Political Protest

The First Amendment should not end at the door of the schoolhouse that teaches it, but in the nineties the U.S. Supreme Court handed down two controversial and conflicting rulings that were supposed to guide teachers, students, parents, and administrators but, unfortunately, made matters worse.

In one (*Hazelwood*), the Court held that school officials may censor the content of student newspapers for any reason. In the other (*Tinker*), the Court said that students may engage in political protest as long as it does not "disrupt the educational process." At the core of both of these decisions is whether people who believe one way have the right to tell (or censor) people who believe another way.

With so much school violence these days, wouldn't it be better if people could exchange opinions instead of gunshots?

Campaign Placards

Whether on lawns, windows, or bumpers, political campaign signs are a patriotic American right—no matter how much of a scoundrel the politician might be! As political speech, campaign signs enjoy full protection under the Bill of Rights. Landlords and condo associations may not remove them from a tenant's window or levy a penalty for displaying them.

AGGRESSIVE ETIQUETTE

*T*he most frustrating dictate of etiquette is that one must be polite to everybody, even people who don't deserve it. This includes the moron neighbor, the bad driver, the manipulative coworker, the overbearing religious nut, and the salesperson who knocks on a door that has a "no soliciting, please" sign on it.

Turning the other cheek may have worked for Jesus and Gandhi, but did they ever have to deal with a woman who pushed her full shopping cart into the ten-item express line?

Contrary to semantics, it *is* possible to be too polite if doing so would:

1. Be lost on the offender
2. Serve no educational purpose for bystanders
3. Inconvenience you for no constructive reason
4. Contribute to a breakdown of the social structure

JUST PLAIN RUDE

Dissing

"Dissing" is slang for showing disrespect. In the palette of teenage culture, this can include anything from the always-inflammatory assertion that a young man has sexual relations with his own mother to accidentally scuffing someone's athletic shoes in the hallway. In the case of the latter, if a simple apology does not suffice, nothing will.

Nakedness

Although the human body may be a temple, not everybody wants to worship there. Nudity not only is inappropriate but also can be offensive, even illegal, when people are not expecting it.

Therefore, guests in others' houses, people in their own houses with guests present, girls and boys on senior class trips, or anyone answering the door should do so fully clothed unless all parties are of an age to consent and have consented.

Wolf Whistles

Life is not a Tex Avery cartoon. Women do not consider it a compliment to be whis-tled at, whether from street level, above it, or below it. Men (for they are not gentlemen) who do so demean themselves, not the lady.

Sexism

Sexism is a political weapon by which empowered men oppress unempowered women. The theory goes that etiquette favors women, but it's sexist to favor women, so why be polite to them?

Haven't we already gone over this? Etiquette is how we agree to behave toward one another to prevent us from having to make it up as we go along. It's just human decency raised to the level of an ethic. Sexism, on the other hand, is human *in*decency lowered to the depth of depravity.

Any questions?

CHAPTER EIGHT

MIND YOUR BUSINESS:
Operating Tips for
the Global/
High Tech Office

It seems that the rate of reported incidents of sexual and racial harassment in the workplace has been falling, proof, according to those who evaluate such data, that office seminars and sensitivity training sessions are working. What a sad state of affairs that it takes organized programs to teach people something they should have learned growing up: awareness of other people's feelings.

> The business of America is business.
> —Calvin Coolidge

Business complicates matters, however. Because of the unequal power between employer and employee, it is essential to observe decorum at all times. That does not mean that boss and worker of whatever gender combination must treat each other coldly. It just means that an act that someone in management may consider a supportive personal gesture (such as a hand on someone's shoulder) may be taken as an assertion of power by the person attached to the shoulder.

How an office functions inside its walls is no less important than how it conducts itself toward the public. Good manners make good business. But business involves more than politeness. It also uses protocol, tradition, and, yes, even sensitivity—not just to make a bigger or better sale, but also to develop long-term relationships and inspire trust.

Such a philosophy may seem strange to a nation that for the last generation has focused on the immediate gratification of the quick buck rather than on the long-range benefits of training, savings, and moderation. Yet from something as simple as spelling someone's name right on a business letter to providing day care for employees' children, the need for business etiquette has broadened considerably.

This is not a self-help text on business philosophy, a chapter on "How to Win at Any Cost," or a motivational text about ways to sell anything to anybody. Rather, it's about how to succeed in business . . . by really politely trying.

Office Issues

The Job Interview

Prevailing wisdom is that if the applicant lets the boss do all the talking during the interview, the more intelligent the boss will think the applicant is and the better chances are he or she will land the job. Nevertheless, job applicants should be prepared to talk. They should research the company prior to the meeting and be prepared to ask questions of their own.

A job interview can be scheduled by phoning the employer, through the company's "human resources" (personnel) department, by sending a resume and cover letter, or by arrangement through a mutual acquaintance. Whatever the means of securing access, the interview is the key part of the hiring process.

The interview itself is an audition, not a first date. The applicant should wear white-collar clothes. Both parties address each other formally and exchange information, primarily about the applicant's previous work experience. Afterward, the applicant should send a letter of thanks for the interview.

The wise employer will hold off making a final hiring decision until she has interviewed all job applicants. Closure is a mark of decency; the employer or an assistant should call or write all the unchosen candidates to advise them that the job has been filled.

The applicant may thank the employer again and ask that his or her resume be kept on file for any future openings. This grace under disappointment may go farther than the original interview in moving the applicant to the top of the pile for next time.

Boss/Secretary Relationships

In the days when bosses were men and secretaries were women, their business relationship was almost completely opposite from what it was in the social world: a boss did not rise when his secretary entered the room; he did not introduce her to visitors; and he did not steady her chair,

hold her door, or refrain from smoking in her presence.

Surprisingly little has changed now that more women are bosses and some secretaries are men (although male secretaries are usually called "assistants," which says something). The following hold true today:

- A boss should rise when meeting personnel for the first time or when meeting someone of higher status.
- A boss has no social obligation to introduce a secretary.
- A secretary and boss should refer to each other by their last names while in public and in front of third parties.
- The boss always enters a room first.
- In private the boss may call a secretary by his or her first name, but the secretary is always correct in calling the boss by his or her last name (unless they *mutually* reach another understanding).
- A female secretary is never referred to as "the girl" or "my girl," and a male secretary is never "the boy" or "my boy." Secretaries should be referred to by their last name.

Mandated Equality

Some companies have policies that state that all employees, of whatever rank, must be on a first-name basis. This sounds egalitarian at first, but not when one realizes that the effect is to create an even more enigmatic structure, not just between management and labor, but also between "those who know the

UNWANTED ADVANCES

*A*ll work and no play may make Jack a dull boy, but it's good advice if Jack wants to avoid a sexual harassment lawsuit. Given the balance of power that exists on the job, the term <u>unwanted sexual advances</u> has no proper antithesis. Legally speaking, any personal relationship that may develop or be desired between an employer and an employee (in any gender combination) is an improper one if it involves even the slightest coercion, whether direct or implied. Merely from a point of office efficiency such a liaison is likewise to be counterproductive.

Any employee who believes he or she is being treated improperly by someone in a supervisory position should contact either his or her union (if organized) or the EEOC (Equal Employment Opportunity Commission), listed in the government section of the phone book, <u>and be prepared to substantiate any charges.</u> Management generally has company lawyers on its side should such charges arise.

If co-workers make sexual advances to each other and there is no question of undue influence, it may still be a matter for legal redress (e.g., if a majority male workplace becomes an intimidating environment to women because of pinups, language, or sexist wisecracks).

In no case is such behavior acceptable. Moreover, it truly exceeds the constraints of etiquette and becomes a matter of law.

way the company really runs" and those who don't. Etiquette should clarify, not obfuscate.

Business Attire

Unless uniforms, safety gear, or work clothes are specifically required (such as for identification, technology, or construction), business attire should be neat and functional, yet comfortable.

Office workers should wear shirts or blouses cut so as not to distract others. Women generally wears skirts that cover their knees while they are seated, and men wear trousers, not jeans. If a jacket and tie are required for a man, it is customary to allow him to hang up his jacket after he has arrived and work in shirtsleeves with his necktie in place. A woman arriving in a suit may likewise shed her jacket.

Shoes should be comfortable and attractive, but running shoes or other sports footwear are not acceptable. People who choose to commute in athletic shoes should keep a pair of "office shoes" at work and change into them upon arrival. Jewelry should be kept to a minimum, especially noisy or showy trinkets.

Some companies, such as restaurants or theme parks, may set their own dress codes, which may require unusual attire. The employee usually does not have a choice in such matters, so if he or she objects, it may be necessary to quit the job.

Punctuality

People are expected to be on the job at, or a few minutes before, their scheduled start time. There is an unspoken custom among office workers that "the first half hour is for me." Employers don't see it this way. If

TABOO TOPICS

Certain subjects are never proper for discussion anywhere, but especially in an office setting. They include:

- *Salary*
- *Commissions*
- *Promotions*
- *Job searches*
- *Your sex life*
- *Another's sex life*
- *Anyone's sexual orientation*
- *Age*
- *Affairs*
- *Criminal activity*

a person is sitting at his or her desk, window, table, chair, or drill press, then he or she must conduct business.

Absence from Work

If you are being paid to do a job, you should be there to do it. Sick pay, vacation pay, leaves of absence, unpaid leave, and other fringe benefits must be negotiated at the time of employment. Activating them once they have been won, however, may be a different matter.

If you know in advance that you are going to be absent, say, for an overnight hospital stay, you should notify your boss as far in advance as possible so that he or she can arrange to hire a temp worker. The company may have a contract with a temp firm, have a pool of fill-in workers, or determine that they can live without you for a short time. If an employee's absences become frequent, it may be grounds for dismissal.

If you discover that you must miss work (accident, flu, family crisis), then either call your boss or contact whomever the company has designated to handle such crises. Whatever the reason for the absence, it is essential that the employee or a designee (parent, child, spouse, etc.) inform the office immediately. Don't just fail to show up.

"Mental Health Days"

Absences on Fridays or Mondays in cases where there is no illness are commonly referred to as "mental health days." In other words, days on which the employee just doesn't feel like coming in to work. These so-called "mental health days" may bolster an employee's self-image, but they lower it immeasurably in the eyes of co-workers who must fill in for their unjustifiably absent colleague.

Hygiene

No matter what the job, one should arrive well groomed to perform it. If the job involves contact with the public, it is essential.

Office workers should not wear strong perfume, cologne, or other aromatic scents that may distract or nauseate co-workers. Body odor is both unpleasant and difficult to discuss, and avoiding one permits avoiding the other. Hair, fingernails, and, where applicable, facial hair should be clean and scrupulously groomed.

It is the responsibility of a worker's immediate superior to discuss matters of hygiene with the employee if complaints have been received. If the problem is physiological (such as diet or disease) rather than cosmetic, this should be determined.

Smoking

In many cities, smoking is no longer permitted in public buildings and less and less so in private buildings.

People who smoke tend not to be terribly considerate of people who don't, and this includes not just the subject of second-hand smoke but also the residue that they carry back into the office on their breath, hair, and clothing. On the other hand, non-

smokers, empowered by the medical and moral facts, tend to be equally inconsiderate of smokers.

Etiquette suggests that smokers smoke where smokers smoke and nonsmokers mind their own business.

Making Coffee

Only if making coffee is within a secretary's job description when he or she is hired must he or she do so. If no secretary is present when a group of managers wants coffee and the person who scheduled the meeting did not have the foresight to order it from a caterer, then the managers can call a break to go out and get some. If the group decides to work through a lunch break and needs to send out for food, the secretary of the hosting manager may be summoned to make arrangements. Needless to say, it is not the automatic job of any female manager present to "go fetch."

The Office Kitchenette

Offices that have sinks, microwaves, drink machines, refrigerators, and hot plates usually have the problem of co-workers who soil the facilities and do not clean them up.

It's easy for the morning crew to blame the night crew. And it's usually the receptionist (or whoever comes in first every morning) who has to scramble to straighten up so that the day crew can get it dirty again.

Unless such janitorial duties are specifically in the job description, every co-worker should clean up after himself or herself or set a schedule to take turns doing it. The polite (and astute) manager notices such things and should take the initiative.

Politeness to and from Secretaries

Politeness to all people is a business rule; politeness to secretaries should be a commandment. Although the boss holds the power, the boss's secretary generally has the key to where the power is kept. Befriend them and you've got priority access; alienate them and you might as well take a number and wait—a high number.

It may feel good to yell at a secretary if the boss has made you angry (if abuse of power turns you on), but it is both rude to the secretary and ineffective. Losing one's temper is never acceptable, but it is even less acceptable to take it out on someone who isn't responsible for the problem and can't do anything about it anyway.

Customer Service

The worker who receives a customer complaint should show his or her manners by remaining polite. If the customer becomes abusive, the worker is under no obligation to endure it and may hang up (if on the phone) or walk away, in each case saying, "It is not my job to be treated in this manner."

On the flip side, some secretaries and assistants believe it is their duty to keep people from talking to the boss rather than to facilitate the boss's business. Others are forced to run interference for the boss and take the heat.

An officious secretary always creates problems for an employer far in excess of the time saved by "screening" people. Did the boss forget to tell the secretary to accept the stranger's call? Did the caller know somebody higher up in the company? Is the caller apt to bump into the boss outside the office and bring it up?

This kind of unfortunate behavior occurs frequently in the entertainment industry where celebrities attract unwanted, even life-threatening, attention. A troublesome secretary can be an employer's downfall, and the employer will be the last to know it.

As for unwanted phone calls, a polite but firm refusal is always the best way to nip them in the bud, before they escalate. Beyond that, the police may be consulted.

APPOINTMENTS

The Business Appointment

When two or more people wish to get together in person, they must agree on a time and location. It can be more complicated than it sounds:

- Both parties must agree on the location. Usually the "seller" goes to the office of the "buyer," which produces the perception that whoever goes to the other's office will be at a disadvantage.

- If two parties meet for lunch, the restaurant should be acceptable to both. People who "do" frequent business lunches should be familiar with a variety of restaurants near their place of business. The person who suggests lunch or does the inviting is expected to pay.
- Both parties should write the information in their office appointment books so that they or their secretaries don't make conflicting appointments.
- If the appointment is more than forty-eight hours away, it should be reconfirmed the morning of the day it is scheduled to take place.
- You should always advise your office where you will be and how to reach you when you leave for an appointment.
- Unless it is established in advance, it is improper to bring along additional people to a business lunch.

Persons should arrive for an appointment a few minutes, but never more than five minutes, ahead of time to allow for parking, security clearance, or just getting lost finding the office or restaurant. If the meeting is at an office, the visitor should check in with the receptionist or secretary of the person he is there to see. If there is to be a minor delay, the guest should be offered coffee or other refreshment and asked to wait. A delay of more than five minutes is rude and should be explained.

GETTING PAST SECRETARIES

*T*hese are old journalist's tricks, but civilians can use them, too, to get past a secretary who won't let you talk to the boss:

1. Write the boss a letter explaining why you've been calling (don't badmouth the secretary, however); the secretary has to show the letter to the boss.
2. Send a telegram.
3. Call during the secretary's lunch.
4. If you have the secretary's direct extension, try adding or subtracting 1 from it: you'll sometimes get right into the boss's phone.
5. Call the next day, and say you're returning the boss's call; the secretary may think the boss called you.
6. Say your job is at stake.
7. Send the secretary flowers or a showy gift.
8. If all else fails, then beg, plead, and grovel.

Handshakes

A firm (not tight or lingering) handshake is the accepted greeting in America. Hugging and kissing is not, except between intimates. Individuals who because of health, disability, or neurosis cannot shake hands should offer their guest the courtesy of an explanation (see Chapters 2 and 12).

Ending Meetings

If the planned business of a meeting has been concluded, the meeting itself is over. The person running the meeting signals this by standing and offering his hand to the guest, by relaxing and thanking the guest for coming by, or by rising and showing the guest to the door. In some cases the secretary may help the boss end a meeting by entering the room on cue. If there was not sufficient time to conclude the business, another meeting may be scheduled. It is never appropriate to leave one meeting for another meeting before it is over unless this has been made known to all parties in advance.

Keeping Business Appointments

Keeping appointments is sacrosanct. If the appointment must be changed, it is a courtesy to do so well in advance. Often one change can create half a dozen counter-changes, not to mention ill will.

Keeping Professional Appointments

Doctors, dentists, and others who earn their living by office visits may have a policy of charging clients who fail to show up for a scheduled appointment.

These are frequently the same professionals who run late themselves and keep patients stacked up in their waiting rooms. Then there's the story of the $450/hour lawyer who sued a doctor for keeping him waiting—and collected.

If a patient has to cancel a doctor's appointment, courtesy demands that he or she do so at least a day ahead of time to allow the doctor to fill the slot with someone else. Likewise, the doctor's office should advise patients if they are running late, just as a patient should phone ahead to check the same thing. Courtesy works both ways. It is never acceptable for a patient not to show up.

PHONE MANNERS

Business calls should be brief, well organized and businesslike. Callers should identify themselves to whomever answers. If it is a receptionist, they should ask for the person to whom they wish to speak. If they do not know the proper person to handle their request, they should ask for guidance from the receptionist (this is why automatic, prerecorded operators are such bad business).

Once callers are put through to the appropriate office, they should identify themselves. In most cases, a secretary or assistant may intercede and "screen" the call, asking for more information if the caller is not immediately known.

Should the recipient wish to speak to the caller, he or she will accept the call. Callers should then reintroduce themselves and immediately explain the reason they are talking. The rest is personal skill.

Personal Calls at Work

Although personal calls are unavoidable as long as human beings work in offices, they should be held to a minimum not only to keep the phone lines clear for important business calls but also so as not to disturb busy (or nosy) co-workers.

Conference Calls

Ganging a large number of people onto the same telephone line can be a time and distance saver; the trick is to juggle everybody's schedule so it can happen.

The highest-ranking member of the proposed teleconference is the one whose schedule must be accommodated, even if she is not the person who suggested the call. Subordinates are expected to rearrange their schedules to oblige.

Flowcharts, spreadsheets, and other visual items should be mailed or faxed in advance to all participants, especially in situations where everybody must share reference. Sending an agenda and participant list is also courteous so people know whom they are talking to.

Speaker Phones

Unless one party has a physical reason for doing so, it is rude to conduct a conver-

sation on a speaker phone. If there are several people in the room, everybody's identity should be disclosed.

Who Gets on the Line First

Some business executives practice elaborate jockeying over who places phone calls, who gets on the line first, who gets put on hold, and so forth. Unless one is the president of the United States or an equally powerful and busy person, it shouldn't really matter who gets on when, only that the conversation takes place. The rest is ego.

Call Waiting

Call waiting is based on the belief that your next phone call may be more important than the one you're on. It is equal parts convenience and rudeness. If you have call waiting that you can deactivate, do so before phoning someone else.

If you are expecting a call, don't phone someone else before it comes. If you are expecting a call but still must phone someone else or are expecting a call when someone else calls you first, tell him or her early in the conversation, "I'm expecting a call; if it comes, I'll have to call you right back."

If a call comes in while you're talking with someone else, ignore it and hope that the other party calls you back later (unless your local phone company has "caller ID" or "call return"). If you can't bear not knowing, tell your caller, "Excuse me, I have another call. Let me check, and I'll stay on the line with you." Then click, tell the interrupting

HOLLYWOOD PROTOCOL

It figures that a town like Hollywood, which creates fantasy for a living, would have its own brand of etiquette. Hollywood etiquette does not necessarily have anything to do with reality—or, for that matter, with good manners. It is a closed society that caters to bad behavior, even rewards it, and aggressively disdains those who would tell it otherwise. Not only does the squeaky wheel get the oil in Hollywood, it usually gets the girl. Here's a taste of what passes for etiquette:

1. *Any business appointment may be canceled without blame up to an hour before it was supposed to take place (the reason is usually that a better appointment came along).*

2. *Never be the first to offer an opinion of anything in case one's superior has a different one ("I don't know what I think about your script," one vice president said with a straight face. "Nobody else here has read it yet.").*

3. *Nothing is ever anybody's fault; it just happens. The grammatical term for this is <u>third person innocent</u>. Examples include "a car just crashed," "a meeting got canceled," "a window broke," and, the most important use of third person innocent, "a film just flopped."*

4. *Never speak badly of somebody in public because someone nearby will overhear you and repeat it to him or her.*

5. *One is allowed to speak to a celebrity in public only if one is either a friend of the celebrity or has worked with him or her in the last six months.*

6. *If you must return somebody's phone call but you don't want to speak to him or her, call during lunch.*

7. *Agents do not make outgoing calls to clients.*

8. *Telephone calls received between 10 a.m. and 5 p.m. mean business; between 5 p.m. and 6 p.m. they can go either way; calls received after 6 p.m. are mere social courtesies, and no business will be conducted (because the secretaries and assistants who write up the deals have left for the day).*

9. *People always want something, they just don't always ask for it.*

10. *Today's secretary or assistant may be tomorrow's studio boss.*

caller that you'll call her or him back, and return to the original caller.

Electronic Receptionists

Answering machines, voice mail, automatic operators, and push-button directories are the wave of the future, as well as a confession that you don't care much about your customers. They are offensive.

Screening Calls with an Answering Machine

Whether at home or in the office, people who use their answering machines to screen calls send others the message, "Sometimes I just may not want to be bothered talking to you." It may be efficient, but it is also rude.

Cell Phones

Okay, they're pretentious. But they're also useful for calling ahead to tell your next appointment that you're caught in traffic or to ask driving directions while on the road. If you call someone's cellular phone, keep the message brief because the recipient pays for it. People who use cell phones should always remember that conversations on them are not private and may legally be monitored—by anyone. It's thoroughly obnoxious to whip out a cell phone in a restaurant or other subdued public place.

Junk Phone Calls

There are computers that call people and sell them things. There are computers that call people and keep them on the line until the live operator can take over. And there are "boiler room operations" full of telemarketers who dial random numbers and try to sell newspaper subscriptions, shares of stock, time-sharing condos, and other schemes. All of them are bad manners and invade your privacy. Some of them are illegal (see Chapter 12).

Businesses who use machines to call people who haven't called them first should be put out of business. If they call, demand that they delete your number and never call you back.

SOLICITATIONS

Home Sales

Before people began dwelling in cities where all the necessities of life (except space) were near at hand, they obtained items they could neither grow nor make themselves from peddlers hawking their wares from place to place.

The modern equivalent of this trade, now that door-to-door salespeople such as the Fuller Brush man or the Avon lady have been ousted by chain stores, is the "home sales party."

Popularized by Tupperware® and adapted by firms as wide-ranging as cosmetics, rubber stamps, home repair items, vacation homes, and marital aids, at-home sales parties are a way for friends to exploit each other even away from the office.

If your checkbook and you are invited to one of these commercial parties at a friend's house, the implication is that you should buy *something*—and, by the way, do you have any friends you could invite to next week's party?

As with office collections (see below), no one should be forced to come to, or buy at, such a shamelessly manipulative occasion. "No, thank you, I really don't see anything I need" is a legitimate excuse for those who do not want to buy.

The "Non-no No"

Nobody wants to say "no" in business. It carries a stigma. But sometimes it is unavoidable. Some businesspeople have devised a way of never saying "no" by making it impossible for the other person to say "yes." This is called the "Non-no no." Here's how it works: Say you don't want to accept a job, but at the same time you don't want to get a reputation for declining work. So you ask for a salary so high that you know they'll never pay it. This is tantamount to saying no, except you didn't say no. Moreover, if they can't meet your salary requirement, they haven't said no either. Of course, if they *do* agree to give you the money you want, you have to work for them. So always ask for enough to make it worthwhile.

Office Collections

In larger offices it is not uncommon (in fact, it is a downright regular occurrence) for co-workers to be asked to contribute to each other's causes. These can include birthday parties for colleagues or the boss, betting pools, political and religious donations, funeral and marriage flowers, church and school raffles, sons and daughters selling greeting cards, seeds, wrapping paper, or candy, or even a needy colleague's upcoming rent. Refuse and you're a sour puss; succumb and you're out good money.

It is never proper to solicit a contribution from a co-worker. If a co-worker wishes to make a donation, he or she should do so privately and without even the slightest coercion.

Although a company should have a stated policy that there shall be no collections of any kind, in point of fact they are impossible to stop. An employee who wishes to decline may say, "I'm afraid my paycheck is accounted for, but if you'll let me know where I can send something in the future, I will see what I can do" or "This is a good cause, but I already have a number of causes I support, so I'll have to pass on this one. Thanks for asking."

That may not do the trick, especially if it's the boss's kid whose school is selling the raffle tickets. Workers pressed into making such buys have been known to write off their expenses and then let the boss explain it to the accounting department. Most simply grin and bear it.

Politics on the Job

There is more likelihood that employees will be asked to make a political donation than a religious one and more chance that they will be held accountable for their response.

Government workers, in particular, are often hit up to support the boss's electoral candidate or the political patron who is responsible for their agency's funding. Even private firms that bid on government contracts have not been immune to this kind of coercion.

Regardless of the illegality of such arm twisting, it persists. One way to discourage the practice is to ask the person making the collection to give you a written bill stating specifically what the donation is for so that you can deduct it from your taxes, and then offer to write a check. If that signal is not clear enough, you are dealing with a coercion level that transcends etiquette, not to mention the law.

Prayer at Work

Just as some businesses provide fitness or quit-smoking programs for their employees, some companies may hold prayer services. If attendance at any such activity is truly voluntary, that is, if no employee is even subtly pressured to attend, there is no problem.

Unless it is an avowedly religion-based company, prayer that is forced on unwilling employees on the job during business hours should be considered an intrusion into their personal lives and thus a violation of manners. On the other hand, where a few employees desire to pray together—say, grace before meals, or a prayer service outside of office hours—friends who do not join in should maintain respectful silence for the brief observance.

GIFTS AND ENTERTAINING

Office Parties and Retreats

It may sound odd to link together the office party, which is a celebration, and the office retreat, which is where management and labor share their innermost feelings. However, both gatherings can turn into minefields—and usually do.

The person with whom you share your intimate thoughts after hours can, and probably will, be the one you will have to face on Monday morning. Fortunately, the sixties' ethic of hiring "facilitators" to run "T-groups" held in "seminar centers" so that co-workers "can get in touch with their feelings" has fallen out of favor. No employee should be required to attend any function outside of business hours, but office politics are such that no rule covers this intrusion.

Business Gifts

Traditionally, at Christmas, companies and individuals may find it to their advantage to give a gift to someone who has served them well. There is another term for this: *payoff*. This may take the form of items, frequently of great worth, delivered to a person's home or office.

Many companies have strict rules about what, if anything, their employees, particularly those in decision-making positions, may accept from those who may benefit from those decisions. Gracious employers, upon receiving edible gifts (fruit, candy, cookies, etc.), may lessen the obligation by sharing them with their employees.

Business Entertaining

Occasionally, it is appropriate to entertain clients away from the office and outside of office hours. However, restraint is always safe protocol. The hosts' behavior reflects not only on themselves but also on their company. Some courts have held the company legally responsible for the actions of their employees while representing the business. In brief, nothing should take place in the course of business entertaining that could not take place in the office.

"Let's Do Lunch"

"We'll have to get together some time," "I've been meaning to call you," and similar empty promises are not only an insult to the intelligence of the person who hears them but also an insult to the company that employs the person who makes them. The worst is "The check is in the mail." Saying it is exactly the same as saying, "I am lying to you." Make such promises at your own risk.

Singing Telegrams and Other Distractions

Anything that disrupts the efficient operation of an office is inappropriate, including strippers (male or female), singing telegrams, birthday tap dancers, and mimes.

Some people are merely embarrassed when a stranger confronts them in an office

setting and performs a greeting that has been designed specifically to do just that: embarrass them. Others are offended.

If it happens, and you object, the best tactic is to walk away without comment, preferably into a bathroom.

NETIQUETTE

Like it or not, the Internet is the communication technology of the future. On one hand, it's reinventing television; on the other, it's de-inventing language. Just ask anybody who thought *cool* went out with the 1950s.

Regardless of its newness, the Internet has developed its own set of rules, called, fittingly enough, "netiquette," to govern the way people treat each other in cyberspace.

SHOUTING

To the rest of the world, capital letters are just capital letters, but in the world of netiquette they are shouting, and shouting is very rude. Perhaps because all caps are harder to read, or perhaps because in a medium that relies on words, capital words stand out, people who use them are first warned, then shunned. Or are they *virtually* shunned?

Staying on Subject

Nothing is more distracting than someone who tries to change the subject in an Internet chat room. If you log onto a specific subject room, you have promised to stick to the topic being discussed. If the people in that chat room wanted to discuss something else, they would leave and find another chat room.

Dissing

They say never speak ill of the dead, but better advice is to never speak ill of the living—because the living can sue. Courts have held that companies who run supervised Internet sites (in other words, censors) are legally responsible for what goes out over them. Their servers are programmed to flag any messages in which certain inflammatory words appear and delay them until a proctor determines whether they are actionable.

Although pressure groups have gotten Congress to pass laws limiting freedom on the Internet, the courts have thus far sided with the First Amendment. Yet freedom of speech and tasteful speech can be different things, and anybody libeling anybody else on the Internet can still be hauled into court. Just because you're typing alone in a room doesn't mean that the whole world isn't watching.

Flaming

Flaming is the (usually) irrational criticism of another person's post. This can be done individually or as a pack, and it is usually way out of proportion to the original post. When using the Internet it is wise to remember that there are people at the other end of your message, even if you're sitting alone in a room typing.

Spamming

Named after the Hormel Corporation's famous mystery meat product, Spam®, *spamming* is the cyberspace term for mass mailings of commercial advertisements, most of which are get-rich-quick scams. The term is also used to describe similar material crossposted to numerous newsgroups. At the risk of stating the obvious, spamming is considered to be extremely poor netiquette.

Spam's most annoying feature is that it is often followed by more spam, which is usually a series of aggravated netizens spamming back replies expressing their lack of desire to receive these unwanted junk e-mails and Usenet postings. When flaming a spammer, remember to not "reply to all," lest you become a spammer yourself.

Anonymity

Because the Internet is private, one never knows whom one is meeting online. One should extend the same courtesy and caution on the Internet as one would to someone one meets on the phone, in public, or in a dark club: *be careful*!

Cyber Stalking

Just as celebrities and ex-lovers are occasionally stalked by people who cannot leave them alone, so it has become possible to stalk someone on the Internet.

This involves making repeated calls to someone's server, leaving endless messages on his or her e-mail, posting information about the person, scanning photographs (often digitally altered) into the system, and hacking into phone records and other accounts. Tragically, the first Internet murder has occurred: a man drew a woman into a personal meeting by chatting with her online, and killed her.

The same laws that apply to telegraph and telephone fraud apply to the Internet, although only within the United States. Prohibitions against cyber stalking across international boundaries, now as easy as calling next door, are less enforceable.

It is tempting when typing on the Internet to write as freely as one would speak. As with any form of personal conversation, it is always best (and certainly more proper) to think first. Maybe twelve-year-olds can't do it, but polite adults surely can.

CHAPTER NINE

BEYOND PLEASE AND THANK YOU:

How to Get What You Really Want

"What's the magic word?"

No, it's not Groucho asking, it's Mother. And the magic word, of course, is *please*.

Children—who, by design, start life thinking only of themselves—must be taught that saying "please" usually helps them get what they want and that following it up with "thank you" will make it easier for them to get it again. Using *please* and *thank you* is part of growing up.

Clearly, there are a lot of people out there who never grew up—people such as the woman who butts into the conversation you're having with a sales clerk, or the guy who makes the whole ATM line wait while he fills out the deposit slip, or the driver who doesn't signal, doesn't turn, doesn't stop, doesn't pull over, just holds up traffic while he looks for a house that just has to be around here someplace.

All of these people have the same problem: they are clueless.

Nobody ever told them how things work, and they weren't able to glean the knowledge by themselves, so now everybody else pays for their being out of the loop. This chapter is about getting in the loop.

> *Nothing is more exhilarating than philistine vulgarity.*
>
> —Vladamir Nabokov

SIMPLE COURTESIES

Applause

Applause is one of the ways in which Westerners show approval: they clap their hands. Applause is appropriate at the end of live public performances, or when excitement at a sports event is so great that a burst of it would be encouraging to the players. It is occasionally permissible at other times, such as when a tenor finishes a difficult aria or a politician tells the truth. It is even used—derisively—when a classmate drops his tray in the school lunchroom.

Applause is not appropriate in church, between movements at a symphony concert, or in a court of law. It's not properly supposed to happen after the national anthem, although it does.

In Russia, the custom is for speakers to applaud their own speeches; in America, it is not. In America, some people resolutely refuse to applaud. Maybe they're critics. Maybe they didn't like what they heard. Maybe they're snobbish and feel they don't need to show appreciation. It's a free country.

Apologizing

People who do something wrong should apologize. This means that they accept responsibility for their actions and agree to pay the penalty. This is the single most basic principle in any system of justice, yet it creates the most controversy. When even John Wayne in *The Searchers* insists, "Never apologize for anything," what are we mere mortals to do?

On the other hand, children learn early on that it is easier to get forgiveness than to get permission. It is only when they discover goals bigger than filched cookies that they revise their morality: "A child is not innocent," wrote William Faulkner. "There is no crime which a boy of eleven had not envisaged long ago. His only innocence is that he may not yet be old enough to desire the fruits of it."

Finally, a newspaperwoman once argued against apologizing for anything. "By tomorrow there will be another edition," she explained. "And all anybody will remember is that you were the person who apologized for something."

Waiting in Line

"First come, first served" is a standard practice whether at the post office or a movie ticket line. What is less well observed is what happens when someone allows a friend to join him in line without consulting those waiting behind him. Ideally, everyone should give consent before cutting is allowed.

Wrong Numbers

James Thurber once drew a cartoon for the *New Yorker* with the caption, "Well, if I called the wrong number, why did you answer the phone?" If you misdial, you should say, "Excuse me, I dialed a wrong number," before hanging up. If you believe you dialed the correct number, you should not ask, "What number is this?" or "Who is this?" If you do, the person at the other end would be unwise to disclose either. Instead, you should ask, "I thought I dialed 555-1212; have I done so?" If you were wrong, try again more carefully.

In large cities where there may be language differences, wrong numbers may result in misunderstanding—or, rather, no understanding. An apology is still called for.

Incidentally, an increasing number of phone systems are offering a "call back" service that allows people to press *69 and dial back anybody who has just hung up on them.

Obscene Phone Calls

Not only are obscene phone calls rude and disturbing, they also are against the law. If this happens, make no response, as the obscene caller desires exactly that. Anyone who receives a phone call he or she considers obscene should contact the phone company for instructions. "Caller ID" allows the recipient of an obscene call to find out the caller's phone number, which may enable some to press charges. This only works for published numbers, however, or for numbers that have not been blocked.

Answering Somebody Else's Phone

Unless the host specifically asks you to do so, it is best not to answer the phone in

ME,ME,ME

ROOMMATES

Regardless of what TV shows such as <u>Friends</u> and <u>The Real World</u> portray, having roommates is just like having brothers and sisters all over again, except without parents around to referee.

Roommates are not only couples living together for romantic reasons. They are people forced for economic reasons to dwell together in college dorms, fraternity or sorority houses, shared apartments, or other arrangements. Therefore, to reduce the risk of mass murder, certain niceties should be respected:

1. Never take either the last beer or the last yard of toilet paper.
2. Save all receipts and put your initials on the stuff you pay for. Everybody can settle up at the end of the month.
3. If you've brought a date home, drape a necktie or bra over your bedroom doorknob to signal privacy.
4. Don't stay in the bathroom for more than fifteen minutes.
5. Rotate doing the chores or pay to hire someone else to do them.
6. Keep the toilet seat down at all times if there is at least one female in the house.
7. Never answer the phone rudely.
8. If you use the last of something, buy more of it (unless it's something nobody liked anyway).
9. Put things back where they belong, rather than where you found them. Always clean up after yourself and your guests.
10. Settle all personality disputes immediately to prevent sulking.

somebody else's house. If so, say "Smith residence" and take a message.

Calling at an Awkward Time

It is thoughtless to phone somebody during meal time or at bedtime. This is espe-cially important when calling long distance between time zones.

If you cannot speak on the phone (because you have company, are taking a bath, are eating, are changing the baby, etc.), ask the caller, "May I call you back in a few minutes?"

or "Would you call me back in fifteen minutes? I'm not able to talk now."

Paying Compliments

Unless you live in a culture that prizes collectivism (such as Japan), it is a gracious gesture to compliment Westerners on the job they, or those responsible to them, have done. A compliment should be freely given—specific enough to demonstrate an understanding of the task that was well performed, yet not so picky that it seems like searching to find something, anything, nice to say. It's never that tough to give a compliment that comes from the heart.

Receiving Compliments

It's always a pleasure being praised, but some people can be too modest. Believe it or not, rejecting a compliment can be as rude as begging for one.

If one receives a compliment one should say, "Thank you very much," and let it go at that. If one was singled out for praise for something to which others contributed, it is fair to add, "I would like to share the compliment with others who worked with me on . . ." It is never correct to accept a compliment for something one has not done.

Fishing for Compliments

It is unseemly to prompt someone to deliver praise. Praise must arise naturally from an act that was performed. On the other hand, one should always offer praise when it is due.

Confessions

The advice that "confession is good for the soul but bad for the reputation" is something that seems widely disregarded today, especially by people who appear on TV talk shows.

Confessing to an inappropriate person is not only of questionable value from a therapeutic standpoint, but also places the listener in an awkward position. People who are appropriate to hear confessions include lawyers, police, judges, psychiatrists, priests, and parents.

Friends, strangers, bartenders, 976 numbers, and Internet chat room participants may provide momentary counsel, but someone who has a serious problem should see a professional.

Talking to Strangers

Children are rightly taught never to talk to strangers, but anyone who plans to function outside of the house sooner or later must deal with someone whom she or he hasn't met before. This can be awkward for both parties.

We are not at all accustomed to having strangers come up to us and start talking. There must be a legitimate reason to engage a stranger in conversation. The seller–buyer relationship is the most common in a commerce-driven culture, as is that of a person seeking information (asking directions, getting a referral, etc.) from someone. In social or business situations, two people may be introduced by a mutual friend and, thereafter, engage in substantive talk. But, by and large, most conversation between strangers is limited to "'Excuse me" or "Hold the elevator door please."

Inappropriate Conversations

Certain subjects are taboo for polite conversation. There are, in addition, places where it is traditionally inappropriate to have any but the most cursory conversation with strangers:

- Rest rooms
- Elevators
- Buses, taxis, etc.
- Airplanes (except, strangely enough, in first class, which is something of a club)
- Supermarket checkout lines
- Cafeterias or lunch counters
- Theaters or stadiums
- Museums or art galleries
- Newsstands

An exception may be made when a common event affects everyone present to the point where he or she may comment on it (e.g., witnessing a car accident, observing unusually rude behavior, complaining about bad service, showing appreciation for a good movie, leaving a worship service). What this says is that people need an excuse to talk with one another, and *that* says something, too.

Listening to Others

As social satirist Fran Lebowitz said, "The opposite of talking is not listening. The opposite of talking is waiting." Unfortunately, she's right; most people don't care what other people say as long as they just get their own views in. Yet the greatest gift one person can give another is the gift of paying attention. Perhaps this explains why there is so much rudeness: it's the only way to make an impression, even if it's a bad impression.

Interrupting Someone

Unless there is a fire or other emergency, it is rude to interrupt someone who is talking. One may say, "excuse me" at a pause in the conversation and then wait to be recognized. Being in a hurry is no excuse to trample the rights or dignity of others.

If you are already speaking with someone when a third party interrupts, you may turn to the interrupter and say, "I'll be with you in a moment." Having aplomb in such a circumstance is a social grace to be acquired and admired.

Making Conversation

Prolonging conversation without contributing to it—in other words, talking just to talk—is both wasteful and rude.

Such words and phrases as "Yeah," "Really," "Is that so?," "No kidding," "Right" and "Know what I'm sayin'?" are insulting to the intelligence of the listener and just downright boring.

In conversation, one should follow the Cheshire Cat's advice to Alice: "Start at the beginning, and when you get to the end, stop."

Me, Me, Me

"Okay, enough about me," the movie star protested modestly, "Now let's talk about my work." Oneself is never a valid topic of conversation unless it is specifically requested by another person, as in "How are you?" There are a few occasions, of course, where one should readily discuss oneself. Two that come to mind are psycho-analysis and autobiographies.

First Names

Unless two people agree on using each other's first names, only last names should be used when addressing others.

Obvious exceptions are made for parents to children, teachers to young students, masters to servants, and celebrities who have only first names, such as Cher, Madonna, Ann-Margret, or the singer formerly known as Prince.

Nicknames

Pity the poor kid who passes wind on the playground when he's six and forever after is known as "Stinky." A nickname is an endearing, familiar term among friends only if the person it identifies expressly wishes to be called by it.

Shortened names are usually acceptable, such as Meg for Margaret, Ed for Edward, Debbie for Deborah, or Jon for Jonathan. Where it may get touchy is when more eso-teric nicknames are devised, such as (and these are real) Spuddy, Shecky, Zero, Skippy, Bluto, Quahog, Bitsy, Muffin, and anything alluding to sex.

Practical Jokes

Pulling a practical joke has no purpose other than to belittle another person. Practical jokes range from the clever to the contrived, the latter of which form the basis for a series of TV specials designed to show that celebrities can be made to look just as stupid as the rest of us from the bottom of a whoopee cushion. In short, practical jokes—and the negative energy behind them—are just plain tacky.

Profanity

Vulgar, suggestive, obscene, or profane language is *never, ever* acceptable in polite society. Even when the listener appears to tolerate it, he or she still thinks measurably less of the person who used it.

It is impossible to avoid offensive language completely when one lives a normal life in the modern world, but one should still not expect to hear such language in certain venues—at a restaurant, for example.

If one is adjacent to people who are cursing, one may properly ask them (even if they are strangers), "Would you mind please not using such language?" They may be so surprised that they will do just that.

Off-color Jokes

It is astonishing that people who con-sider themselves civilized will tolerate racist, ethnic, sexist, and off-color jokes made at the expense of others. There is even a series of best-selling paperback books, *Truly Tasteless Jokes*, that codifies them.

If one does not want to participate in such humor, one should inform the would-be comedian, "I do not care to hear that kind of joke." Although those present may agree with you, they may not have the good manners to say so.

Peer Pressure

The foregoing having been said, it is admittedly difficult for young people, or those in a work situation involving comradeship, to stick by their moral guns when demeaning jokes are flying around. If one cannot actively dissuade them from being told, the least one can do is not participate (or laugh), on the belief, however introspective, that "it stops here."

Tolerance

Tolerance went by the boards in the eighties, a result of the glorification of greed and a growing philosophy of "I'm all right, go fend for yourself" (only not in those exact words). To some people, *tolerance* means "permissiveness." To others it means "acceptance." At the very least we should follow Mrs. Patrick Campbell's advice that anything should be accepted "so long as one doesn't do it in the street and frighten the horses."

In America, everyone can have an opinion, even though there's nothing that says everybody's opinion is of equal worth. Should you disagree vehemently with

someone's opinion, you can either oppose it or ignore it, keeping in mind that you will be weighed against your success in doing either.

There is one specific exception to civility in differences of opinion: courts have held that when someone threatens a group of people ("the blacks," "the Jews," "the Arabs"), he is exercising free speech, but should he threaten an *individual* black, Jew, or Arab, he may be prosecuted for assault.

Helping the Elderly Cross the Street

First, make sure he or she wants to go. Then offer your arm (a lady or a gentleman may do this). You may have to encourage oncoming traffic to slow or stop to permit both of you to cross.

Joggers

People who jog have a fear of stopping for traffic. "I'll get cramps," they say. Joggers have the same right-of-way as pedestrians. They may cross with the "walk" light in marked crosswalks, they must not run in the street, and they may not, in many states, wear personal stereos.

Testosterone and the TV Remote Control

Men are hunter-gatherers. Women are nurturers. Men hunt and gather TV stations. Women nurture a particular show. There is a story about a wife who was so fed up with her husband hogging the TV remote control all the time that she broke it in half.

Pet Peeves

Who would want a peeve for a pet? It is never proper to criticize someone's habits if they pose neither a threat nor an inconvenience to you. Someone who cracks his knuckles, constantly clears his throat, uses the same trite expression all the time, whistles "Melancholy Baby" incessantly, clicks his Bic, says "Yessss!" when pleased, or puts ketchup and mustard on his scrambled eggs may test your patience, but not your etiquette.

Etiquette, after all, is about forgiving people for their faults in the hope that they will forgive you for yours.

COMPLAINTS

Although "You catch more flies with honey than you do with vinegar," it is often difficult to know just which government or retail fly handles complaints about service, conditions, or products.

Unfortunately, as government abdicates its regulatory responsibility and retailers downsize, the first people who get laid off are the ones who look out for the consumer. This explains lawyers, litigation, and the mercurial marketplace. It also places more of a burden on individuals to settle scores themselves. Here are some hints on how to do it.

Working the Phone Book

Even if a special "Complaint Department" isn't listed for an organization, there usually is someone on staff capable of settling consumer problems.

First, clarify what your complaint is about. Then write it down concisely so that you won't ramble on while describing it. Most misunderstandings occur because one person was thinking "round" while the other person was thinking "square." If you have receipts, account numbers, or merchandise, keep them within reach.

Then look up the company's or agency's main number in the phone book. Most directories have separate residential, business, and government listings; choose whichever is appropriate and dial carefully. If you get a live operator, ask who handles complaints. If no one does, ask for the public relations department. An electronic operator sometimes can direct your call as well. If you don't hear what you want on the directory, wait for the recording to end; most of the time, you will then be transferred to a live operator. For government problems, ask for "information" or, failing that, a case worker.

Have a pen and paper handy, and keep notes during the call. Get the name and direct-dial phone number of everybody you speak to. It will all come in handy.

No matter how much incompetence you encounter, do not lose your temper. It only steels others against helping you. Accept that you may not be able to solve the dispute on the phone and might have to write a letter.

Letters of Complaint

A letter of complaint can be either a mad tirade or a helpful, coherent guide to

TOLL-FREE NUMBERS

*J*ust as dialing 4-1-1 will ring up local directory assistance and 1-(area code)-555-1212 will connect you with long-distance information, so will 1-800-555-1212 put you in touch with every organization that maintains a toll-free number.

Nobody really publicizes this fact. But the diligent dialer can ask toll-free directory assistance for all kinds of consumer help lines, corporate outreach lines, and even government fax-polling documents.

When seeking satisfaction from a company, it's always easier to start off on their dime.

RING

solving a problem. First, get over your anger. If you write a letter (of any kind) in anger, put it aside for a day or two until you cool down. Never name-call or threaten anyone, especially in writing. If saying "I'll take my business elsewhere" isn't enough to goad someone into action, threatening their first-born will be completely counterproductive.

As you did when you phoned, provide a brief description of the problem in the letter. Do not try to be sarcastic or guess how they erred; they probably won't get it. Just state the facts, and ask them to call you to advise you what to do next. If you don't hear from

them in two or three weeks, follow up with another call or letter.

Taking It to the Top

If you cannot get satisfaction from the foot soldiers to whom you've been complaining, try the boss. Make another call to the switchboard to get the name of the president of the company (or of the division). Now that you have built a phone and paper trail, you may enclose copies with the letter you write inquiring why such a big company can't correct such a small problem.

Nine times out of ten, the boss will lean on his or her underling to solve the problem if for no other reason than to get you off his back. Just remember: use honey, not vinegar.

Complaining to a Broadcaster

Radio and TV stations arrogantly believe that they are operating in the public interest, yet they do their best to make the public feel that nothing the public says or does will have any influence on them.

Nonsense. Broadcasters are scared to death of the public, despite FCC deregulation. Broadcasters' dirty little secret is that each letter that they receive is worth a thousand that were thought of but not sent. Phone calls don't count; they are spur-of-the-moment outbursts and usually made in anger. But a reasoned, literate letter from an individual sent to a local station can cause high-level meetings. Ten can cause firings. And fifty letters sent to networks can do . . . *anything.* ("Individual" means just that: one person's thoughts. Never mention that you're part of a group; E-mail, faxes, or form letters circulated by pressure groups mean zip because they're mindless.)

Complaining to a Newspaper

Unlike broadcasters, newspaper and magazine publishers do not operate under federal license, and complaints will have little or no effect on them. This holds true whether the complainant is a lone nut case or a U.S. senator, so take some comfort in that.

EMPOWERING INFO

"There is no physical gulf between the philosopher's classroom and the bull ring," Shaw wrote in *Man and Superman*, "but the bull fighters do not come to the class room for all that." Sadly, the same might be said for people whom American society has bypassed. Fortunately, it's not a permanent condition if one simply learns how to use the system to one's advantage. This doesn't mean that one should milk the system for benefits or entitlements. It means learning how to take part in the system.

Voting

It's easier to vote now than ever before in the nation's history thanks to the "motor voter" laws that have been passed in most states. One registers to vote when one applies for a driver's license (as well as in the traditional grass roots manner of signing up at tables at shopping centers or by dropping in at the local election commission).

A frightening statistic should convince anybody to vote who is doubting the effort: in any given election, only 30 percent of those who are eligible to vote actually do vote. That means that all the bad guys need to win is 15 percent plus one.

Bad Debt

People can't meet their bills for a variety of reasons. Some even go further into debt by signing with commercial debt-consolidation services (frequently pledging their homes to do so). But some people go into debt because they simply don't know how to make a phone call.

If you're in arrears with a creditor (gas, electric, phone, fuel, doctor, dentist, etc.), don't ignore the bill; call the company's credit office. They usually are happy to discuss a schedule of payments that you can afford to make. After all, they would much rather get *something* from a customer than spend even more money chasing a total default. Just ask.

Call First

As with all business and social appointments, if you must cancel or be late for one, it is essential to call ahead and inform those who are waiting for you. A little thing like making such a call will "keep the door open" with the people involved. Of course, you should never make a habit of this. Knowing how to plan your time is very important and proves that you are trust-worthy.

Be on Time

If a meeting is scheduled to start at 10 A.M., be there at 9:55 A.M. It is unprofessional to keep others waiting for you. Even if you're a big movie star and can decide not to show up at all, it will ultimately work against you.

Legal Obligations

Some people who had minor scrapes with the law (say, traffic violations) discover later on that there are arrest warrants for them and they can't figure out why. Didn't they know that ignoring a court summons would result in a warrant being sworn out?

They probably didn't. Even people who have had a brush with the legal system can remain ignorant of how it actually operates, or perhaps they figure, "Out of sight, out of mind." Justice is blind, but cops aren't. Advances in computer and Internet technology are making it harder to jump warrants or elude parking fines. In a society where so many people are caught in the penal system, ignorance of the law is no excuse.

Taxes

If you have ever filed income taxes, you must continue to do so, even if you made no income in a given year. Even if the income you earned was illegal, you have to file taxes on it! And, no, that's not a violation of the Fifth Amendment because the government's right to tax supersedes the individual's right against self-incrimination.

Alimony and Child Support

Court decrees on alimony and child support must be paid. Not doing so will result in default, garnishment of wages, cancellation of visitation or custody rights, and public embarrassment.

Your kid will also grow up hating you. Alimony and child support issues, just like warrants, debt, and taxes, don't just go away without being settled.

CHAPTER TEN

THE LONG
GOODBYE:

*Leaving This
Earth, Your Job or
Your Marriage*

I n this world we can be sure of only three things: death, taxes and reruns of *Star Trek*®. Of the three, death is the one we fear most, and, as the ultimate "final frontier," it is fraught with considerable ritual and etiquette, probably as a way of lessening its terror for those who must observe its trappings.

In our society there are other kinds of death, however—*petit mal* by comparison, perhaps, but just as discomforting. Separation, divorce, job loss, the death of a beloved pet, and even moving away are all attended by their share of shock, depression, and anxiety; in other words, they, too, are rife with ritual. How does etiquette address issues that are this unpleasant?

Contrary to popular misconception, etiquette does not attempt to deny the emotions or cover the pain and grief. Rather, etiquette tells us precisely what to do under confusing circumstances and often in punctilious detail. Here's why: people going through trying periods in their lives do not think rationally; more to the point, they often flail around emotionally and may find themselves at the mercy of those who might take advantage of them. (This explains, for example, why the funeral industry is regulated by law.)

> *Nothing in his life quite became him like the leaving it.*
> —**William Shakespeare,** **Macbeth**

As for divorce, there are resentments to deal with as well as a highly complex set of new considerations that have nothing to do with community property: Who gets the kids? The friends? The cat? First dibs at party invitations? What happens when everybody shows up at the same place at the same time?

Leaving a job (whether voluntarily or involuntarily) also is an invitation to confusion, and at such a stressful time it's good if somebody has a clear head and all the AK-47's are under lock and key.

Bearing in mind that etiquette's first duty is to reduce friction rather than heal psychological wounds, the reader who is bereft over any of the contentious and disturbing issues addressed in this chapter might do well to consult counseling professionals specializing in those areas.

JOB SEPARATION

"Never trust anybody who hasn't been fired at least once." That may not sound encouraging, but firing should be taken as a rite of passage, something to be endured, surmounted, corrected, . . . and then not repeated.

Firing can take several forms: *corporate downsizing*, a perverse phrase that managers use when they eradicate other people's jobs to prevent the stockholders from eradicating theirs; *laid off*, a term meaning that the job has been removed but the person holding it hasn't, although the net effect is the same; *riffing*, a government acronym for "retired in force," also meaning mass layoffs; and such additional euphemisms as *cut back, early retirement, discharged, sacked, booted, dismissed, terminated*, and one that the British use with characteristic understatement, *redundant*. But it all means getting fired, and here's how to deal with it.

Reasons to Fire

An employee may be fired for failing to perform his or her duties or for engaging in unsuitable behavior. The firing should be done face to face and in private by the employee's immediate superior. If it is necessary, for legal reasons, to have witnesses, then this fact should be disclosed to the employee at the start of the meeting at which the firing is to take place.

There may be additional reasons for firing, such as office politics, companies in corporate trouble, patronage, but, strictly speaking, these have nothing to do with an employee's competence.

Second Chances

The need to fire an employee should be balanced against the cost (in both money and time) of training a replacement. This does not mean that an errant employee should be kept on just because his losses are consistent ("The czar we know is better than the czar we don't know"); sometimes a "stern talking-to" can help a worker shape up.

Notice Versus Firing

Two weeks' notice is customary when an employee is to be laid off for financial reasons or where there is no question of his or her honesty or competence. It also is generous to offer the employee a choice of two weeks' severance pay or two weeks' notice when allowing him or her to remain on the job might facilitate his or her landing another one more easily. In some cases the amount of severance pay is commensurate with the number of years the employee has worked for the company.

Doing the Actual Firing

Some bosses enjoy telling employees that they are being fired, but most find it an unpleasant, if necessary, task. It is helpful to fire someone at the end of a business day, preferably on a Friday, to allow you the weekend to get over it. There may be some buzzing in the office come Monday morning, but far less than might happen if the sacking happened on a Monday.

Matters of severance, notice, and interim continuation of employee benefits (such as medical insurance) should be established during the firing session. It may help if the employer has a list of such things to refer to or to hand to the employee.

In no case should an employer act in anger, even if the employee does so. If there is a question of instability, building security should be notified to stand by.

An employee who must be immediately dismissed for "cause" (drinking, drugs, sexual harassment, theft, repeated tardiness, unexcused absence, insubordination, etc.) is not, of course, offered a choice. He or she may even be escorted from the building.

Job Recommendations

Anything less than a full and glowing recommendation of a former employee will be taken as a negative reference. Unfortunately, an outright negative letter of reference may be legally actionable under libel laws. What's an ex-employer to do?

If the employee was a good worker and it would be a credit to you and your company to endorse another company hiring him, by all means write the letter. It should contain evidence of your familiarity with the employee and his skills, your assurances that the employee is competent and honest, and a clear indication that you would encourage hiring him.

If you cannot provide a positive recommendation to an employee who requests one, you must tell him so when he asks for it. This will enable him to decide whether to use you as a job reference.

You may also wish to give only a half-hearted reference and allow the next employer to read between the lines. There have certainly been instances when an employer, seeking to get rid of an employee he cannot fire because of seniority, a union, an affirmative action, zealously recommends him to a competitor in the hope that the competitor would hire him away. This is clever, but wholly dishonest.

Disgruntled Employees

Although journalists seek out disgruntled former employees to provide juicy news about ex-employers, a worker who trashes his former boss also trashes himself. Nobody likes a tattle-tale.

Consoling Someone Who Has Been Fired

It's embarrassing to be fired. It's no great ego boost being laid off, either, but getting sacked is the pits. The fallout from a firing can be profound. Often it affects not only the breadwinner, but also those who depend on him or her. Furthermore, a firing can shatter self-confidence, break up marriages, and occasionally lead to suicide.

Those close to someone who has been fired should be supportive and noninflammatory. There is bound to be anger, but the more important task is to allow the victim to rebuild his or her self-confidence and go out to look for another job right away.

Getting Even

Seeking retribution against a boss for a firing or layoff is bound to be fruitless, as the first suspects the authorities check are those employees who have just been fired. It is also tempting to write a letter giving one's ex-boss "a piece of my mind." Remember, writing is forever. If one is compelled to compose such a missive, it should be stored in a locked drawer for at least a week or until anger subsides.

Quitting

As with a firing, how an employee voluntarily resigns a position also is an indication of his or her character. If the resignation is to take a better job elsewhere, to leave the field entirely, to relocate, or for other reasons, it should be broached to one's immediate boss in person, and later, if requested, confirmed in a brief letter of resignation.

One should never quit a job in anger (except as a planned tactic, which means it wasn't really anger, was it?), and the wise boss dissuades a valued employee from doing so.

In most cases two to four weeks is a considerate notice to allow for a smooth transition between old and new employee. The departing worker might be expected, and should offer, to train his or her replacement.

Thank-you Notes

Whether one resigns, is laid off, or, yes, is even fired, it is a thoughtful gesture to write a letter to one's former employer with thanks for having had the opportunity to work under him or her.

Even when the parting has been acrimonious to the point of being just short of a duel, a gracious letter can go a long way toward defusing an incipient reprisal. Better yet, if your old boss ever speaks against you, you will already be on record as praising him, and, boy, will he look stupid.

DIVORCE, SEPARATION, AND BREAKUPS

Like marriage, divorce shouldn't be entered into lightly. At its worst, divorce forces former lovers to become combatants, coldly quantifying every element of their soured relationship as a prerequisite to dismantling it. At the very least, you get your monogram back.

If a marriage is failing and counseling has not worked, it is better if both parties can come to a mutual understanding without placing blame. If this is not possible, as in the case of marital infidelity, then it's time to call in the lawyers. Meanwhile, there's etiquette.

Ground Rules

Prevailing wisdom suggests that the partner who wants the divorce should break the news to the other partner in an expensive restaurant, the reasoning being that one is less likely to yell, cry, or turn violent in a fancy public setting. The presumption is that anyone hearing awful news will maintain decorum. Yeah, and the Chicago Cubs will win the pennant. Call a lawyer.

Social Obligations

Once a couple has decided on a separation, they must not appear socially at the same event (family gatherings excepted, provided they remain civil, especially if there are children). The couple may continue to wear their wedding rings until the divorce decree comes through. They also may date other people.

A Woman's Name

Until the divorce is final, the woman continues to use her married name. Afterward, she may revert to her unmarried name if she wishes. If her marriage was annulled, she returns to her unmarried name. The choice is hers.

If she and her husband joined their last names with a hyphen, she may remove her husband's name, although if their children had hyphenated last names, she may choose to keep hers hyphenated until the children turn eighteen.

Children

Because children are, after all, children, they will most likely view their parents' divorce in terms of themselves: "What did I do to make Mommy and Daddy stop loving each other?" Both parents should assure children that the divorce had nothing to do with them and that both parents continue to love them very much and will continue to spend time with them. During the divorce process, parents must avoid forcing the child to take sides (about as easy to do as putting hair spray back into the can). Strictly speaking, this has nothing to do with etiquette, but it has a great deal to do with not raising axe murderers.

DIVIDING MARRIAGE PROPERTY

Where state community property laws are not in effect, some rules will apply to divorcing couples who must divide their joint possessions.

1. Whatever either party brought into the marriage (school books, comic collection, pets) should remain with that person after the divorce.
2. Wedding gifts become the joint property of the couple and should be divided according to who can better use them.
3. Heirlooms presented to the bride by the groom's mother should be returned to the groom (and likewise the bride).
4. Items that would clearly be more appropriate to one party than the other (favorite lamp, chair, computer, appliances, etc.) should be ceded to him or her.
5. Jointly held securities should be liquidated at maturity (for short-term); at optimum value (for long-term, and the penalty shared); held in escrow; or used as leverage against other items.

Taking Sides

People who know both parties seldom adjudicate their friends' divorce, they just wind up taking sides according to whom they like better. How sad, since it's friendship that helps friends get through their divorce. Rather than be caught in the middle, one can tell the divorcing peers the following: "I am fond of both of you and want to stay friends, but I refuse to be caught in the middle. Whatever one of you may say to me about the other will remain with me, although I would prefer that neither of you speak ill of the other in my presence." It is both tacky and dangerous to ask friends to testify in a contested divorce; doing so will invariably build walls on both sides.

Engagement Before a Divorce Is Final

A man and woman involved in a relationship may not become engaged so long as either has a divorce pending. There may be legal and ethical reasons for them to refrain from living together during that same period as well. Consult a lawyer.

Formal Notice of Divorce

As tempting as it is to buy an ad, hire a skywriter, or send a chain letter announcing a divorce, it is improper to do so. Family and friends should be notified personally (phone is okay); others may glean as much from the change-of-address form that each party should issue. There should be no formal newspaper announcement, although in rare instances a routine "legal notice" may be run if there is any question of credit rating or other joint liability.

Party Invitations

If your large celebration (wedding, christening, bar mitzvah, etc.) involves inviting a divorced couple, each should be informed of your intention to invite the other, allowing each to make the decision to attend.

For smaller functions, such as dinner parties, only one partner should be invited. In that case invite only one, and if he or she declines, invite the other. If the first friend has a change of plans and calls after the other has accepted, explain the situation and suggest another get-together.

Weddings: When the Immediate Family Is Divorced

The proud mother and father should not be excluded from their daughter's or son's wedding (or any other happy occasion), even if they are divorced. In all cases, decorum and good behavior must apply (see Chapter 4).

Accidentally Encountering a Former Spouse or Lover

Nothing can dampen newly kindled flames of love than to be on a date and bump into the person who poured water on your previous flames. In other words, you run into your ex. Don't panic. On such occasions (if the breakup was unpleasant), pay no attention. Ignore each other.

If ignoring the other person is impossible, a simple, icy "Hello" will discourage any further conversation. Should the ex-lover try to make an issue of the encounter, rebuff him or her with, "We have nothing to say to each other," and walk away.

Divorce Decree Parties

Although divorce announcements should not be sent out, divorce parties have come into fashion.

What will you serve at such a function? Split pea soup? Fork-split English muffins? Frozen dinners for one? One Musketeer bars? In short, get over it! Such gatherings are in the worst possible taste.

Staying Friendly with Ex-In-Laws

Although a divorce severs the family ties between a person and his or her now-ex-in-laws, often a bond of friendship may remain. This is particularly important where there are children who may never see their grandparents again.

In-laws are grown-ups who are fully capable of choosing their own friends, even if the divorce makes it obvious that their child couldn't. Although the in-laws would not be included as family in a second wedding, they may still be invited as friends.

Religion and Divorce

Different religions have different ways of addressing the subject of divorce and remarriage. Most, if not all, encourage a troubled couple to seek counseling to try to reconcile their differences rather than dissolve the holy marriage bond.

- Catholic: No divorce is permitted between Catholics married in the Church. There is only annulment, which holds, after the fact, that there never was a marriage in the first place.
- Protestant: Divorce is permitted.
- Jewish: For Orthodox Jews, a religious divorce is granted if both husband and wife agree and a civil divorce has been obtained first; for Reform Jews, a civil divorce is sufficient.
- Eastern Orthodox: Divorce is permitted with a religious decree.
- Quaker: Divorce is rarely permitted and only after dissolving the sworn and witnessed marriage certificate.
- Mormon: Divorce is permitted for civil weddings but rarely for temple weddings, which are "for time and all eternity."
- Christian Science: Divorce is permitted.
- Islam: Divorce is permitted.

FUNERALS

Church or Synagogue

If the deceased or the immediate family are members in a specific church or synagogue, the officiating clergy can arrange the ceremony, usually in tandem with the funeral director and the family.

The clergy will help determine the time and details of the religious service. If, for some reason, the facility cannot be made available, then a service may be held in the chapel of the funeral home and a memorial service scheduled at another time in the chosen house of worship.

Funeral Home Versus Residence

A funeral home is a commercial establishment designed to coordinate the many details of burying the dead. They have chapels in which services can be held, viewing rooms, and private gathering rooms. They can arrange for clergy, transportation, cemetery space, and even, in some cases, mourners. Funeral homes can be sectarian or nonsectarian.

Viewings and funerals also can be held in the home of the deceased, although this is less common today. If the wake is held in a residence, the family may "hang the bell" in purple, black, or white ribbons, which is to say that the doorbell or knocker is muffled. This signifies a house of mourning.

Interment, Mausoleum, and Cremation

If a burial plot has been purchased by the family, interment may be in a reserved place. If there is no plot, the funeral director or clergy can help the family make the purchase. A mausoleum, or structure,

also may be a repository for the remains. It, too, must be procured or erected if it does not exist.

Cremation, or the incineration of the remains, is as old as civilization. In modern times it has become a highly personal matter and should be the choice of the deceased by prior declaration. Some religions object to it. Whatever the decision, provision must be made for who shall receive the urn (containing the ashes) and where they will store it.

Chapel and/or Graveside Services

Some families desire a full chapel funeral with songs, prayers, full mass, and many mourners. Others choose an intimate service held at the graveside. Often the deceased specified his or her wishes ahead of time. Whatever the choice is, it will be made known in the newspaper notice or will be available by calling the funeral home.

Fees for Funeral Homes

The funeral director will outline all costs of any work performed. Regardless of the compassion shown them, the bereaved must remember that they are entering into a business arrangement. All costs and responsibilities must be clearly delineated before any agreement is reached. This is why it is helpful to have a trusted friend serve as liaison between a grief-stricken family and the funeral home. Fees can range from $2,000 or $3,000 to $10,000 and include a wide range of variables.

Fees for Clergy

The officiating clergy, sexton, choir, and/or organist may charge a fee, which varies widely, for holding a religious service with the facilities of the institution. These fees usually are established by the church or synagogue board and must be disclosed and payment arranged, in advance.

Protestant Funerals

The casket is placed in front of the altar shortly before the service starts, and the immediate family waits in a vestry to the side of the altar. Mourners gather in the pews, but the pews immediately to the front are reserved for the immediate family, who enter once the others are in place. In some churches the immediate family remains in the vestry during the service.

Afterward, pallbearers carry the casket to the hearse for the procession to the cemetery. The family follows. Only after the family has left do the mourners leave.

Jewish Funerals

Jews bury their dead as quickly as possible on the first non-Sabbath day following the death.

Visitors dress as for any religious service. The traditional skullcap (*yarmulke*) is worn to observances at the temple and the cemetery, even by visiting Christians. The *kaddish* (a prayer for the dead in which the word *death* is never mentioned, incidentally) also is recited.

At the cemetery, once the casket is lowered, mourners may drop a handful of soil into the open grave. The mourners then retire to the late residence to sit for a Jewish mourning ceremony of *shiva*.

Catholic Funerals

Catholic funerals are always held in church where a formal procession is held according to a precise protocol. The procession begins with the spouse, with the oldest children next, and so on (this is changing). Family and friends wishing to commemorate the deceased may buy a mass card from the priest, who will fill in the date and time a mass will be said for the soul of the departed. The card, in lieu of flowers, will be sent to the bereaved before the funeral.

Hindu Funerals

The body is cremated on the day of death if this is at all possible. A holy man, however, may be entombed in a *samadhi*, or crypt, where his soul can pass to its higher state of consciousness.

The deceased is cleaned, anointed, shaved, wrapped in a cloth, and carried to the place of cremation by males chanting *Rama*. The corpse is laid on a funeral pyre with its feet pointing south to the god of death (*yama*) and its head pointing north to the god of wealth (*kubera*). Three to ten days after the pyre is lit, the remains are gathered and placed in a sacred area or, if at all feasible, spread on the Ganges River. The bereaved are comforted by memories of the deceased and by the reminder of the transitory nature of life.

Baha'i Funerals

Because the Baha'i services do not follow ritual, the funeral service is dictated by those who were closest to the deceased. Physically, however, there are restrictions: no embalming unless demanded by law, and the body may not be moved more than an hour's distance from the place of death. Baha'i also forbids cremation (on the tenet that the body was its spirit's temple).

During the funeral itself the casket may be open or closed, there may be music or none, and any who wish to do so may speak. The only essential part of the service is a reading of the Prayer for the Dead, which must be spoken by a believer while all present stand.

Muslim Funerals

The body is prepared by ablution while someone reads from the Qur'an. There is no embalming, for the body must return to the earth, and the cleaning is done under the strictest conditions. The body is placed in a coffin and removed to a mosque.

The funeral procession varies by country; mourners may precede or follow the casket, and women may or may not participate. The mosque service is open to all.

At the cemetery the body may be removed from the coffin and laid to rest with its head pointed toward Mecca. Muslims believe that the prophet proscribed

mourning, so grieving may take place by hired mourners or by women of the family, who typically will wail over the deceased.

Water Burials

If a death occurs at sea where there is no way of preserving the body, a water burial may be performed. In this ceremony the captain officiates and the remains, enclosed in a coffin or a body bag, are slipped into the sea. Viking lore provides that the deceased is placed on a ship or raft and set adrift afire. In both instances, water is both a form of purification and a symbol of immortality.

How Close Friends Should React When Informed

Close friends of the family, on hearing of someone's death, should phone the deceased's house and ask whomever answers (it probably won't be the immediate family, but a relative running interference) to offer sympathy and to ask how they can help. The family may need food, drink, extra chairs, or help making phone calls to let others know the news or the arrangements.

Obituaries

The newspaper "death notice" is run as a matter of fact, at minimal cost, and is arranged by the funeral home. An *obituary* is an article especially written by the newspaper and is produced if there is sufficient space that day or if the notoriety of the deceased warrants it.

Private Services

Families sometimes request that funeral services be private. This is frequently the case when celebrities die, but also if the family desires to keep its grief within its own unit. Such wishes are to be observed absolutely.

The Procession

The mourners, led by the hearse containing the casket and cars with the immediate family, proceed from the funeral service to the cemetery for interment. If there is no service at a chapel, the mourners follow the hearse directly from the funeral home to the cemetery for a graveside service.

En route, all mourners turn on their car headlights and proceed in a line. This funeral cortege is protected by state law, is often guided by hired policemen, may pass through red lights, and may not be interrupted by outside drivers. Members sometimes sport dashboard signs or bumper tags that read "mourner."

Acquaintances

Those who knew the deceased only casually or who knew the deceased but not his or her family may better serve them by leaving them to their grief and checking the "death notices" section of the newspaper.

If funeral arrangements have been announced, and if the funeral is not private, the particulars will be given. Hours of mourning will also be given. The named funeral home can provide details.

Flowers

Flowers, if sent, should include a gift card with the donor's name on it, but no mention of death. Instead, "Praying for you" or "With sympathy" are useful phrases. Flowers sent to the house a week or so after the burial with a "thinking of you" card may also be appreciated.

When flowers are received at the funeral parlor or house of mourning, a friend should collect the gift cards so that the family can acknowledge the gesture.

In Lieu of Flowers . . .

If flowers are not desired by the family, they will say so by stating "no flowers" in the published death notice. Their wishes should be respected. Families who feel that money spent for flowers might be put to better use if given to a charity may write, "In lieu of flowers, please favor the such-and-such fund." In such a case, send the flower money to the charity with a cover letter designating it in the name of the deceased. The charity will send both you and the family an acknowledgment.

The Funeral Home

Most professional funeral homes have living rooms, viewing rooms, and chapels so that several funerals may be handled at once. Visiting hours are posted, will have been published, or may be gleaned by phone. When guests arrive, they will be greeted by a member of the staff and directed to the proper room where the family will be in attendance. Some families arrange to hold preburial visiting hours and viewing hours at home, in which case the same procedures apply.

What to Say

You wouldn't be there if you weren't expressing sympathy, so the best thing to say to grieving family members is "I'm so sorry" or "My prayers are with you." Chat a few moments about the deceased and then move along unless the mourners ask otherwise.

Suicide

There is never only one victim of a suicide; the survivors also suffer. Suicide is disdained by most religions and by many individuals. Some newspapers also refuse to report suicides, preferring to use the expression, "Died following a sudden illness."

Persons sending condolences should not, of course, mention the suicide, but should acknowledge the "passing" or "loss" of the family member. It also would be inappropriate to refer to an "accident" where common sense suggests otherwise. Better to just let it be.

Manner of Death

At the family's request, the manner of death or the age of the deceased may be withheld from published death notices. This may particularly occur if suicide or AIDS is involved. It used to be that way with cancer and tuberculosis, too.

If one does not already know, one should never inquire or comment on the manner of death. It is absolutely never appropriate to say, "It's better this way" or "At least his suffering is over."

DEATH OF A PET

The loss of a pet is no small thing to a family or individual who has enjoyed the animal's company. Although a religious burial would be improper, interment in a pet cemetery may ease the person's pain (backyard graves are generally prohibited by law). A note of condolence may also be sent.

This may also be a good time to discuss the concept of death with small children. The best way to get over the loss of a pet is with the passage of time, not by rushing out and getting another pet. Some people, however, insist that this will help the bereaved owner "get over it." Hardly. Would they tell a woman to hurry and conceive another child if the one she just had was stillborn?

Funeral Attire—The Living

People should attend wakes, viewings, homes, and funerals dressed in respectful suits or long dresses, as though going to church. Clothing should be dark but need not be black. Children are not dressed in black.

As a matter of practicality, it is usually helpful to carry a small package of facial tissues or an extra handkerchief.

Funeral Attire—The Deceased

Different religions dress the body in differing ways, which the funeral director can advise. Christians, for example, may be buried in good clothes, usually provided by the family from the deceased's wardrobe. It may sound grisly, but check the pockets first. Jews favor a burial shroud. Children are generally buried in white. If married, the deceased may be buried with the wedding ring on, but all other jewelry should be removed.

Viewing the Body

Some religions permit an open casket, others do not. Visitors to funeral homes should follow the dictates of their own faith regarding kneeling and genuflection and their own sensibilities about viewing a dead body.

Behavior of Mourners

Funerals are the time to show grief, not help people get over it. That will come later. It is not anybody's duty to crack jokes, sing songs, or lighten the mood.

Wakes

For at least a day, and sometimes three days, the deceased may be "waked" either at the funeral home or at his late residence. Wakes are social gatherings (sometimes loud, sometimes not) at which the good times are discussed and people are encouraged to carry on.

Wakes vary in raucousness with religion and ethnicity. Some cultures hold that life is slavery and that death is liberation, so it should be celebrated with music and happiness. Others are more dour. Custom prevails.

Shiva

In the Jewish religion, a house of mourning sits *shiva* (meaning "seven") for a week following the funeral.

The family returns to a house loaded with mourners. A vessel of water is just outside the front door for ritual cleaning of the hands. Inside, mirrors are covered (so that people in mourning will not be concerned with vanity), food is served, and great energy is spent reminiscing about the dead. It is a busy and even frantic time; its purpose is to distract the bereaved.

The Guest Register

As you leave the funeral home or house, you may sign the guest book. Since the stream of faces will likely be a blur to mourners, the book is a way to pay your respects. Sign your name legibly and the way it would appear in a phone book so that acknowledgment cards can be sent out. Write "Mr. and Mrs. Steven Langan" instead of "Steve and Amy Langan."

Ex-spouses at Funerals

The ex-spouse of the deceased may attend the funeral, sitting far enough back so as not to encounter the new family. However badly the divorce went, there is always a vestige of the relationship that must be addressed, if only for the sake of closure.

Children of Divorce at Funerals

If the deceased had children by a previous marriage, those children do not sit with their stepparent, they sit with their other parent (the deceased's ex-spouse). If this may cause pain to the new family, the ex-spouse sits to the rear of the chapel and the children sit with their grandparents.

Sympathy Cards

A written expression of sympathy to a grieving family is a tangible form of comfort at a terribly trying time. Prepared sympathy cards may be purchased in stores, but they must never be merely signed and mailed "as is." Handwritten notes and letters containing a few personal, meaningful memories of the deceased are far more appreciated.

An expression of sympathy may be nothing more than, "I am so very sorry for your loss" or it can be a more flowery, "I will always cherish the exciting times we shared. He (she) had the remarkable gift of making all around him feel special, and the memory of his joyous spirit will forever be with me."

Acknowledging Sympathy Cards

No matter how distraught the grieving family may be over their loss, they have an absolute obligation to acknowledge the cards, letters, and flowers sent to them. Do not degrade the memory of the deceased by acting thoughtlessly in his or her name.

Preprinted cards supplied by the funeral home are unacceptable to send to family and friends. They may be sent only when they include an additional, handwritten message such as, "Thank you for lending your memories of Jack at a time when we miss him so much."

If the family cannot answer each and every expression of sympathy, a close family member may be asked to do it in their name, to wit: "Mary and the girls asked me to thank you for your moving memories of Jack."

Pallbearers and Ushers

It is an honor to be asked to serve as an usher or pallbearer (actual or honorary) at a funeral. The funeral director will instruct such participants in how to do their duties during the ceremony. Often it is only an honorary designation.

Unlike weddings, no gift is given to ushers or pallbearers, but a handwritten thank-you note from the immediate family is expected.

Wishes of the Deceased Versus Survivors

Many people, when approaching old age or if they are aware of a terminal condition, plan their own funerals. This may include everything from prepayment to choosing verses and music. These instructions must be obeyed to the letter.

The funeral of a beloved relative or friend is neither the time nor the place to launch into a protest over religion, burial customs, or family feuds. It does not honor the deceased to countermand his or her last wishes.

Memorial Services

If the deceased was a professional person, if he died out of town, if the services were private, or if there are a large number of people who want to pay respect, a memorial service can be arranged at a later date. This can be coordinated among friends and family, there can be speakers, and the life and achievements of the departed can be celebrated.

There always is a danger of memorials becoming too showy. Restraint should be exercised to ensure that the event does not besmirch the memory of the deceased.

Addressing Survivors

The surviving wife is called a widow, or the surviving husband a widower. Each may continue to wear a wedding band until or unless he or she is ready to consider dating new people. The widow will continue to use her married name, as in "Mrs. Charles G. Forbes" rather than "Mary Forbes."

The Mourning Period

Strictly observed mourning dictates that men wear black armbands and women don black veils to signify their grief. Depending on the culture, this may continue for weeks or months. Italian widows may dress in black for a matter of years; Jews will rend (tear) their clothing at the funeral, usually symbolically, by cutting a small lapel ribbon to show that a loved one has died; other faiths may burn candles, attend regular mass, or confine themselves to the house.

It is traditional, although severe by modern standards, to conduct one's mourning correspondence on black-bordered stationery or to present black-bordered calling cards.

The late residence generally is given two or three weeks before those in it are disturbed.

Markers Versus Tombstones

A "marker" is a small, ground-level stone placed, as soon as possible after interment, at the foot of the grave. It bears the name and dates of the person buried. A year after the burial, a larger, more ornate tombstone can be erected or unveiled to mark the grave.

CHAPTER ELEVEN

GOOD FORM:

The Written Word from Invitations to Recommendations

nyone who has ever gotten a form letter, or tried to decide which fork to use, or wanted to know if purple was okay for a cummerbund, knows how frustrating, even maddening, convention can be. Trouble is, some societal baselines are essential.

Consider the form letter. The idea itself is contemptuous: that a stranger would think he can sell you something by sending you the very same thing he's sending to 100,000 other people, even if he's told his computer to put your name in! Nothing could be less spontaneous or more insulting.

Yet the direct mail industry (which is what junk mailers call themselves) makes a ton of money, and the people in it have created sophisticated systems that can spit out a form letter that looks as if it was written expressly for you . . . well, almost.

The rest of us have a much better way of writing letters: we just pick up a pen and paper and do it—or should. The gift of a letter, and the importance such a gesture means to a lasting friendship, cannot be overstated. The very act of touching a sheet of paper that a friend has also touched can strengthen the bond between them. Even when it's an engraved invitation, a typed letter, or the product of a word processor,

> *Igor, the scalpels go on the left . . . with the pitchforks.*
>
> —Buchanan and Goodman, "The Flying Saucer Goes West"

there is, well, a *substance* in a letter that cannot even be approached by the transience of a phone call. This is why society has developed guidelines, not only in writing but in other endeavors.

There is good form, and then there is bad form, which is to say no form. Just as life goes more easily for people who know which fork to use at a formal dinner, things also go more smoothly for those who observe etiquette in social encounters. Over the centuries, civilizations have apparently taken the fun out of parties by inventing specialized silverware, constricting clothing, stiff forms of address, and elaborate behavior, and for what? To make people feel out of place? On the contrary, it has been to make people free, for if all questions are answered about what to do in a given social circumstance, the participants can get past their awkwardness and start having fun.

Fun with manners? You bet. But it starts when you know the basics.

STATIONERY

Personal and Business Correspondence

Tradition exists surrounding paper, envelopes, number of folds, color of ink, borders, and how correspondence is inserted and sealed. Fortunately, custom has eased since the days when replies to formal invitations had to be written in black or blue ink on white or ivory paper, and notes had to be sent on engraved rather than merely printed letterhead.

Although strict decorum designates separate forms and sizes for ladies' versus mens' stationery, some concessions may be made to the modern reality of both men and women working and enjoying a less rigid social life.

One caveat: writing etiquette is now in service of the U.S. Postal Service as to envelope size, position of address, and clarity of printing.

Basic Stationery

The following presents the most common types of stationery and their purpose:

Foldover cards. Used for informal notes, they measure 4" x 5" when folded (8" x 5" flat) and have matching envelopes. There is a monogram on the very top of the front page and a return address on the back flap of the envelope.

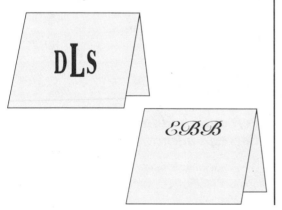

Personal stationery. Used for letters, sheets measure 7" x 9" and bear the sender's full name, address, and phone number printed at the vertical top; additional pages are blank pages of the same paper. Matching envelopes are for a one-third fold.

Business stationery. Sheets measure 8½" x 11" with name, address, and phone number printed at the vertical top (there is some allowance for artistic layout). Matching No. 10 envelopes are for a one-third fold.

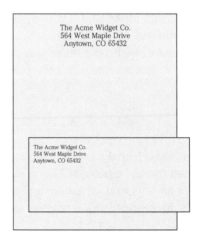

Post cards. Used for quick notes, they measure approximately 4" x 6" on heavy card stock printed with colored border and the sender's name only on the top. These can also quite properly be sent in matching envelopes.

Ms. Melanie Mackinaw

Memo pads. Single or bound ("perfect binding"), they measure anywhere from one-third of a page to one-quarter of a page, are printed with "Memo" on the top and the sender's name on the bottom. Use of the phrase "from the desk of" or "stuff I thought of" (or anything else) is considered tacky. Quite often memos are attached to other documents in lieu of writing a cover letter.

MEMO

SUSAN BEALE

Celebrities frequently choose stationery with either their name or address (but not both) printed on the envelope to avoid extra eyes learning their address. A single woman may also properly use only her address, and not her name, on the return address printed on an envelope.

Businesses, of course, may have far more elaborate stationery carrying corporate logos, subsidiaries, names of their board of directors or ranking counsel, international offices, and so on.

Borrowed Stationery

Travelers using the hotel's stationery rather than their own, or businesspersons writing from one location on office stationery printed at another location, may write "as from" below the letterhead and add the appropriate address:

International Widgets
14 Clewer Crescent
London SW1, England
[typed:]
as from: 200 West 70th Street
New York, NY 10023

Inappropriate Stationery

One should never mix business and pleasure, at least not in writing. Personal use of business stationery may reflect on the business itself and, in addition, may offend the recipient who is due a strictly personal note.

It is also incorrect, not to mention hurtful, for a businessperson to have a secretary type personal correspondence. Many is the child who has been distanced from his or her "too busy" parent by such a practice.

Finally, one should never return a letter to its sender by writing on it with the excuse of saving time and paper, even though the government and some mail order companies employ the practice. A letter of request requires a separate and complete reply. The only exception would be a contract or a writer's manuscript where emendations are required by the nature of the transaction.

Greeting Cards

Despite advertising claims, a prewritten, mass-produced commercial greeting card is never as personal or appreciated as an individual letter. The proof is that nobody looks on the back of a letter to see how much you spent for it.

Commercial greeting cards can be ornate or clever. Some even play music or sound like cows. But they aren't letters.

It helps take the onus off of using commercial greeting cards to add a handwritten note to the blank side facing the printed message. The only part of a personal note that may be typed is the envelope (out of respect for the post office).

Writing Personal Letters on a Computer

Formal letters must be written only by hand. Modern technology, however, has made it increasingly acceptable—and certainly faster and easier—to write personal letters on word processors or E-mail, and even to fax them instead of mailing them. It's a tough call; strictly speaking, it is a shame to take the personal touch (literally) out of correspondence. On the other hand (also literally), a letter written on a computer is better than none at all.

Dual Signatures

When one member of a couple writes a letter for both of them, only the actual writer signs it. Postcards, telegrams, and gift cards may be signed by both parties.

First Name Versus Full Name

Business letters are signed with a person's full name unless a friendship or informality exists between the sender and recipient. One should not sign only one's first name as a means of ingratiating or obligating a recipient whom one does not know.

Married women signing business letters should sign them by the name with which they conduct business, such as "Eleanor Botkin." If she is signing a business letter concerning a matter involving both herself and her husband, she may sign "Eleanor Botkin (Mrs. George Sand)."

Personal letters, of course, are signed with one's first name. Additional guidelines on signatures can be found in numerous books and guides, as well as in the back of office dictionaries.

INVITATIONS AND ANNOUNCEMENTS

Sample Engagement Announcement for a Newspaper

The following are examples of engagement announcements to a newspaper:

Mr. and Mrs. Adam Claypool of Hillandale, Maryland, announce the engagement of their daughter, Miss Justine Claypool, to Mr. James Brendan Danielson of Dallas, Texas. Mr. Danielson is the son of Dr. and Mrs.

Roger Wakefield Danielson, also of Dallas. A November wedding is planned.

Miss Claypool is a graduate of the University of Maryland and is a development executive for National Public Radio. Mr. Danielson is a graduate of the Rochester Institute of Technology and is a biochemist with the Naval Ordinance Laboratory.

SALLY LOUISE SMITH
TO WED JOHN F. JONES

Mr. and Mrs. Harvey Smith of Palmersville announce the engagement of their daughter, Sally Louise, to John F. Jones of Waynesville. The couple will be married on November 1.

Miss Smith is a graduate of Palmersville High School and the Choate Academy and holds a B.A. in Art History. She is an instructor at the Museum School.

Mr. Jones, son of Mr. and Mrs. Chester H. Jones, earned his Bachelor's degree from Hunt College and his law degree from Scott University. He is an associate in the firm of Dewey, Cheetham, and Howe.

A photograph of the bride-to-be may accompany the release.

Sample Wedding Announcement for a Newspaper

A wedding announcement to a newspaper can read as follows:

Mr. and Mrs. Adam Claypool of Hillandale, Maryland, announce the marriage of their daughter, Justine, to Mr. James Brendan Danielson of Dallas, Texas. Mr. Danielson is the son of Dr. and Mrs. Roger Wakefield Danielson, also of Dallas.

The bride, who will retain her last name of Claypool, is a graduate of the University of Maryland and is a development executive for National Public Radio. The groom was graduated from the Rochester Institute of Technology and is a biochemist with the Naval Ordinance Laboratory.

The couple will reside in Bethesda, Maryland.

Wedding Invitations

Given all combinations of married, widowed, and divorced parents, plus the wedding details, there are many variations on standard invitations and announcements. A wedding consultant can compose one that fits the particulars, but here are those that occur most often. The basic wedding invitation is quite formal:

Mr. and Mrs. Adam Claypool
request the honour of your presence
at the marriage of their daughter
Justine
to
Mr. James Brendan Danielson
on Friday, the ninth of November
One thousand, nine hundred and ninety-seven
at twelve o'clock [or: half-past noon]
Church of Our Savior
Hillandale, Maryland

Notice the British spelling of *honour* and the complete spelling of numbers, except for long addresses, which would be awkard. Use of *Miss* also is generally reserved for invitations sent by the bride herself or where she has no relatives. There is no punctuation save for the period after *Mr.* or *Mrs.* The invitation is engraved on fine card stock, enclosed in an inner envelope on which the recipients' names are written by hand in black ink only, and enclosed in a larger envelope for mailing. The mailing envelope, too, is addressed in ink by hand, preferably by someone skilled in calligraphy.

Where a recipient may also be invited to a reception following the wedding ceremony, a separate and smaller card is enclosed:

Reception immediately following the ceremony
Red Rim Country Club
Briggs-Chaney Road
Hillandale
The favour of a reply is requested
594 Beacon Road, Silver Spring, Maryland 20903

If the wedding ceremony has been private, guests may be invited to the reception only:

Mr. and Mrs. Adam Claypool
request the pleasure of your company
at the wedding reception of their daughter
Justine
and
Mr. James Brendan Danielson
on Friday, the ninth of November
One thousand, nine hundred and ninety-seven
at one o'clock
Red Rim Country Club

Briggs-Chaney Road
Hillandale
The favour of a reply is requested
594 Beacon Road, Silver Spring, Maryland 20903

There are numerous permutations that address such issues as divorced parents of the bride, divorced parents of the groom, one or more deceased parents of either the bride or groom, divorced and one remarried parent of either, or someone other than a parent giving the bride away. Here follows an assortment of wordings (courtesy of The Everything® Wedding Book by Janet Anastasio and Michelle Bevilacqua); a wedding consultant can also specify which is appropriate.

When both the bride's and groom's parents sponsor the wedding:

Mr. and Mrs. Roger Parker
and
Mr. and Mrs. Robert Clark
request the honour of your presence
at the marriage of their children
Beth Elaine Parker
and
Mr. Justin James Clark
on Saturday, the fifth of August
One thousand, nine hundred and ninety-seven
at two o'clock
Center Street Baptist Church
Fairview, Pennsylvania

Alternate:

Mr. & Mrs. Roger Parker
request the honour of your presence
at the marriage of their daughter
Beth Elaine Parker
to
Justin James Clark
son of Mr. and Mrs. Robert Clark
Saturday, the fifth of August
One thousand, nine hundred and ninety-seven
at two o'clock
Center Street Baptist Church
Fairview, Pennsylvania

When the groom's parents sponsor the wedding:

Mr. and Mrs. Robert Clark
request the honour of your presence
at the marriage of
Beth Elaine Parker
to their son
Mr. Justin James Clark
Saturday, the fifth of August
One thousand nine hundred and ninety-seven
at two o'clock
Center Street Baptist Church
Fairview, Pennsylvania

When the bride and groom sponsor their own wedding:

The honour of your presence is requested
at the marriage of
Miss Beth Elaine Parker
and
Mr. Justin James Clark . . .

Alternate:

Miss Beth Elaine Parker
and
Mr. Justin James Clark
request the honour of your presence
at their marriage . . .

When the mother of the bride is sponsoring and has not remarried:

Mrs. James Parker
requests the honour of your presence
at the marriage of her daughter
Beth Elaine Parker . . .

When the mother of the bride is sponsoring and has remarried:

Mrs. David C. Hayes
requests the honour of your presence
at the marriage of her daughter
Beth Elaine Parker . . .

When the mother of the bride has remarried and she is sponsoring the wedding with her husband, who has not adopted her daughter:

Mr. and Mrs. David C. Hayes
requests the honour of your presence
at the marriage of Mrs. Hayes's daughter
Beth Elaine Parker . . .

When the father of the bride is sponsoring and has not remarried:

Mr. Roger Parker
requests the honour of your presence
at the marriage of his daughter
Beth Elaine . . .

When the father of the bride has remarried and is sponsoring:

Mr. and Mrs. Roger Parker
request the honour of your presence
at the marriage of Mr. Parker's daughter
Beth Elaine . . .

When the mother is deceased, the father has not remarried, and he is sponsoring his daughter's wedding:

Mr. Roger Parker
requests the honour of your presence
at the marriage of his daughter
Beth Elaine . . .

When the father is deceased, the mother has remarried, and she is sponsoring with her new husband, who has not adopted the daughter:

Mr. and Mrs. David Spencer
request the honour of your presence
at the marriage of her daughter
Beth Elaine Parker . . .

When both parents are deceased, a close friend or relative may sponsor (note no use of *Miss*):

Mr. and Mrs. Frederick Parker
request the honour of your presence
at the marriage of their granddaughter
Beth Elaine Parker . . .

Alternate (the bride may wish to include the names of her deceased parents as long as the invitation does not appear to have been sent by them; also note the use of *Miss*):

Mr. and Mrs. Claude Salt
request the honour of your presence
at the marriage of
Miss Beth Elaine Parker
daughter of the late Mr. and Mrs. Roger Parker . . .

Wedding Announcements to Friends and Relatives

An announcement of the nuptials may be sent after the fact to people who, for whatever reason, were not invited to the ceremony itself:

Mr. and Mrs. Adam Claypool
and
Dr. and Mrs. Roger Wakefield
announce the marriage of
Justine Claypool
and
Mr. James Brendan Danielson
on Friday, November 9
one thousand, nine hundred and ninety-seven
Hillandale, Maryland

Wedding Shower Invitations

Although handwritten notes are preferred, preprinted invitation cards are being used with increasing frequency. As long as the host and mode of gift are stated, there is no problem:

Dear Rebecca,

Margaret Weitz and I are hosting a wedding shower for Pam Matthews on Sunday, August 3, at 4 p.m. at my house. She and Ron are registered at Bloomingdale's and Crate and Barrel, and Margaret and I are also keeping track of who's giving what in the "major gift" department, if it's at all helpful to you.

We look forward to seeing you here on the third. Let me know if you can come.

Sincerely,
R.S.V.P. 555-2345

Baby Shower Invitations

These can be quite informal, but still require written notice. Of course, they apply to the first baby only, as the second baby is showered with the hand-me-downs of the first baby, if gender allows. They are hosted by friends:

Come to Mary Litwak's Baby Shower!
on
Sunday, September 23 at 4 p.m.
at
416 Niemann Place, Apartment 6, Cornishtown
R.S.V.P. Cindy Memelstein, 555-5545

A notation about gifts can be added at the bottom of the card (in handwriting if it is printed).

Birth Announcements

Commercial announcements can be formal, in which a small card bearing the newborn's name is tied with ribbon to a larger one showing the parents' names:
Small card:

Charlotte Ann MacGregor
March 25, 1997

Tied to a bigger card:

Mr. and Mrs. Addison MacGregor
49 Shawn Drive
Wheaton, MD 20902

To the less formal (single card):

Our Home Has New Joy!
Name: Charlotte Ann MacGregor
Weight: Six pounds, ten ounces
Length: Twenty inches

Carole and Addison MacGregor
49 Shawn Drive
Wheaton, MD 20902

It is especially appropriate to announce adoptions:

Mr. and Mrs. Addison MacGregor
are pleased to announce the adoption of
James Michael
Age: eighteen months

Child's Birthday Party Invitations

There are tons of commercially printed, festive invitations for kids' parties. They are sent to the child in care of the parent (mother):

Please come to Shelley's Fifth Birthday!
on Saturday, April 19, at 4 p.m.
at Showcase Shake 'n' Pizza
6556 Glendale Parkway
Glendale, California
R.S.V.P. to Shelley's Mom (Wendi), 555-6666
Ice cream, cake, and pizza

Anniversary Party Invitations

Formal anniversary observances (at twenty-five or fifty years) may be grand events with hired ballrooms and orchestras, or they can be friends and family. The situation dictates the invitation, as does the host of the celebration:

1972–1997
Mr. and Mrs. Paul Frederick
request the pleasure of your company
at a reception honoring their
silver wedding anniversary
Sunday, October 18, at 7:30 p.m.
Bombay Yacht Club
R.S.V.P.
3601 Connecticut Avenue, NW

An invitation sent by children might read:

1947–1997
Buddy Frederick and Celia Frederick Collins
invite you to honor their parents
Mr. and Mrs. Paul Frederick
on the occasion of their
golden wedding anniversary
Saturday, October 18, at 7:30 p.m.
Bombay Yacht Club
R.S.V.P.
286 Ashdown Street (Buddy)

Christening and Baptism Invitations

Christening invitations are kept informal (as for the Jewish circumcision) as they occur so quickly after the child's birth. A phone call or handwritten note will suffice, although printed invitations are certainly correct.

Dear Kietryn and Keith,
   Our adorable Becky is being christened on Sunday at St. Ambrose's at 2 p.m. We would love for you to join us and come back to the house afterward for a light buffet.
   Yours truly,

First Communions

There is no formal invitation for a communion. Phone calls and notes may advise friends and relatives of the occasion before hand. The post-communion party is generally attended as a group by the girls, boys, their parents, and godparents, all of whom have just celebrated their first Communion.

Bar Mitzvah Invitations

Mr. and Mrs. Samuel Snyder
invite you to the
Bar Mitzvah of their son
Edward Amram
Saturday, November 23
at 10 o'clock in the morning
at the
Congregation Jacob Ben Utz
6600 Galway Boulevard
Shaker Heights, Ohio
R.S.V.P.
10406 Fawcett Avenue
Shaker Heights, Ohio

Marriage Vow Renewal Invitations

The couple electing to renew their wedding vows will send out their own invitations, which can be informal (handwritten) or formal, but more usually informal:

Donna and Buddy Joe Becker
request the honor of your presence
as they renew their marriage vows
on the occasion of their
tenth wedding anniversary
Thursday, May 18, at 6 p.m.
Christ Church, Cambridge
R.S.V.P.
555-1667
Reception following the ceremony
at the Church meeting room

Second Baptism Invitations

There is no general precedent for a formal invitation to an Evangelical Baptism at which one embraces Jesus Christ as Lord and becomes "born again." An informal or telephoned invitation may be extended, although a handwritten one is appropriate:

Praise God
and witness the rebirth in Christ of
Jean James Munson
at the Church of the Holy Redeemer
on Sunday, February 2, at Noon
Reception afterward in
Church family room
R.S.V.P. 555-1122

Invitations with Strings Attached

When the purpose of throwing a party is to raise rent, solicit charitable contributions, sell plastic food containers, hawk cosmetics, or anything other than to celebrate, this must be disclosed to the guests when they are invited.

The same holds for B.Y.O.B. (bring your own bottle) or B.Y.O.F. (bring your own food/pot luck) gatherings. It is especially true for bachelor or bachelorette parties held in expensive venues where those attending may be asked to ante more than their means will allow. No one should feel pressured into attending a party that, in essence, he or she has to help throw!

ACKNOWLEDGMENTS

Formal Reply: R.S.V.P.

R.S.V.P. is a notice that the host or hostess requests a response indicating whether an invited guest will attend the function. A reply is mandatory as soon as the invitation is received to allow the host or hostess to set plans.

Accepting Informal Invitations

An acceptance repeats the pertinent information so that there is no misunderstanding:

Dear Linda,
    Scott and I gladly accept your luncheon invitation for Tuesday, December 3, at your home at Noon. We look forward to seeing you and Earl again.
        Kind regards,
        Susan

A similar message also is sent for regrets, again so that there is no misunderstanding:

Dear Linda,
    I am so sorry, but Scott and I already have plans for Tuesday, December 3, and so won't be able to join you and Earl for noon lunch. I hope we'll be able to see each other another time soon.
        Kind regards,
        Susan

Accepting Formal Invitations

As with an informal invitation, a formal invitation demands a response. Often there will be a response card enclosed with the invitation, a sad, but pragmatic, commentary on the times.

Formal responses can be letters:

Dear Mrs. Southwaite:
    Mr. Bradford and I will be honored to join you and Mr. Chumley at your home for dinner on Tuesday, December 8, at 7 o'clock.
    We look forward to seeing you then.
        Sincerely,
        Susan Crumb
        (Mrs. Scott Bradford)

They may also be a repeat of the invitation, except with the word "regret" added:

Mr. and Mrs. Scott Bradford regret that they will be unable to accept the invitation of Mr. and Mrs. Earl Chumley on Tuesday, December 8, at 7 o'clock at 1616 Beverly Boulevard.

Acknowledging Gifts, Cards, and Deeds

Although one may say "thanks" in person (such as when receiving a gift or leaving a dinner party), it is always proper to repeat those thanks in writing immediately after someone has done something nice. The person who accepts another's generosity without thanking him or her for it is, very simply, unworthy of receiving more.

Invitation to a Formal Dinner Party

An invitation to a formal dinner party can read as follows:

Mr. and Mrs. Nutley Rose
request your presence at dinner
to honor Judge and Mrs. William Winship
at eight o'clock on Thursday, July 5
103 Ames Drive
Rockville, Idaho
R.S.V.P.
Formal dress
555-1212

Bread-and-Butter Notes

A thank-you letter sent to a hostess after attending a dinner, or after staying over in her house, is sometimes referred to as a "bread-and-butter note." It needn't be elaborate, but it must be sent (on personal stationery):

Dear Gladys,

Tom and I had a marvelous time with you and Jim last night. Your meal was sumptuous, and the company was equally nourishing. I don't know how you manage to make us feel at home and to do it all so easily! I'll phone in a few days to invite you and Jim over to our house. I can't wait!

Sincerely,
Ruth

It is essential that the guest of honor at a dinner send written thanks.

Positive Letters of Reference

A letter of reference reflects on its writer as well as its subject and should be considered a public document. Although, in modern times, a telephone call by a prospective employer to a former one often substitutes for a letter of reference, it may be convenient to put it in writing.

To Whom It May Concern:

Mary Reilly has been my faithful domestic servant for many years. During that time she has proved herself industrious, efficient, and, above all, trustworthy. I am forced to let her go at this time because my living situation has changed and she is redundant to the household, but I lose her knowing that whoever employs her will be engaging someone of extraordinary skill and discretion. I trust that person shall be you.

Sincerely,
Henry Jekyll, M.D.

Noncommittal (Negative) Letters of Reference

Unlike a positive recommendation, a negative letter of reference is as notable for what it does not say as for what it does say. It must be neither libelous nor misleading, yet clear enough so that the reader should get the picture without having it drawn for him. Be positive but vague; it is preferable to damn with faint praise than to praise with faint damns.

To Whom It May Concern:

Uriah Heap was in the employ of my firm for several years, and he ably performed his duties throughout the entire time. My business partner and I were no longer able to use his services.
Sincerely,
Philip Pirrup

Letters of Introduction

The formal letter of introduction introduces someone you know to someone else you know, although the two of them do not know each other. Such a letter is, in effect, a blank check drawn against your good reputation and should never be written lightly.

Such letters establish a connection, tell a bit about the person, and subtly acknowledge an obligation in both directions. A copy should be given to both parties:

Dear Pierce,

My writing partner, Betty Crawford, is moving to Columbus with her family where she will be finishing her latest book and accompanying her husband, Tom, who is starting with the Zigler Agency.

Both Betty and Tom are great friends of Cynthia and mine, as are you and Chelsea, and I would dearly appreciate it if you could help them make early contacts in the new city.

I appreciate your time and look forward to seeing you and your family this summer at the beach.
Sincerely,
Ellen Wilkins

WRITING TO STRANGERS

Writing to a Celebrity

Actors, sports figures, television newscasters, and other highly visible people receive an enormous amount of mail, some of it connected with the work they do, the rest merely enamored of it. The average person would feel put out, even threatened, to get an unsolicited letter from a stranger, yet celebrities get them all the time, sometimes with intimate or insulting contents.

No celebrity is required to respond to any correspondence that does not pertain directly to his or her work. Many choose to do so because they are aware that their fame depends on their continued favor with the public.

Some must go to considerable trouble and expense sending autographed photos (in the case of retired or cult figures, this can involve financial sacrifice). If writing to a celebrity one should be brief and benign. If you send something to be autographed, include a self-addressed, stamped envelope for its return.

Writing to a Politician

Correspondence with an elected official is likely to be handled by his or her staff and will usually provoke a form letter that barely answers your inquiry. Of course, it differs depending on the individual politician. Generally speaking, however, politicians respond (without necessarily *answering*) to all reasonable correspondence.

Writing to a Stranger

A phone call can be dismissed, but a letter commands attention; moreover, in a legal dispute, it serves as proof. Yet some people can't write letters; or they can write friends but not strangers. Still others, who couldn't compose a personal note to save their lives, find that they can write anything to a complete stranger.

Writing a company, requesting brochures, filing complaints, commending an employee's good deed, summarizing an agreement reached during a phone call, and ordering merchandise are only a few reasons to write a stranger. This is sometimes called a "cold" letter, meaning that it comes with no prior relationship.

Be clear. The mistake that most people make is, quite literally, to start at the second paragraph. When writing, first *tell the recipient what the letter is going to be about.* Then say it. Then suggest how you might like to resolve the matter. Then say goodbye. For example:

Dear Mr. Mendez:

An encounter with one of your sales clerks yesterday has left me uneasy over the way your bookstore treated me.

I was having trouble finding a particular book and asked a man, whose name tag identified him as Mr. Smith, where the philosophy section was. He told me it was on the lower floor. I asked him where the store directory was, and he said that the directory was on the lower floor, too. My response was to ask why the store doesn't have a directory on the second floor as well to prevent customers like me from having to climb the stairs every time we want to know something. Mr. Smith replied that I should have looked before I went upstairs.

There are two issues here: first, is Mr. Smith paid to help customers or to lecture them? Second, why don't you have directories on both levels? As far as I am concerned, you could ameliorate both problems with an apology.

Sincerely,
J. Hegelius

Salutations

"Dear Mr. Gable" sounds a little presumptuous for a business letter, especially between two men, but tradition insists it is nevertheless correct.

There are only three other forms, each less acceptable: "My Dear Mr. Gable" sounds condescending; "Dear Clark Gable" or just plain "Clark Gable" are both cold; and "Dear Sir" is rude, as the letter is addressed to Mr. Gable.

General letters to unknown people that begin "Dear Sir," "Dear Sir or Madam," "Gentlemen," "Ladies," "Dear Friend," or some other vague vocative (from the Latin *to call*) also are improper. Even "To Whom It May Concern" is dicey and impersonal, if useful. And "Dear Credit Manager" is pushing it. If you don't know to whom you're writing, either call to find out the name or don't write the letter.

When writing someone you don't know, and whose name gives no indication of gender (such as to Chris Pond, Jan Amos, Pat, or a person with an unfamiliar foreign name), if you have no way of finding out, use "Dear Chris Pond." Such a vocative is not strictly proper, but it is functional, and when "Chris Pond" responds, he or she may give you a hint.

Signing Off

The valediction (adapted from the Latin *vale*, meaning "farewell") is the message used to end a letter. The usual valedictions are "Sincerely," "Sincerely yours," or "Very truly yours."

Others, such as "Regards," "Kind Regards," "Fondly," "Best regards," "Best wishes," "With affection," and those that may be even more personal are best reserved for letters between acquaintances, friends, or intimates.

DEPORTMENT

Behavior in a Court of Law

One stands when a justice, judge, or magistrate enters the courtroom and stands again when he or she leaves. The bailiff will announce this.

The judge has absolute authority to call, eject, silence, or cite for contempt anyone present. Chewing gum, talking, drawing, tape recording, reading, and even taking notes can be prohibited, and complaining about not being allowed to do so can be met with a contempt citation.

Court Clothes

Those appearing in court to respond to charges should be dressed for the occasion. A full suit for men or long dress for women is not required, but a neat appearance can greatly benefit one's circumstances.

If one has been arrested and detained, a change of clothes may not be possible. Since not everybody is O.J. Simpson, an indigent defendant may be loaned "court clothes" from a supply the jail or courthouse has for such contingencies (like fancy restaurants that keep a supply of ill-fitting jackets and ugly ties). Relatives of defendants may also furnish court clothes.

Curtseying and Bowing

Americans are proud of the fact that they need bow to no one (unless they're acting on the stage, of course, which says something). Because of this, bowing or curtseying voluntarily can be a demonstration of respect, even if the recipient does not realize how un-American it is.

It is never done when being presented to elected officials in this country and need not be done when being presented to visiting royalty. Socially, though, it can be charming (if a little affected).

A bow can be anything from a slight nod of the head to fully bending over from the waist, and from covering the heart with one's right hand to bending and covering one's stomach with one's left hand braced behind the waist. A Middle Easterner may show respect by touching his forehead, lips, and heart with his hand while slightly bowing. Asians may press their hands together in front while bowing slightly.

Western women curtsey, in which one pulls the sides of one's skirt slightly aside, crossing one's feet while dipping, and also while bowing one's head (it performs better than it describes!). There is no counterpart if the woman is wearing jeans or shorts, but then such attire would not be worn anywhere curtseying might be expected.

Men and women bow to each other at a formal dance, before the lady takes the gentleman's arm to the dance floor, and bow again as the dance ends. A gentleman also may bow slightly with the head when he is presented to a lady and she offers her hand.

The Chinese custom of *kowtowing*, incidentally, is widely misunderstood here; most people think it means to defer or obey. In fact, a *kowtow* is a deep bow from a kneeling position touching one's head to the floor.

Dance Cards

A lady may decide with whom she will dance at a formal ball by listing her beaus' names on her dance card. The first and last dance must be reserved for the gentleman with whom she arrived at the dance. Whom she dances with in between is entirely her choice.

Cutting in at Dances

If a gentleman wishes to dance with a lady who is already dancing with another gentleman at a formal dance, he may approach them, tap the gentleman on the shoulder, and ask, "May I cut in?" This is an awkward custom that defies logic; perhaps this is why modern dances make it impossible to tell who is dancing with whom.

A lady may not refuse a cut-in. The initial dancer may not cut back in until the next dance; a third person may cut in at any time; the three cutters may not make a game out of cutting in on each other.

DINNER PARTIES

Seating

Dinner parties honoring an individual or couple need not involve a dais (DAY-us) or raised head table. The average home dining room can easily be set to honor a guest. Seating always alternates male and female; the man sits to the left of the woman he escorted.

- *Man and woman host a dinner for ten.* Clockwise from top of vertical table: hostess, male, female, male, female guest of honor, host (at bottom of table), female, male, female, male guest of honor.
- *Woman alone hosts a dinner for eight.* Clockwise from top of vertical table: hostess, male, female, male, female guest of honor (at bottom of table), male (acting host), female, male guest of honor.

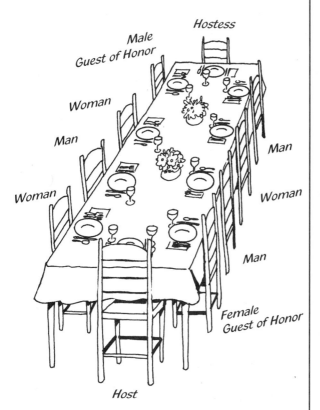

Hostess

Male Guest of Honor

Woman

Man

Woman

Man

Woman

Man

Female Guest of Honor

Host

Note that, in each case, the guest of honor is seated at or near one end of the table, but never in the center.

Engaging Servants

If one does not have one's own servants, one may engage a professional catering service for a large, formal affair. For informal functions, temporary hiring agencies or the local hotel and restaurant union are good sources of trained personnel. In college towns, student employment agencies can often provide competent servers.

Planning the Menu

Professional caterers know to the ounce how many bottles of wine, how many heads of lettuce, and how many hors d'oeuvres a function will require based on the time of day, number of guests, and even season of the year.

The wise host or hostess keeps tabs on food and drink consumption, even if it has been carefully planned, and is prepared to bring out back-up food or instruct the bartender to pour short shots if inventory gets limited.

Spending Time with Guests

It is the gifted host or hostess who can make each guest feel that he or she is the only one present, despite the size of the crowd. That having been said, it is the selfish guest who tries to monopolize a host's or hostess's time at a large party.

The host or hostess must greet each guest individually and make introductions to those nearby, all the while keeping a sharp eye out for stranded guests and duties that need looking into. Some formal affairs (such as at the White House) specifically provide garrulous men whose sole job is to facilitate introductions and to see that no solo guest is left alone.

Dress

It is mandatory that the invitation to a formal dinner party indicate the dress required. If it should omit such information, the guest may inquire after the mode of dress when accepting the invitation.

For Men. Depending on the time of day and the occasion, formal attire can vary. Gone is the era of cutaway, mourning coat, frock, beach wear, lodge wear, and so on. Those modes may still apply in high society and diplomatic circles, but those that most men are apt to encounter include:

Black tie (this is what is meant when "formal" attire is announced on an invitation). A black tuxedo with black trousers, solid black shoes, a white shirt, and a bow tie are worn. Either a waistcoat (vest) or cummer- bund is acceptable. Suspenders (braces) may also be worn instead of a belt; black socks, and solid black shoes are appropriate. Fashion is easing up a bit to allow double-breasted jackets and even colored jackets, although not on strictly formal occasions.

White tie. Attire includes a white tie, a wing collar, a tailcoat, black socks, and solid black shoes. This type of affair is very rare these days; think Fred Astaire.

Semi-formal. Attire includes a white jacket, black or dark trousers, a bow tie, a white or ruffled shirt, a cummerbund, and solid black shoes. Increasingly, all items but the shoes may be selected in colors and patterns.

Business. Attire includes a suit with dress shirt, a full-length necktie, dark socks, and black or brown shoes. (Red neckties are power ties.)

Informal/casual. Business attire or good slacks, a sport jacket, a dress shirt, dark socks, and black shoes are appropriate. A tie is optional the farther west you go.

For Women. Just as no one is supposed to notice a man's attire, *everyone* pays attention to what a lady wears. Women today have far more leeway than in the past; fashion and social change have done wonders in that area. The only point to remember is that a lady's mode of dress should match that of the gentleman escorting her. Here's where to start:

Formal (evening gown to accompany man's white tie). Attire includes a full-skirted dress (off-shoulder if desired), suitable for dancing, length not quite to floor; long gloves reaching to elbow, elegant shoes (heels), and jewelry; and a shoulder wrap if needed. Never wear a hat with an evening dress.

Formal (dinner dress to accompany man's black tie). Attire includes an on-shoulder, mid-calf to floor-length dress; long sleeves, shoulder wrap, and long gloves; elegant shoes (heels); jewelry; and no hat.

Semi-formal. Attire includes a mid-length dress or gown; elegant shoes; and a shoulder or full wrap. Dress attractively and comfortably (low shoes).

Informal. A mid-length dress or pant suit is appropriate.

Business. A mid-length dress or pant suit is appropriate. Suits with jackets are seen as "power" clothes. Dark shoes are worn.

Casual. Whatever.

Before and after 6 P.M.

Formal attire is never worn before 6 P.M. If the occasion calls for afternoon arrival, the host should provide a dressing room and the guest should bring along an appropriate change of attire. In practice this is seldom, if ever, done anymore.

Before and after Memorial Day

In some communities one wears light-colored or white clothing after Memorial Day, marking the beginning of resort season and warmer weather. This fashion continues to Labor Day, after which dark clothing is the rule. This applies only to people whose lifestyle permits them to use "summer" as a verb.

Shoe Color

Comedian George Gobel once described himself as being so alienated that he felt like "a pair of brown shoes and the rest of the world is a tuxedo." Lonesome George is gone, but the question of shoes is not. The answer is: black. Always wear black shoes for formal dress (evening: shiny or patent leather; daytime: Oxford). Business or informal daytime shoes can be brown, but

never after 6 P.M. Of course, for country, boating, golf, club, ballet, hockey, or athletic wear, rules of comfort and practicality apply.

Athletic Shoes

Athletic shoes are never proper attire for formal occasions, except, at the very remotest, the wedding of the president of Nike.

A Wardrobe Hint

It is said that by the age of forty, a man gets the face he deserves. Unfortunately, that's also when most men stop buying new clothes. Men and women can prune their everyday wardrobe by going through it from time to time. A rule of thumb to keep *au courant* is to toss out anything you haven't worn for at least a year.

Arrival Time

Nobody wants to be the first to arrive at a party, but somebody has to be. Local custom, rather than strict etiquette, addresses this thorny topic. Of course, the host or hostess should be prepared by the time of the arrival of the first guest and may even "break the ice" by inviting a few people to "come early so we can spend some time together before the others get here."

However, the person throwing the party has the obligation to be ready at the stated time. Generally speaking, guests for a dinner party should arrive within five minutes of the time printed on the invitation. Guests for cocktails, where a span of time is given, may arrive anywhere within it. More pragmatically, other parties begin to boogie half an hour to an hour after the given start time.

Crossed Legs

Ladies over ten wearing dresses are expected to sit with their knees together or their legs discreetly crossed; gentlemen, who presumably wear trousers, may sit however they wish, although allowing one's legs to spread in public is equally rude.

Seeking Professional Advice in Social Situations

Doctors, lawyers, and other professionals are constantly being cornered at parties and asked advice, usually by people who don't want to pay for it. A polite tactic to deflect such encounters is to tell the questioner, "Your problem sounds interesting, but I really can't make a reasoned decision now. Why don't you call me at the office tomorrow and we'll set up an appointment?"

CHAPTER TWELVE

FAUX PAS:

*Etiquette Tips
You Can't Live
Without*

There may arise a time when one commits a gaffe so offensive that it seems impossible to apologize for it. This may include inadvertently inquiring after the health of someone's recently deceased relative, making a pass at a man or woman in the presence of his or her spouse, laughing out loud during a funeral, shattering a hostess's priceless vase, running over someone's pet . . . or worse.

Hollywood, where culture clashes can be as conspicuous as a spider in the punch bowl, boasts innumerable shows of bad manners and at least one heroic self-rescue. One story recalled by conversationalist Dick Cavett, who described a Hollywood dinner party at which the conversation turned to former child actors. One guest asked, "Whatever happened to that obnoxious child star Dickie Moore?" The man sitting across from him said, "That's me." Without batting an eye, the offending guest turned to the hostess and said evenly, "Excuse me, but do you happen to have a revolver handy?"

As a diversion, that line can cover a multitude of sins. It enables the user to admit publicly that he has made a horrible mistake in manners, permits witnesses to laugh at a witty rejoinder, and allows him to apologize by offering to take the "gentleman's way out"—confident, naturally, that he will not be called upon to do so. Of course, if anyone within earshot has lost someone to suicide, all bets are off.

Humor aside, nothing takes the place of an honest apology. Contrition should be offered immediately, or at least as soon as the opportunity presents itself, and if it doesn't, it should be sought. Do not be fooled by stoicism; frequently someone whose feelings have been hurt will not reveal this, but will sulk in silence, waiting for an apology that never comes. It is safer to be contrite than cavalier; on the other hand, showing too much remorse can be a further insult. It all depends on what you've done, to whom, how close you are, and the repairs involved.

Lawyers frequently remark that a good number of the lawsuits they bring are on behalf of clients who feel wronged and only want an apology; failing that, they resort to legal action. Unfortunately, the law only makes social matters worse, which is why an increasing number of judges are instructing litigants to consult mediators rather than juries. In the end, it usually boils down to manners. As a help, then, here is an emergency guide to etiquette.

> *Silence is the most perfect expression of scorn.*
>
> —George Bernard Shaw, *Tragedy of an Elderly Gentleman*

SEPPUKU

Many's the movie in which a discredited officer or disgraced mogul is handed a revolver along with the message (spoken or implied) to "do the decent thing." In real life, however, suicide is usually reserved for the despondent, not the merely dishonored.

Unlike Western culture, which has honed the art of the apology to a fine point, Japanese society provides the ultimate way of saying you're sorry: _seppuku_. This Asian concept of "saving face" is oft-cited but never fully understood by non-Asians, who may consider it a form of inflated ego. Yet in such a rigidly structured culture as the East, where people have learned how to get along over centuries of close contact and frequent friction, any tear in the fabric can have repercussions across society.

Seppuku (or hara-kiri) is ritual suicide committed to preserve one's honor in the belief that a good death will redress a grievous life or at least an inexcusable transgression. It typically involves a sword or dagger that is inserted into the abdomen and pulled across so that one disembowels oneself. It is not a spontaneous act, but rather a reasoned one for which the subject prepares himself through meditation, cleansing, and, of course, by importuning one's ancestors to accept one's spirit.

One of the most famous _seppuku_ adherents was Yukio Mishima, Japan's ultra-right-wing writer and poet, a militarist who yearned for his country to rearm itself despite its postwar prohibition to do so.

In 1970 Mishima and four of his cadets took over the office of Tokyo's commanding general, intending to force his country back into militarism. Almost immediately his coup failed and, deluded by visions of patriotism, he cut himself open.

His final speech was made to a jeering crowd: "Long live the Emperor!" Inside the office, however, he uttered his last words: "I don't think they even heard me." Mishima's flamboyant life and death fused a lifelong obsession with the old and the new, between Japan's samurai past and its corporate destiny.

Personal Hygiene

Bathroom Habits

Some people, for reasons known only to themselves, refuse to flush the toilet after they have finished using it. This is not a matter of the handle not working or there being drought conditions; it is a phobia, and when they do it in your home, it is also rude.

But remember that etiquette teaches us not to be rude in return. Forget it. Go in afterward and flush for them.

Belching or Passing Wind in Public

Regardless of the pleasure that children derive from announcing bodily functions among peers, adults try to avoid such subjects. In certain Middle Eastern countries, a well-timed belch after dinner signifies enjoyment and is a compliment to the host. If you're not in the Middle East, though, and an irresistible force occurs in public, a simple "excuse me" will suffice. No further notice should be paid by anyone present.

Fly Open or Button Undone

It happens to everybody eventually, not only a zipper or button left inadvertently open, but also how to break the news. The best action is the direct and discreet one—"Sally, your button is undone" or "Paul, your fly's open"—simple and neat.

This is harder to do in a crowd, say, when the after-dinner speaker is unaware that he's in danger of revealing too much of himself. If this case, someone near him should stand in front of him, slip him a note, or rise to whisper in his ear, after which he will turn his back on the audience, make the adjustment, and continue as though nothing has happened.

Kids used to have a code they would shout at one another: "X-Y-Z." It stood for "eXamine Your Zipper." One television interviewer had a generous way of dealing with the barn door question. He asked his guest to stand, and then both men turned away from the audience. The host then said, "One of us has his fly open."

Food Between Teeth

The best way to tell someone that he or she has something caught between the teeth is to tell them, "You've got something caught between your teeth." Public picking and flossing is unacceptable; if need be, retire to the washroom.

Incontinence

The inability to control one's bowels or bladder is variously a function of age (low or high), disease, or, ahem, sobriety. Soiling oneself in public or soiling a host's furniture or bedding should be treated as an accident, not a plot. As with spilling food on a carpet, the person responsible should discreetly offer to make reparations to the host or hostess.

Enuresis (bed wetting) will certainly be discovered by the hostess or servants when making the beds. It is wise to bring the matter to the hostess's attention privately and matter-of-factly: "I'm terribly sorry, but I had an accident overnight; I would like to pay for cleaning [or replacement] of the sheets [or blanket, etc.]."

Littering

Ever since Arlo Guthrie got busted for littering in the sixties, this symbol of disregard for propriety has been a subject for discussion—but, let's face it, not at the top of anybody's agenda. Littering is, plain and simple, a form of arrogance and immaturity, an indication of a bigger problem. It blights our cities and disgraces our highways. Statutes against it are rarely enforced, and, when held to it, people would very likely pray that of all society's problems, this is the one they'd rather have.

Manners suggest that one hold on to trash until it can be thrown away in a proper receptacle. It would be amusing if one could hand the trash back to a person who littered, saying, "Excuse me, you just dropped this."

Sleeve in Food

The best way to tell someone that he has his sleeve dangling in the food on his dinner plate is, "Watch your sleeve, it's in the gravy." This also works with syrup, sauce, au jus dishes, and salad dressing.

Torn Clothing

Neglected clothing is one issue, but if you or a guest is unlucky enough to split a seam in public, there are two ways to deal with it. If no one has noticed, excuse your-self to the appropriate rest room and ascertain the damage. Can it be held with masking tape or a staple until you get to the tailor? Is there another piece of clothing (jacket, sweater) that will cover it?

Or ask the hostess (or whoever might know) if she has a needle and thread. If the problem is massive, ask to borrow an old article of clothing.

If you are among friends, it will not be a major issue; it can even be converted into an amusing topic of conversation, and then dismissed. Should such a rip occur in public, however, the only thing to do is excuse yourself and ask the butler/maitre d', concierge, or limousine driver (limousine drivers are amazingly resourceful) for assistance. A tip is then discretionary.

Uncontrollable Coughing

Coughing was dramatic and romantic when it happened in *Camille*. A person who, for whatever reason (a cold, smoking, a food crumb), finds himself in a prolonged spasm of coughing or wheezing should leave the room immediately and not return until it ends. This does not apply, of course, to life-threatening emergencies (vacating good seats for a hot Broadway show does not count as an emergency).

Wet Spots and Other Embarrassments

Men sometimes encounter embarrassment in public washrooms where the faucet has either been improperly adjusted or vandalized. The result is that they get water splashed onto their trousers that makes it look as if they had an accident while urinating.

If the gentleman cannot button his jacket to cover the wet spot or dry it on the hot-air blower, his only move is to return to the table—smiling to make people look at his face rather than his crotch—and continue the conversation long enough for the spot to evaporate.

Adolescent boys and pubescent girls sometimes develop spontaneous erections— boys of their penises, girls of their nipples— and always at the wrong time. If they are wearing revealing clothes, this can cause no small degree of embarrassment if it happens in the school cafeteria line, in the hallway, or while giving a report in front of the class. Additionally, teenage girls who have not as yet settled into a monthly schedule may experience the onset of menstruation at inconvenient times.

It does no good to implore understanding from one's peer group. The best emergency action is for the affected child to excuse himself or herself for the lavatory until the matter passes. Junior and senior high school teachers are well aware that these things happen, that they are nothing to be ashamed of, and that life goes on.

EATING LIKE A HUMAN BEING

Chewing Gum

Provided one disposes of spent chewing gum safely and discreetly, there is nothing wrong with enjoying it in a public situation where one does not plan to conduct extended social interaction, such as rock concerts, driving, or grocery shopping.

It is not polite to be chewing one's cud in an office, a school, or a press conference, on the phone, or on the sales floor. The teacher's admonition, "Did you bring enough for everyone?" also applies away from school. Gum chewing is a solitary endeavor, and when solitude is lost, so should the wad. Chewing should be performed quietly, with the mouth closed, and the gum inside at all times.

Chewing Tobacco

Why would anybody invent something that you put in your mouth, gets in the way of your speech, makes you sick if you swallow it, dribbles down your shirt until you get it right, and causes you to spit brown liquid in public? Oh, and it gives you cancer.

Unlike smoking, chewing tobacco (and its nasal cousin, snuff) pose health risks entirely to the user. They also raise an immense etiquette liability: excretory functions are a private matter, but the spitting and sneezing caused by chewing tobacco and snuff are very much a public issue.

Expectorating phlegm and sneezing into a handkerchief are ways that people parry the body's accidents. Making them happen on purpose is offensive as well as stupid (unless you're a multimillionaire baseball player).

Gristle at Dinner

If a dinner guest cannot chew a piece of food, he should, using his fingers, remove it discreetly from his mouth and place it on the edge of his plate. One may also remove the food, with a paper napkin, but not a cloth napkin.

Gurgling Soda Straws

When the drink is gone, so is the need to keep sucking on the straw. Besides, do you want everybody to think you're too stupid to know your own glass is empty? Some people also find it annoying to hear others eat the ice after they have finished their drink. If it helps, mention that some dentists advise that crunching of ice carries a high risk of chipping or cracking teeth.

Hair in Food

"Excuse me, may I have a comb for my potatoes?" is not the best way to call attention to the presence of a hair in one's food. If one discovers an errant item (hair, bug, stone, glass shard), one should try to ignore it as well as one can and eat around it. This may not be possible if one is truly repulsed. If the hair is floating in soup or otherwise raises suspicion about the whole meal, one may stop eating and trust the hostess to notice.

It would be rude to make a scene ("Eeeeeeooooowww" comes to mind) in a private home. In a restaurant, of course, you should summon the waiter.

Seasoning a Meal Before Tasting It

Some restaurants do not put salt and pepper shakers on the table in the belief that because they prepare the meal properly in

the kitchen, it shouldn't need any augmentation. Nevertheless, some diners routinely salt and or pepper their food without sampling it first. This is an insult to the chef or hostess.

There is a story about a major corporation that invites prospective management candidates to lunch following their job interview. Unbeknownst to the applicant, lunch is the final part of the interview. If the job seeker puts salt or pepper on his meal before tasting it, the hiring panel reasons that he is operating with a closed mind and passes on employing him.

Spills at Dinner

There was an old rule that if a guest spilled his wine glass at the dinner table, the hostess should also spill hers to make the guest feel less embarrassed. Great—two wine stains.

The guest who spills wine (or anything else) should try to blot it up with his napkin. The servants (if present) or the hostess should help. A simple, "Excuse me, I'm sorry," will do for the moment. On the way out, the guest should offer the hostess payment for the dry cleaning. If it turns out that the tablecloth cannot be cleaned, the guest should offer to replace it. The hostess can decide whether to accept.

PESTS AND OTHER PROBLEMS

Car Alarms

In most cities, the car alarm has replaced "The Star Spangled Banner" as the national anthem. What a car alarm does is wake people up, scare animals, create an unpleasant neighborhood atmosphere, and make installers rich. There is no proof that they catch car thieves.

In most cities a car whose alarm that goes off for fifteen or more minutes may be impounded by police and towed. In many neighborhoods, car alarms whose sensitivity is set at too low a threshold may be plastered with signs from angry neighbors or even vandalized. A malfunctioning car alarm is what might be called a passive insult that inspires active revenge.

Cockroaches

Cockroaches are probably the oldest surviving species on earth, which may be interesting in the abstract but not at all pleasant when you see one crawling up the wall or along the floor when company's visiting.

If you're the first one to see the culprit, a few subtle steps and a slight move of the foot will eliminate the problem. This can be done whether the spotting is in your home or someone else's; the purpose is to stop the problem, not the conversation.

If you are not the first to notice the roach (and hearing someone say "Eeeewwwww!" will tip you off), do the same footwork, and clean up the resulting mess with a piece of tissue. You might then announce, "Oh, dear, that must have come in with the delivery. I never have these around here."

Do not attempt to capture and rehabilitate the cockroach. But do call the pest control people the next day.

Cutting in Line

During the gas crisis of the mid-seventies, fights would break out at filling stations when a driver dared to cut in line. Similar fracases have resulted in school lunch lines. Make no mistake about it: as much as Americans enjoy getting special favors, it is never accepted to barge ahead of somebody else in a waiting line.

Of course, it still goes on. If someone tries to usurp your place in line, start by assuming that he or she did so by mistake: "Excuse me, but I was ahead of you." A more indirect, "The end of the line is that way," may also work. If you're dealing with an incorrigible person, you might ask the cashier or teller (or whomever you're standing in line to see) to intercede.

Should you encounter a situation where somebody several places ahead of you allows a friend to cut in line in front of them, the ante is upped considerably, as the offender now has reinforcements. All you can do at this stage is to hope somebody closer to them asserts himself—or seethe and remark to those around you how much rudeness there is in the world today.

Leaf Blowers

What could be a better symbol for the nineties that the emergence of leaf blowers: an invention that takes your problem and

MAILING LISTS

*I*f you register to vote, have a driver's license, use a credit card, or subscribe to a magazine, you are probably on a mailing list. And not just one; like a virus, your name, address, and other vital statistics will spread throughout the junk marketing industry.

Some people enjoy receiving direct mail and phone calls; others find it an invasion of their privacy, an abuse of their name, and, if nothing else, a waste of paper and energy.

The direct marketing industry supports a trade organization that can add or delete your name from the lists of participating members. They are extremely helpful at both. Write or call for the appropriate forms:

Direct Marketing Association
11 West 42nd Street
New York, NY 10036
(212) 768-7277

The DMA cannot ensure that you still won't be bugged by junk mail by nonmember organizations, so if you are seeking revenge or are particularly bothered by one company in particular, there is a private organization that can help.

Private Citizen, Inc., was established to urge legislators to enact laws protecting privacy and to enable individuals to bring action against junk mailers who violate that privacy. For a small fee, they will notify the major mailing houses to delete their members' names—or else. Contact:

Robert Bulmash
Private Citizen
P.O. Box 233
Naperville, IL 60566
(800-CUT-JUNK)
(800) 266-5885

makes it somebody else's problem, plus noise. People using blowers must properly collect and dispose of the trash they amass. A growing number of municipalities are passing laws to restrict their noise; others have outlawed gasoline-fueled blowers. Local police can tell you the permissible hours during which noisy equipment may be used, usually from 7 A.M. to 10 P.M.

Mailing Lists

It was bad enough when McCarthy made lists in the fifties, but the advent of computers and junk mail (called "direct mail" by people who like it) make it highly likely that you will receive things in your mailbox that you don't want. Some of them may even come because of friends!

Giving somebody else's name to a mailing list is a betrayal of trust, not to mention a waste of resources. In some states (notably California, where celebrities are a powerful bloc), it may even be legally actionable under laws that protect an individual's use of name for exploitation.

Just as one should not add another's name to a mailing list, one should also never add, without permission, a friend's name to a charity fundraising list. This has nothing to do with the legitimacy of any particular charity, all of whom depend on public supporters for their livelihood. This has to do with giving your personal appraisal of a friend's financial worth, allowing someone who is a stranger to them to call to ask for money, and expecting to continue the friendship untarnished.

"Spam" or junk e-mail on the Internet, is likewise intrusive and rude.

Panhandlers

It's funny, but what used to be a quaint touch in old Ali Baba movies ("alms for the blind") has become a national disgrace in present-day America. More to the point, panhandling, especially aggressive panhandling, has become such an urban blight that even righteous people have taken to blaming the beggars rather than the system that produced them.

That having been said, what does one do when approached? Whether one chooses to donate, the panhandler must be accorded his or her common dignity. Yes, it's true that many are just street hustlers (a widely posted sign in Los Angeles warns, "Some of Hollywood's best actors aren't on the screen") or slackers. But a great number also are distressed people, many of them Vietnam veterans, who, for a variety of reasons, can't cut it. A large number of street people eschew shelters not for the "love of freedom" as some ignorant politicians have waxed but because in shelters they can be robbed, beaten, molested, or worse.

If you decide to give money, remember that it is a gift, not a contract. The recipient can do with it as he pleases. You might, instead, offer to buy him a sandwich or soft drink. If you choose to ignore him, a simple, "No thank you" is a nonconfrontational response. If the panhandler persists, pay no further attention unless, of course, your personal safety is threatened, in which case call for assistance.

Pests

Everyone knows the chatterbox, the bore with nothing worth hearing, or the person who always calls you and never grasps why you never call him. Being a pest is not a criminal offense, but it is a breach of etiquette. It shows that the person is more concerned about himself or herself than about others. Your tolerance only reinforces his annoying habits.

Unless you wish the pest to continue, you may tell him politely, "I can't talk to you now; I have important business to attend to," and rebuff any further inquiry such as "So when can I call back?" with "I'll call you." Then don't.

(There's a classic *New Yorker* cartoon that shows a businessman on the phone, looking through his appointment book, and telling the caller, "No, Thursday's out. How about never? Is never good for you?")

If the pest persists, you will have to say, firmly, "Please understand that you and I don't have anything in common, and that I prefer you didn't call me any more." If this doesn't do the trick, we are approaching the threshold of "stalker," for which there are criminal sanctions and for which you may bring in the police.

Racists

Intolerance for others must never be tolerated. Racists, bigots, hate mongers, and other exclusionists only cheapen themselves when they attempt to cheapen others. As the admonition goes, evil triumphs when good men do nothing.

People who hold intolerant views are seldom open to learning the truth. When a conversation turns offensive, a nonconfrontational response is a straightforward, "Sir [or Madam], I do not wish to hear that kind of talk."

Talking in Movies

Why should somebody's movie ticket entitle them to more than somebody else's? Why should what an audience member says be more important than what a screen character is saying?

Nevertheless, people talk in movies. This has nothing to do with short attention spans or the advent of home video; it existed long before Betamax, VHS, and laserdiscs.

Sociologists refer to it as "a cultural phenomenon." Some movie critics celebrate it as "hearing right from the people."

The logic is formidable: if a person keeps quiet in a movie, he isn't disturbing anyone else; if someone talks, he is. Add to that the intimidation factor (the presumption that a talker disrespects the rights of others and, therefore, by extension, may be prone to violence), and this is a major issue. It may also explain why going out to a movie in many cities has become an unpleasant experience and why the home video market is growing.

Talkers in movies should be given a loud "shhhhh." When (not if) that doesn't work, they should be specifically asked to talk in the lobby. When that fails (or after you've been insulted), get the theater manager. Ask him to eject the talkers. If he won't, ask him to give you your money back, plus parking, plus the cost of your baby-sitter because your evening has been ruined.

Telephone Solicitations

Many states are passing laws against companies or charities who phone people at home, often during the dinner hour, to beg for charity or sell them merchandise. This is tantamount to saying, "As you won't come into my store of your own free will, I am going to force you to pay attention to me." There are anecdotal reports of sick or elderly people hurting themselves while hurrying to answer a ringing phone, only to learn that it was a salesperson or, worse, a computer voice, who placed the call.

Your name gets on a phone list the same way it gets on a mailing list: somebody puts it there or perhaps you do by buying something over the phone. But usually it's just someone calling from a directory listings or, for those whose numbers are unpublished, randomly.

Hanging up is not enough. By law, salespeople within the state must delete your listing if asked to do so. Across state lines it may be another matter.

There is still no excuse to threaten or be vulgar to someone who calls to sell you something. There is also no reason to buy anything, either.

THE RULES FOR INANIMATE OBJECTS

Baseball Caps

Clothing styles are in a constant state of change, and, for the moment, baseball caps are part of the national fashion statement. Girls as well as boys top their heads with caps, often turned around—and frequently look very attractive and stylish.

Of course, haberdashery has been part of ladies' and gentlemen's ensemble for centuries. The practice has been that ladies wear their hats indoors while gentlemen do not.

How does the baseball cap fit in? Men should remove them when indoors, or in the presence of a lady or an elder. What about girls? Girls should remove their baseball caps, too. This is because baseball caps are not ladies' hats; they are men's hats that are being worn by ladies.

Boom Boxes

Nothing is more boorish than to have someone force others to listen to his conversation, except perhaps someone who forces everyone around him to listen to his music. Aesthetics aside, it isn't the tune, it's the venue.

The "boom box," "ghetto blaster," or whatever it may be called is a cultural affectation. It also is a joke, a confirmation of a stereotype for those who note its presence and reject its noise.

In the last ten years the personal tape player has more or less replaced the boom box, except for people who have converted their car radios into portable, and even louder, sound systems. These also are intrusive.

Furs

The wearing of coats made from genuine animal fur is rapidly losing acceptance in American life, almost entirely through the efforts of individuals and groups who disdain, often with confrontational tactics, the way they are made.

From the point of view of etiquette, it is as impolite to comment on what somebody is wearing as it is to wear something that would be inappropriate to the circumstances. From a moral point of view, it might also be said that it is as incorrect to destroy someone's property as it was for that person, or her furrier, to destroy animal life.

Offensive Gifts

When someone knowingly gives a vegetarian a gift box of sausages, it can only be interpreted as an insult. Emotions run high at such times, but having good manners demands that the response on the part of the recipient should remain, "Thank you." A more pointed response would be, "Thank you. Although I don't eat meat, I will give these to someone who does." Remember, even though it's sausage, there don't have to be *two* pigs in the room.

Personal Stereo Etiquette

The great thing about personal stereos is that they have replaced the boom box, so the streets are safe for people who don't want to be forced to listen to somebody else's music.

Unfortunately, folks who play their personal tape machines too loud are likely to lose their hearing. And the original problem isn't quite solved; some of the sound leaks past the headphones and can continue to disturb others on airplanes, buses, offices, and other areas. It is illegal in many municipalities to wear personal tape players while driving, jogging, biking, or operating heavy machinery because the music blocks out the sound of traffic and sirens.

Unwanted Gifts

Playwright George S. Kaufman detested licorice, and when a dinner guest once presented him with a box of it, he responded dryly, "It's nice to know that there will *always* be licorice in the house." In other words, be gracious until the gift giver leaves. If there is a chance that he or she will come back, put the gift away. That's what attics are for.

Bicycle Etiquette

Except for rural areas, most cities and towns have ordinances that prohibit bicycle riding on the sidewalks. Except for very small children whose parents instruct them to stay near home (in which case driveways and sidewalks may be permissible, the latter

ME, ME, ME

LAST WORD ON THANK-YOUS

*W*hen is enough enough when it comes to thank-you notes?

The scenario is typical, and tragic: the grown-up relative is frustrated that she has been sending birthday and Christmas presents to a nephew since he was born. But she has never received a thank-you note from him since he was old enough (eight) to write them, even haltingly, himself. He is now thirteen and common sense would tell the relative to stop sending them. Thing is, she doesn't want to hurt his parents' feelings or create a rift in the family. His next birthday is staring her in the face. Should she send a gift that she knows will not be acknowledged?

Tough call. It's the parents' fault for not making the kid sit down and thank Auntie, but it's not their birthday coming up, it's his. The solution? Send the money that would have been spent on his gift to a charity, and write in his card, "In honor of your birthday, I have sent a check to the XYZ Foundation." The charity will notify the kid (and send a proper thank-you to the aunt), and when, after a month, the aunt hasn't heard from the kid, she can write him to ask, "Did you get a notice from the charity?"

Will he get the idea? Will the parents make him write his thanks? Will the charity appreciate it more than he will?

---

only with careful observance of pedestrian traffic), biking should take place in the street.

It is indeed tempting to ram a broom handle through the spokes of a bike whose rider insists on ignoring the driving laws and your personal safety. As a matter of fact, bike messengers in New York City rack up an impressive number of injuries each year not only from accidents but also from assaults by pedestrians and car doors.

YOU KNOW BETTER THAN THAT

Accidental Eavesdropping

This is a trick question. There is no such thing as accidental eavesdropping, as eavesdropping is the purposeful listening-in on somebody else's conversation.

The best thing to do if one accidentally overhears dialogue that one would rather not share (shouting neighbors, an answering machine playing at full volume, unavoidable discussion in the next office cubicle, a door left open, etc.) is to ignore it. Make no remark to the person you overheard, and keep it to yourself.

If this is impossible (say, you're on a speaker phone or can't easily close the door) then interrupt the intrusive conversation in a businesslike manner and say, "Perhaps you didn't know your voices were carrying," and let it go at that.

If there's nothing you can do (for example, the couple upstairs are happily enjoying their couplehood) then mind your own business. As the nineteenth-century actress Mrs. Patrick Campbell advised, anything should be accepted "as long as one doesn't do it in the street and frighten the horses."

Asking Somebody's Age

Age, income, religion, political affiliation, and sexual orientation are the Big Five topics that are never brought up in the second person. There are professional exceptions to not asking someone's age: medical reasons, ordering alcohol, signing a legal document, applying for a driver's license, buying children's movie or airline tickets, and so on. But age is never a fit subject for discussion in a social or job-related setting unless the person raises it himself or herself.

Bragging

As the saying goes, "Self-praise is no praise." Braggarts are seldom open to sar-castic suggestions to stop from the people they offend, so they continue. The most polite way to deal with a braggart or with someone who continually turns the conversation back to himself to the exclusion of all else is to make no response, not even an "Is that so?" or "Really?" When there is a lull in the conversation, change the subject. Next time, change the guest list.

Calling Attention to Bad Grooming

If one's hair is unkempt or one's clothing is disheveled, it may be taken as a character statement. If the person, however, who may be otherwise rational, has more pronounced problems, such as failing to bathe, bad breath, soiled or torn clothing, then discreet action may be taken. He or she may be pulled aside and asked, as though it was of no import at all, "You probably aren't aware of this, but there's something the matter with your clothing [or hair, or teeth]."

Poor hygiene is more troubling, especially as people cannot smell (or do not mind smelling) their own body odor. There is a major movie star who consistently offends those he meets by, in the words of one person, "having no acquaintance with a bar of soap." In this instance the only way is to be direct, yet sensitive, in private: "I'm sorry to have to say this, Mr. Yeti, but there seems to be a problem with your cleanliness." In such cases, it's not a question of bad manners, but of better manners.

Character Assassination

Although gossip may be a preoccupation of ignoble minds, one occasionally hears negative information about others that cannot be ignored. Unfortunately, repeating the information or using it to make business decisions is both unfair and might lead to a nasty lawsuit.

Motion picture executive Dore Schary had a novel way of stopping rumors when someone brought him a defamatory report. He suggested that they immediately summon the third party and straighten out the matter face to face. Schary found that it always worked.

Another way to stop chatter about someone is to interrupt the conversation to announce, "I don't want to hear that. All of my friends are perfect." The gossiper should get the picture.

Children Commenting on Persons with Disabilities

Children are curious. They want to know about things they have never encountered before. To most children, seeing a person in a wheelchair, or on crutches, or bearing some other disability inspires them to ask why and, sometimes, to wonder whether they, too, might become disabled.

Often the person with the disability himself will be able to answer the child's question, as he has very likely been in this position before. A very valuable lesson in humanity can then take place.

It is incorrect for the parent to scold the child or say, "Don't look at him," or to make any disparaging comment. Truth, delivered at the child's comprehension level, to be sure, is always the best response. These are tough, tough questions:

Question: "Mommy, why is that man shaped funny and riding in a chair?"
Answer: "He's in the chair so he can get around more easily. He had something happen to him that makes him look that way, but there is no difference inside."
Question: "Will I be like that?"
Answer: "I don't know and neither can anyone else. What is important is that you should act toward other people exactly as you would like other people to act toward you."

Comments on Cosmetic Surgery

Just as it is never proper to comment on somebody's medical condition, it also is improper to inquire after cosmetic surgery, hair transplants, toupees, or hair extensions. It also is impolite to stare or to speculate about it with others. When caught in a situation where the subject comes up, a useful response may be, "Oh, doesn't she look wonderful?"

Ethnic, Racial, and Other Jokes

Jokes that demean a particular group of people, no matter how funny they are, have no place in polite society. They contribute to the general cheapening of life and the lowering of respect for our fellow human beings.

OFFENSIVE WORDS

*E*verybody knows that the epithets *nigger, faggot, kike, spic,* or *gook* (among many others) are hurtful; after all, that's why they are used. But some terms have become so much a part of American slang that most people may not know what they mean or the extent to which they offend those they target. These are not an example of political correctness but of social ignorance, and the list is only partial:

- *Gyp (cheating someone in a business transaction) is drawn from "gypsy"*
- *Paddy wagon (the proper term is police patrol wagon)*
- *Dutch treat/going dutch (splitting the cost of a meal)*
- *Welsh on a bet (deny an obligation)*
- *Indian giver (wanting something back after giving it to someone)*
- *Jew somebody down (haggle with a seller to reduce a price)*
- *JAP (Jewish American Princess)*
- *Chinese Fire Drill (scramble from a stopped car)*

The question is often raised whether a specific group (blacks, Jews, gays, etc.) may make such jokes at their own expense while chastising others for doing so. The answer is that they do so at the cost of spreading and strengthening the stereotype.

The Enemy Next Door

It is the obligation of every dinner guest to speak equally with the person to his right and left. The conversation also must be cordial. If you find yourself seated next to an apologist for Hitler and you happen to be a Holocaust survivor, however, that may be quite impossible. This is why it is the host's or hostess's vital responsibility to balance the guest list to avoid such gaffes.

When two enemies happen to be at the same social event at the same time—and both must remain—they should either avoid eye contact or, if this proves difficult, both should mutually back off so as not to disrupt the event. If even that is impossible and a personal meeting is inevitable, nothing says more than stony silence or disarms an opponent more than politeness.

Freudian Slips

Comedian Jonathan Katz says, "I was having lunch with my father the other day and I committed a classic Freudian slip. I meant to say, 'Please pass the salt.' But what came out was, 'You prick, you ruined my life.'"

Every now and then everybody accidentally says what they were really thinking rather than what they meant. Dr. Sigmund

Freud referred to these as "slips," instances where the unconscious mind overpowers the conscious mind and the truth shoots out like soda on a hot day.

If you've made an inadvertent slip of the tongue, take a page from the politician's book: plow ahead as though nothing has happened. If you hear titters at the unintentional joke you've just made, go back and repeat the correct phrase as though nothing has happened.

The attempt to correct one small Freudian slip could explode into a full avalanche:

. . . Oh, did I say that polka dots make you look fat? What I meant to say was that at least you didn't wear stripes because then you'd look like the Ringling Brothers big top. Not that there's anything wrong with circus elephants, other than they have big noses, too. Oops, I mean, don't you just love peanuts? Did you know that one in four people can't digest peanuts and they pass right through whole?

In such cases, shut up. Then defuse the situation by laughing at yourself, adding, "Well, when I make a mistake, I don't cut corners, do I?" or some other self-deprecating remark. One famous choreographer told his dancers, "If you make a mistake, smile and do it with gusto—it just became your solo."

The person who calls attention to his own major gaffe and quickly apologizes for it will almost always salvage his respect.

Irritating Habits

People who whistle, tap their feet, crack their knuckles, and make other repetitive noises are usually not conscious that they are doing so and would be appalled to know the extent to which such habits bother others. The subtle approach is for someone to ask, in a crowd, "What's that noise?" It is certain to stop for the moment, but also bound to recur. "There it is again . . . it sounds like someone's cracking his knuckles [or whistling, or whatever]."

If the subtle approach doesn't work, try escalating your complaint: "There's that noise again! Does anyone else find it annoying?"

The last tactic is the direct one: "Blanche, please stop doing that; it's driving me crazy."

"I'm sorry," Blanche may say, who has ignored your three previous hints. "I had no idea I was doing it."

"Well, now you do."

Pointing

Actual (as opposed to metaphoric) finger pointing is a violation of another person's dignity. It can also be a threatening gesture; perhaps this is because it so often arises in a criminal setting ("Will the witness identify that person in the courtroom?").

Film director John Ford had a good rule that's still a pretty safe one to follow: "There are only three things that you can point at—let me get the billing right—the producer, the privy, and the French pastry."

Public Discipline of Children

Kids rounding puberty often do things that displease their parents. The parent who admonishes her child in front of a friend risks not only embarrassing him but also making him resist correction, by not accounting for peer pressure.

It also places the friend in an extremely awkward position. Does he leave the room? Go home? Get in the middle? What the friend should say is, "Perhaps I should leave until you two have finished this discussion. I'll be outside." As no kid on earth would ever think of that, however—and if the berating parent does not take it as a clue to pull her child out of the room to finish the instruction—the best thing a friend can do is say, "Excuse me," and head for the bathroom.

Afterward, when they're alone, the friend should not acknowledge the incident unless his buddy brings it up, and then only to say, "Are you all right?"

Returning an Insult

Given that etiquette is designed to reduce the incidence of insult, when is it appropriate to return one? Sarcasm seldom works in the face of total stupidity. If you are asked a question you feel to be invasive, an even-handed response is, "I beg your pardon?" spoken in a cold, firm voice.

If the inquisitor persists, reply in a likewise even (and not raised) voice, "Was it your intention to ask such a personal question about something that is none of your business?"

Speech Disabilities

Many people have difficulty understanding others who have international accents or speech impediments (stuttering, cerebral palsy, stroke, hearing-related muteness, etc.).

Usually, people with these disabilities have learned the patience and technique needed to deal with others who do not share them. Non-speech-impaired people can assume some of the burden, however, by listening closely and making an attempt to understand. It's amazing what concentration and politeness will do. Do *not* finish someone's sentence for him.

Spitting in Public

Expectorating demonstratively—that is, spitting—is unacceptable public behavior. It also is disgusting and unsanitary. If one must expel phlegm or other matter from the mouth, one should use a handkerchief or tissue or remove oneself to the bathroom or, if outdoors, expectorate behind a bush or tree. Rolling down the car window and letting it fly is risky, even dangerous: your expectorant could land on somebody's person or vehicle.

Socializing with the Physically Challenged

People in wheelchairs and people who are blind report instances in which they have been sitting with friends in a restaurant and the waiter or waitress has leaned over and spoken to them in a loud voice, as though they were deaf, too. At other times

BACKSTAGE

There is etiquette in legitimate theater that borders on superstition: never whistle in a dressing room, never throw a hat on the bed, tell people to "break a leg" as a good-luck charm, and never mention the title <u>Macbeth</u> when referring to the Shakespeare classic—always refer to it as "the Scottish play."

The most uncomfortable theater etiquette involves going backstage after a performance to greet friends who are acting in the show. If the play is bad, or they are bad in it, what do you say when tradition demands that you compliment them?

Some suggest the diversion technique (spoken with great enthusiasm):

"What can I say? The curtain went up and <u>there you were</u>!!!"
"I've seen a lot of plays in my life and, wow, <u>this</u> was one of them!"
"I'll <u>never</u> forget tonight!"
"Do you want to talk about a play? I tell you, <u>do you want to talk about a play</u>?!"

But the best thing to do when faced with what you are sure will be a critical disaster once the reviews come out is . . . lie like a rug. After all, this is friendship, not brain surgery: "<u>Darling, you were wonderful!</u>"

---

they may be simply ignored, as though their disability renders them invisible.

Needless to say, a person is supposed to be defined by who he or she is, not by what kind of chair he or she sits in.

Supermarket Hogs

The checkout line clearly says "Limit ten items," but the customer ahead of you has twelve, twenty, or more. This is a matter, first, for the cashier. If he or she does nothing to inform the customer of the limit—and if the length of the line makes it important—bring the matter up to the store manager's attention on the way out of the store. A confrontation would be neither productive nor polite, as it would only slow the line down even more.

Telling Someone Off

It is never proper etiquette to give someone a piece of your mind. Hurting someone or making him or her feel embarrassed is a mark of bad manners.

On the other hand, why do we have to be concerned for the feelings of someone who clearly has no concern for ours? What can be so wrong about telling a thoughtless, obnoxious person to go take a long walk off a short pier?

Etiquette books differ on this. Some insist that the other person's feelings are always paramount and that merely by showing someone the right way to behave, he will change his manners.

This book, however, takes a more aggressive view. When someone wantonly transgresses the constraints of good manners, he consciously commits to operating outside the bounds of propriety. One is not compelled, therefore, to use good manners when dealing with him. Use your best judgment to defuse an unpleasant situation peacefully.

"The Thing That Wouldn't Leave"

The late John Belushi, on *Saturday Night Live*, as well as apparently in real life, was known as "The Thing That Wouldn't Leave," for his matchless energy and persistence at parties.

When it is time for your party to break up, several signals can be given. Announce "last call" and then end the liquor service. Turn the music off. Turn the lights up. Start clearing glasses and plates. If all else fails, hand people their coats and say, "It's getting late. Thank you for coming."

For smaller, more intimate evenings that have run on longer than the host or hostess can bear, yawns (which may be naturally occurring anyway) are a good signal. Then look at your wrist watch. If something more assertive is required, a simple, "It's getting late. Thank you very much for coming, but I've [we've] been up since very early this morning. I [we] would hate to fall asleep on you, so let's get together again soon and pick up where we left off."

Unintended Insults

Occasionally a slip of the tongue or a lag in learning personal information can result in an unintentional insult. A woman who recently became a widow may be taken aback if a friend whom she hadn't seen in a while asks her, "How's your husband?"

As obviously no harm was meant, it behooves the insulted person to inform the accidental insulter of the news: "We've been out of touch, so you couldn't have known that my husband passed away last month." When faced with such a gaffe, the best way to make amends is with a simple, clear, and unqualified apology: "Oh, dear, I'm dreadfully sorry; there's nothing I can say to excuse myself, so please accept my apology."

children in, 12
funerals, 193-96
weddings, 68, 69-71
See also specific faiths
remarriages, 192
children and, 55, 62
informing ex-spouses, 63
resignations, 190
resorts, all-inclusive, 125
respect, 137
restaurants
abroad, 128, 130-31
arrival at, 89-90
children in, 12, 91
clearing places, 93
complaints, 90, 93
discrimination by, 94
disturbances in, 90
doggie bags, 94
maitre d's, 90, 95
menus, 91
ordering, 91-92
paying bill, 94-95
reservations, 89
tipping, 94, 95-96, 108
waiters, 88, 90
wine, 92-93
retreats, office, 167
reunions
class, 47-48
family, 57
ring-bearers, 76-77
rings
engagement, 64
wedding, 74
road rage, 113
Roman Catholic Church. *See* Catholic
Church
roommates, 175
royalty, 141
R.S.V.P., 72, 216
rude behaviors, 152
See also faux pas
rumors, 243
Russia, 130-31, 133

S

salads, 105
salt and pepper, 104, 234
same-sex marriages, 80
Scandinavia, 129, 130
school
behavior in, 12, 17-19
cheating, 18
dress codes, 19
homework, 18

intentional failing, 18
parent-teacher conferences, 18-19
political protests in, 151
school colors, 19
secretaries, 160
getting past, 161
relationship with boss, 156
typing personal letters, 207
senior citizens. *See* elderly
separation, marital, 190-91, 192
See also divorce
seppuku, 230
servants, 88-89
engaging for dinners, 222
letters of recommendation, 89, 217
tipping, 108, 146
service workers, 87, 107-8
See also tipping
sex
age of consent, 34-35
dating and, 30-31
sexism, 152
sexual harassment, 155, 157
shiva, 195, 199
shoes
athletic, 157, 225
for business, 157-58
colors, 224-25
shopping, express checkout lines,
247
shotgun weddings, 84
showers
baby, 4, 5-6
bridal, 77-79
silverware
European use of knives and forks,
100
in place settings, 101-2
removing, 104
specialty, 104
in trousseau, 67
skycaps, tipping, 108-9
sleepovers, 43-44, 144
smoking
abroad, 127
at dinners, 101
during pregnancy, 5
on public transportation, 117
when visiting, 144-46
in workplace, 159
Society of Friends. *See* Quakers
soda straws, 234
solicitations
fund raising events, 215
home sales parties, 165-66
office collections, 166
telemarketing calls, 165, 239

sommeliers, 92-93, 95
soup, eating, 105
spamming, 169, 237
speaker phones, 163
speech disabilities, 246
spitting, 246
spousal abuse, 37
stationery, 205-7
borrowed, 207
business, 206, 207
personal, 206, 207
stepbrothers and sisters, 55
stepparents, 55
subways. *See* public transportation
suicide, 198
supermarkets, express checkout lines,
247
surprise parties, 46
Sweden, 129
Sweet Sixteen parties, 42-43
sympathy cards, 200
synagogues. *See* Judaism

T

taxes, 183
taxicabs, 121, 130
teachers, 18-19
teacups, holding, 107
tea service, British, 131
teenagers
birthday parties, 43
dating, 34
parties, 34
proms, 44-45
spontaneous erections, 233
Sweet Sixteen parties, 42-43
telemarketing calls, 165, 239
telephone manners
answering machines and voice
mail, 165
in business, 162-65
calling at awkward times, 175-76
call waiting, 163-65
cell phones, 165
for children, 16
conference calls, 163
of house guests, 147, 174-75
obscene calls, 174
pests, 238
speaker phones, 163
telemarketing calls, 165, 239
toll-free directory assistance, 181
wrong numbers, 174
television
complaints to stations, 181-82
remote controls, 179